David Jansen is a psychologist with a doctorate in the field of marriage and family therapy. For thirty-seven years he has practised in California, Canada and Australia. Since 1968 he has been a leader in the education of couple therapists and psychotherapists. In 1971 he co-founded the California Family Study Center (now Phillips Graduate Institute), which offered the first masters degree in marriage and family counselling in the United States. After moving to Australia in 1978, David founded the Relationship Development Centre in Sydney. In 1981 he was joined by Margaret Newman, and as co-directors they further developed the centre. Now the Jansen Newman Institute, it offers counselling services as well as tertiary education in counselling, psychotherapy and couples therapy. David now lives mostly outside Sydney and maintains a practice called Australian Couple Coaching, in Laurieton, New South Wales. He continues to develop new and innovative approaches to couple therapy and is available for intensive counselling for those wishing to have a holiday while working on their relationship.

Margaret Newman is a psychologist who for the past twenty-three years has practised as a psychotherapist, couples therapist and couples educator. During this time she has worked extensively as workshop leader in a wide range of courses for the general public and the corporate sector. Together with her husband, David Jansen, she is co-director of the Jansen Newman Institute in Sydney, and lectures and supervises in the area of couple counselling. She is the author of *Stepfamilies*, published in Australia, the United States and Canada (French edition), and various cassette series, including *Becoming an Assertive Communicator*.

Claire Carmichael taught English as a secondary teacher for twelve years in Australia, and is a prolific writer of educational texts and fiction. She resides in California, where she pursues her busy writing career.

Acknowledgement

The authors wish to acknowledge the contribution of Interpersonal Communication Programs, Inc. to their work over the last twenty years. Further information on their programs is available at 7201 South Broadway, Littleton, Colo. 80122, USA.

REALLY RELATING

HOW TO BUILD AN
ENDURING RELATIONSHIP

David Jansen
Margaret Newman
with Claire Carmichael

Random House Australia Pty Ltd
Level 3, 100 Pacific Highway, North Sydney, NSW 2060
Sydney New York Toronto
London Auckland Johannesburg
and agencies throughout the world
First published 1989
This edition published 1998

National Library of Australia
Cataloguing-in-Publication Data

Jansen, David.
   Really relating.

   ISBN 978 0 09184 006 8

   1. Interpersonal relations. I. Newman, Margaret. II. Carmichael, Claire. III. Title.

158.2

Designed by Anna Warren
Printed by The SOS Print + Media Group, Australia
11

Dedicated to

All our clients, students, radio listeners and School of Marriage
participants who encouraged us to write this book.

Contents

Step One   WHY MARRY?   1

Why has marriage changed?
What are the forces for change?
Reasons for marriage
Pre-marriage checklist
Really relating in marriage
• Myths about marriage
• The four stages of marriage

Step Two   WHAT IS THIS THING
CALLED LOVE?   14

Where did the ideas of romantic love come from?
Why do we have to analyse romantic love?
Why is romantic love so powerful?
What are these hidden forces?
The advantages of romantic love
The disadvantages of romantic love

Step Three   WHAT CAN I DO ABOUT MYSELF
TO BE HAPPY IN MARRIAGE?   23

The importance of a well-developed self
What makes us the way we are now?
Roots: Your family of origin
Your individualised programme for survival
    or coping
The pseudo self
The real self
The four types of marriage and why developing
    your real self is vital for marital happiness
Why do so few of us develop the H-type marriage?
Self-defence mechanisms. What stops us
    knowing our real selves?

Step Four   SKILLS FOR REALLY RELATING I   45

The three ways of relating:
• Relating in a non-assertive way
• Relating in an aggressive way
• Relating in an assertive way
Speaking for self
The value of assertive communication
Dealing with issues and problems
The awareness wheel

Step Five   SKILLS FOR REALLY RELATING II   68

Putting the self-awareness wheel to work
Setting procedures
Why don't we see things the same way?
Inviting disclosure of your partner's
   self-awareness
What makes it difficult for a person to express
   her/his real self?
Checking out
Sharing a meaning
Styles of communication
Blocking communication by failing to listen
Creating a sense of being understood

Step Six   IS THERE A CONSTRUCTIVE WAY
                  TO RESOLVE CONFLICT?   95

The damage caused by unresolved conflict
Power struggles — achieving peace, not war
Approaching conflict constructively
Ten steps to resolve conflict
The real reason behind conflict

Step Seven   DO I RULE MY EMOTIONS
OR DO THEY RULE ME?   109

Reasons behind strong emotional reactions:
- Experiences in your family of origin
- Contracts and emotional over-reactions
- Rules and strong emotions
- Crazy-makers and over-reactivity
- Anger as a weapon
- Anger as a cover-up
- Displacement of anger
- Anger as a tension release

When is anger justified?
Jealousy: An emotion that destroys

Step Eight   HOW TO BUILD MATURE LOVE AND
ROMANCE INTO YOUR MARRIAGE 130

Transactional analysis: foundation for the mature
love program
Constructing an egogram
Using the mature love program
But I still want romantic love in my life
The three R's of marital success
This is all too hard!

Step Nine   INTIMACY AND SEX   151

How to receive love
Developing intimacy
Destroying and discouraging intimacy
The vital importance of time
Sex: A way of being together
The most common complaints
What can sex be like
Overcoming the sexual complaints and building
intimacy
A good sexual life ...
What frequency is normal?

Step Ten   BLENDING YOUR LIFE
WITH ANOTHER   172

The blending process
Steps on the path to blending

Step Eleven   HOW TO GO ABOUT WORKING
ON YOUR MARRIAGE   187

What it means to work on a marriage
Mistakes people make when conflict arises
Destructive ways of trying to change a
    relationship
Constructive ways of bringing about change in a
    relationship
What you cannot change in a relationship
What you can change
How long does it take?
Starting over again
What to do when you cannot achieve resolution
Divorce — When is divorce a failure?

HOW TO APPLY 'REALLY RELATING'
TO YOUR PROBLEMS   212

When the partner won't relate
I don't want children
Relating with children
The curdled family
Marriage the second and third time around
The ex-partner

REBOUND RELATIONSHIPS   219

THE AFFAIR   221

Prologue

The response to the first edition of *Really Relating* has deeply moved us. People have come to us again and again and told us how helpful the book has been in their lives. Many have followed up the reading of the book by attending a School of Marriage course at the Jansen Newman Institute or by seeing a relationship counsellor. Over time, the book has been adopted by many relationship teachers as a standard text in marriage and related university courses. Counsellors frequently assign the book to their clients, some counselling centres have given a copy to every client. As a result of the ongoing feedback from clients and counsellors we are confident that this book will make a major impact on your life.

Please keep the following suggestions in mind as you read *Really Relating*.

- Treat *Really Relating* as an important resource. Read the book more than once. Assimilation of the contents in one reading is virtually impossible. One way to experience the benefits of the book is to first read the whole superficially, perhaps scan it and get the highlights. Then go back and read those parts which relate to you. We have always marvelled, however, how one sentence, paragraph or case history has illuminated the inner workings of people's confusing relationship problems. So just when and where you will find the help as you read and consider is unpredictable.

- Remember that all of us become the way we are as we are growing into adulthood. Our beliefs, habits, attitudes, living patterns and values become very fixed. How we relate becomes automatic. So changing ourselves is a challenge which takes some awareness of how we are and then what can be changed in ourselves. One important principle is to be open to changing your beliefs about reality. As a child it is all too easy to adopt certain approaches to life which we cling to in adulthood in spite of much evidence that it may no longer work for us. Our perceptions of reality are like a trance state in which we live and we create illusions of reality which persist even when life is screaming out that there is something wrong. We want to encourage you to experiment with new ways of relating. See for yourself whether what you learned in your family of origin and your childhood environment was really the best way to find fulfilment in life.

Really Relating gives you the direction to change your patterns of relating and provides the impetus for you to try different ways of being, communicating and relating. As you read you will learn that information gathering is not the same as changing how you have learned to relate up until now. You must face the anxiety which goes with new behaviour. You will not always succeed the first time.

Be patient, persistent, and like any great athlete practise, train, overcome the injuries and create better times. It is worthwhile for some to find a coach much like an athlete, for external input and feedback. Ask 'The Shark', Greg Norman, Australia's own. He too develops bad golfing habits which only a professional coach can help him correct. Robbie Burns, the Scottish poet, made it so clear that we need the gift to see ourselves as others see us. This is where a professional marriage counsellor can be helpful.

- Another major fact has emerged since the first publication of this book. People are busier than ever. Many people complain about a lack of time. People are taking less time for their marriage and families. Even during the holiday breaks people are spending less time with each other as families. Our society has created more wealth for some, often at the price of *physical and relationship health*. We must also be mindful that some are suffering from a financial redistribution which favours some at the price of others. Worry over one's financial state also puts a strain on relationships. So whether you are well off or struggling financially there is always the need to stop and think about how you can give time to each other for what can be the most important thing of all — your relationships.

Creating more efficiency and responsibility in the workplace has its benefits but we have to face the next challenge and that is how to live with this culture. In a way, confronting your weaknesses in relationships at home and elsewhere is running counter to a culture which is focusing so much on productivity and wealth creation. Many of us have to stop and come to terms with a way to get balance in our lives. What good is it to 'gain the whole world and lose your own soul?'

What are your priorities in life? This book assumes that for many people relationships are still one of the highest. For many it is *the highest*. If you are one of these people, then assimilating the contents of this book will be especially valuable and that requires making time.

- Since the first edition of this book was published many books have appeared which might lead you to believe that there are simple answers to the complex problems of marriage. Harville Hendrix's book *Getting the Love You Want* leads us to believe that marriage is a crucible for discovering how we have developed personality flaws from our childhood hurts and life experience. As adults we go on to select a partner, from our unconscious self who will inevitably be the right catalyst for our flaws to surface. Marriage or coupling thus becomes an opportunity for learning about and healing ourselves. When troubles emerge in a relationship it is a signal that for reasons unknown to our conscious mind at the time we chose that person because living with this partner will highlight exactly what needs to be healed in us.

This kind of simple answer satisfies a lot of people. But does it prove too much with too little evidence? Is it really true that we marry or couple with our chosen partner for some unconscious reason having to do with our own damaged self and therefore our own need for healing? Where is the evidence that we marry our chosen partner for such a therapeutic intention? This looks more like an assumption which stabilises a relationship for some people while they pay attention to their own unfinished business. In that way it serves a good purpose but is the assumption that we are so unconsciously clever really based on any solid facts? And are we really going to believe that our selection of a marriage partner is so often based on our deficits and not on our adequacies. This theory might only be a diversionary tactic to avoid looking at other possible causes of difficulty.

Another idea which has been latched on to by people is the idea that the major source of marriage conflict can be traced to the differences between men and women. The most popular of the books espousing this belief is *Men Are from Mars and Women Are from Venus*, written by John Gray. This book and other similar books encourage people searching for answers to their relationship pain to buy into the idea that men and women are just different. So different in fact that it explains the frequency of marital discord. On the basis of generalisations Gray in particular has created a plausible fairytale. But have he and others proven too much with too few facts?

We believe that Gray and others have carried the facts of gender differences much too far and in doing so made this new edition of *Really Relating* more important than ever. In this book we attempt to teach how to relate from your 'real self' to another person's 'real self'. In Gray's world of relating one is taught how to activate the pseudo self and how to relate from the pseudo self. Or you are taught to relate from a stereotypical female to a stereotypical male. The uniqueness of the individual gets lost and people are not related to as they are.

In Gray's world a man's sense of self is defined through his ability to achieve results. A woman's sense of self according to Gray is defined through her feelings and the quality of her relationships. In *Really Relating* that concept of the sense of self is seen as a pseudo-self mostly dependent on what is happening externally. The research of the most distinguished scholars of psychology and family therapy look internally for the basis of a strong sense of self. Gray's stereotypical men and women are externally focused, immature, insecure, manipulative and needing someone to instruct them how to behave.

Another message of Gray's book that has become quite popular and often alluded to in humour and cartoons is that men go to their caves and women talk. This contradicts most other relationship research. People's psychological caves have been studied for over a hundred years of psychological research and are known as ego-defence mechanisms. The reality is that *some* women go to their caves and *some* men go to their caves. Under stress, *some* women talk and *some* men talk. This book deals more fully with this reality in Step 3 (What Can I Do About Myself to be Happy in Marriage).

In the light of so much long established and new knowledge, many in the marriage education and counselling field have been scratching their heads in disbelief over so much uncritical acceptance of the current gender fairytale and the Imago Therapy of Hendrix. Many questions are arising. Why so widely accepted? Why so popular in religious circles?

Perhaps the most obvious reason for the popularity of the single idea theories is that we live in a time of rapid change and massive marriage breakdown. There is so much marriage distress that people would love to have some simple explanation for this widespread marital unhappiness. It would be a great discovery to find a single key. For many of us it seems like another instant gratification solution to very complex relationship conflicts. Single idea theories might sound good but they rarely solve real problems.

In spite of our protestations, those of us who work in the practice of couple therapy have experienced some couples being helped by accepting simplified explanations. Experienced marital therapists, however, are usually wary of easy change based on flimsy theories and beliefs. We have heard hundreds of times from enthusiastic couples about change brought about by a new philosophy, religious belief, theory, formula, new house, trip, whatever. But time has nearly always shown that the couple was pasting cardboard over the holes in a sinking ship.

People turn to all sorts of theories, religious beliefs, easy answers to the riddle of marriage conflict, dissatisfaction and breakdown. But in the full light of day the truth comes out, the illusory improvement comes unstuck and we have to go back to basic truths about what creates lasting intimate relations. It is only truth and workable change methods which can free us of the human tendency to seek the easy route or the one which gives temporary or instant gratification.

When all has been said and done the reality for us is that blending two lives into a relationship is a people problem not a gender problem. Neither does it go down well that we have marital problems because we have found just the right person to help us heal ourselves. An approach which over emphasises our wounded self sounds all too cynical and negative as there can be so many positive aspects of ourselves which help us find a person with whom we can further mature and grow. Conflict is normal and necessary for growth not necessarily a result of childhood wounding.

So now you have read some background reasons why we believe this updated edition of *Really Relating* is so timely and important. The basic truth of *Really Relating* must be re-emphasised — every single man and woman is marvellously different. To relate authentically you must respect and appreciate the uniqueness and special nature of your self and every other person.

To build a rewarding life with a marriage partner you have to first secure the blending process by accepting the uniqueness of your partner. You must never stereotype. You must never look for simple explanations which take you away from the real problems which beset human relationships. If you generalise, or stereotype you will miss out on realising the special dignity of your partner. When you do that you have failed to *really relate*.

This book teaches you about the art of relating to others but most of all with your special partner. This task is not simple. There is no magic formula, no simplistic idea which can create this, no interesting fairytale to give you false hope. It is only your dedication to learn all you can about yourself and your partner which can create the magic of a life of *really relating*. There might be times of despair but when you know what you need to know and you focus your efforts on the right issues, you will be able to turn despair into joy.

Introduction

Every working day we listen to stories of how relationships, which started out with great promise have turned into great pain. This decline from promise to pain is so common in history that it prompted Robert Louis Stevenson to write: 'Marriage is like life in this — that is a field of battle, not a bed of Roses.'

The content of this book began to incubate fifty years ago when David became fascinated by the many different concepts about love. Even then, it was obvious that confusion reigned. Not much was written to genuinely help anyone make sense out of this powerful human experience. Forty years ago the situation was no better as David began constructing courses for high school students in the area of love, sex and marriage. Useful books were scarce. Since then a large number of books based on much research have been published. So why then are we writing yet another book on relating?

To be honest, it is because of pressure. We are busy people with clients, students, classes, workshops — all that is involved in the practice of and training of marriage therapists. When we began the School of Marriage, however, we found ourselves having to pull together years of experience and knowledge to make the course a relevant and powerful experience. The rich storehouse of research and information from scholars needed to be put into useful form. Our own discoveries and new material were not in print. Hence we felt the pressure to write and put into photocopy form some of this information.

We were also encouraged by some of the listeners to David's daily radio talks. Again and again, we were asked for transcripts. We had none as those talks are made from notes only.

Margaret's ever-popular communication courses taught to thousands of students were often followed by requests for a book.

Clients repeatedly asked for information which we had in book form. So many of their problems had arisen from lack of information and skills in the past and they were currently making bad decisions and hurting each other on the basis of myths and misinformation.

Thus the pressure has mounted from many sides to put into print what we had learned over many years. When Claire Carmichael agreed to work with us to help pull together all that we had in print or on cassette tapes of talks and lectures, we jumped at the offer. Her energy, intelligence and writing ability made her the perfect person to accomplish such a difficult task.

At that very time we were being interviewed by TV, radio and press reporters regarding our School of Marriage Course. It seemed the right time to buckle down and provide in a single volume the information people wanted for building real relationships. People were, after all, calling us from a long distance wanting to know where they could take our course outside of Sydney.

There is another important reason for this book. It comes out of the experiences of our own marriage relationship. Much of this book is based on what we have found important to help us really relate. The 'ups and downs' of marriage are as well known to us as to anyone else. We are from drastically different cultural backgrounds. We have the normal differences of wants, ideas, expectations, values and interests. We know conflict as you do.

The skills, information, and challenges of this book have been practised by us daily. Without those skills, the same skills we have taught to thousands of clients and students, we would have been in the same kind of pain that many other people are experiencing.

Everything in this book is based on real life — on the real lives of people who have struggled with promise turned to pain or pain turned to joy. They have enriched our lives and helped us to know in depth what it means to really relate.

Stories of people in this book are so disguised that you cannot possibly know who we are talking about. Some of those come from Canada, the United States, and Australia. In many cases we have seen hundreds of couples much like the two anonymous people mentioned as examples.

We ourselves are still putting into practice what we have written about in this volume. Hence we do not place ourselves above you readers as people who have arrived. We, too, are on the journey — learning what it means to really relate. Join us in life's greatest adventure.

DAVID JANSEN
MARGARET NEWMAN JANSEN

Further reading and listening

All of the following learning resources are available from Edumedia Books, 125 St Johns Road, Glebe, NSW, 2037. Telephone toll free: 1800 809 502 Fax: 02 9660 0345

***Indicates university and professional level.

Stepfamily Realities by Margaret Newman, New Harbinger (USA)
Every stepfamily can use this book to understand and help the process of blending two families.

Family Ties That Bind by R. Richardson, Self-Counsel Press (Canada)
A practical and useful guide to developing your real self. Very highly recommended. The best supplement to Really Relating.

I Never Knew I Had A Choice by Gerald and Marianne Corey, Brooks Cole (USA)
An excellent book for personal development.

Intimacy and Solitude by Stephanie Dowrick, Random House Australia

Intimacy and Solitude Self-Therapy Book by Stephanie Dowrick, Random House, Australia.

Passionate Marriage: Sex, Love and Intimacy in Emotionally Committed Relationships by David Schnarch, Norton (USA)

***Basic Concepts in Family Therapy* by Linda Berg-Cross, Haworth (USA)

***Couple Therapy* by Linda Berg-Cross, Sage (USA)

***Family Therapy* by Goldenberg and Goldenberg, Brooks Cole (USA)

***Feminist Visions of Gender: Similarities and Differences* by Meredith Kimball, Haworth (USA)
This might be the most scholarly work available on gender issues. A masterpiece.

Books and cassette tapes by the authors of *Really Relating*

Books

Stepfamilies: How to Overcome Difficulties and Have a Happy Family (ISBN 1876451 521), by Margaret Newman, Finch Publishing, 2004
This new edition of Margaret Newman's highly acclaimed book addresses the major issues facing stepfamilies. These include: managing the complications of stepfamily life; understanding how to help children through difficult times; and ways to maintain a loving relationship.

Cassette tapes

The following cassettes are available from Balanced Living Books, PO Box 244, Laurieton NSW 2443, Australia. Tel (02) 6559 6033; or e-mail david-jansen@fasternet.com.au

Really Relating: How to Build an Enduring Relationship (for the hearing impaired or non-reader)
Contains the entire text of *Really Relating*. An eight-tape series available in local libraries or from the above address for purchase.

How You Can Really Relate
A 90-minute cassette that demonstrates the skills taught in *Really Relating*. A demonstration in which two couples work on real issues using the awareness wheel and other skills brings the book alive.

Becoming an Assertive Communicator, with Margaret Newman
A three-tape series that condenses a 16-hour course. This lively series illustrates Chapters 4 to 6 of *Really Relating*.

Step One:

Why marry?

Love and life were exciting and rewarding for Shirley and Neville. Their friends and families saw them as the perfect couple and everyone was sure their marriage was the beginning of a wonderful life together. Now, six months later, Neville and Shirley look at each other with the same thought:

'This isn't the person I should have married. I've made a terrible mistake!'

Philip and Zoe have been married for ten years. It may not be the most exciting marriage in the world, but Philip is reasonably satisfied with life — he has a dutiful wife, two children and a demanding, well-paid job. Yet tonight, without warning, Zoe has blurted out, 'I don't love you any more. I don't want to be married to you. I want a divorce.'

Henry and Florence are proud grandparents. This year they will be celebrating, with the entire family, their twenty-seventh anniversary. Florence is busy with the arrangements for the party when Henry drops a bombshell — he's sorry, but he's found someone else, and he's leaving to make another life for himself.

What's gone wrong in each of these relationships? Didn't each couple start out with optimism and high hopes for the future? How is it, then, that disaster has been the end result?

There are reasons for every failed relationship, just as there are reasons for every successful one. Together, in the Eleven Steps of this book, we will examine the factors that can lead you to greater balance, happiness and growth, both in your personal life and in your relationship with your partner.

These Eleven Steps form a package deal: they provide information, skills and insights to allow you to take out insurance against your emotional future.

In this book we have used the word 'marriage' to cover all forms of pairing relationships which are intended to be permanent.

We are living in a time of change — a transition period where the attitudes and values of the past are subject to tremendous stress. Everything has changed, socially, economically, technologically — and the pace of change has accelerated in the last twenty years.

'Old' social structures, such as marriage and the family, creak and groan as the currents of contemporary thought ebb and flow, the flood of innovative ideas challenging many of the ideas previous generations held dear. How people relate, what they expect from marriage, their personal aspirations — all are dramatically different from the generations before them.

Yet, in all this revolution, many people still treat marriage as a rock that will stand immovable, unaffected by this sea of change.

In many respects we live in a throw-away society, where everything must be new! fresh! modern! In this throw-away world, when a marriage doesn't live up to expectations, there is a tendency to throw it away too, because it isn't working.

But for each of us this period of change can be an opportunity to break new ground in our personal lives, to look at our relationships with fresh eyes, to develop new skills so that we are enriched in many dimensions.

Why has Marriage Changed?

To appreciate the tremendous changes in the concept of marriage, it is necessary to look at what marriage used to be. There are several common denominators that have existed through many centuries.

Traditionally marriage was based on a hierarchical structure: the husband was regarded as dominant and superior, the wife as inferior and submissive. And the inferiority of the female was reinforced by lack of training and education: without these no woman could be independent.

The economic base of society was marriage and the family, property and money were inherited by males, meaning that for many centuries it was virtually impossible for women to have any financial independence. In many cultures a dowry was used as a 'sweetener' to encourage a man to take a daughter off her family's hands.

Marriage provided a form of protection for women and children from the harsh realities of a world which took little social responsibility for its individual members — any type of government assistance for the unemployed or destitute is a very recent innovation.

Traditions and ideas of the appropriate behaviour and responsibilities for each member of the family were passed from generation to generation: the husband was expected to be the head of the family, protecting, supporting and providing discipline; the wife's role was to run the household, providing comfort and nurture to her husband and children.

These attitudes towards marriage and family worked well in the past, and for some people, particularly in conservative religious groups and certain ethnic communities, it is still the preferred structure. Preferred it may be, but the impact of the modern world makes it more and more unlikely that such ideas will survive unscathed and that traditional families will be unaffected by what is happening today.

Where once roles were clear, and patterns of behaviour and expectations were settled and agreed upon, now, most of us must find new norms and new philosophies to make sense of our lives.

Our world is moving towards equality, in which any individual — whether male or female, black or white, young or old, healthy or infirm — can expect to be treated as an equal to anyone else.

What are the Forces for Change?

There are many factors at work. These are some of the most important.

Over the years the availability and quality of education has improved so much that more and more people now reach high levels and thus have more expectations than before.

The explosion in technology has destroyed some job areas and created opportunities for new careers that did not previously exist.

The status of women has risen as the roles women can play have broadened — women are no longer restricted to housewife/mother etc.

Careers are changing. Again, for women in particular, the opportunities have become wider.

The cost of living means that households now often depend upon two incomes to be financially viable.

Women have become more financially independent, partly because of work opportunities, partly because of the impact of the welfare system.

Within society, people are more mobile, and, as they become less settled, they become isolated, especially from extended families. This places much more pressure on marriage as it is expected to fill the gap left by the absence of traditional family structures.

The cost of housing and a declining standard of living is causing many young people to postpone starting a family, move in with parents, or move away from the cities where housing is expensive. Dwellings are becoming smaller, a source of more stress in the home. We are going to pay an enormous price in marital conflict due to this emerging problem.

We live in what could be called the Age of Psychology: the emphasis is on the *individual* and people flock to courses to find answers to questions such as: Who am I? Where am I going? What makes me tick? How can I be happy? Rich? Fulfilled?

The change in the influence and impact of authority, religion and of once unquestioned social standards has made us the first generation in history to have a widespread need and opportunity to really understand ourselves, to be more fully aware of our potential, and to find our own personal meaning to life.

Many men, also now have an increasing awareness of their inner selves — the emotional part and searching part of their self. As they explore their real self, they also wish to be with a partner who can do the same. This reciprocal sharing is no longer seen as a thing that only women do.

And What Are the Implications for Us and for Our Society?

- Marriage has a whole new meaning.
- Marriage has a new set of 'rules'.
- Marriage gives us the opportunity to understand our deeper selves and therefore to know another person on an intimate level.

REASONS FOR MARRIAGE

There are both positive and negative reasons for marriage. Often a person avoids examining the real reason behind the desire to marry because there is a HIDDEN AGENDA operating — the rationale behind the decision is not the most common socially acceptable one of: 'I'm in love!'

Negative Reasons for Marriage

Although some of the following reasons might seem quite extraordinary to base a partnership upon, they occur again and again as a rationale for marriage. People might not be at all conscious or aware of these reasons.

1. 'I haven't got a very good self image ... but look! Someone's chosen me! Now the world can see I'm worth something because this person thinks I'm good enough to marry!'

   If a person has a low self-esteem, he or she receives a considerable boost by the very fact of being 'worthy' of being chosen and having a public acknowledgement of that fact.

2. 'I'm so unhappy ... but he/she will change that!'

   This person is unwilling (or unable) to face the reasons for unhappiness, so the marriage partner becomes the solution — 'Someone to make me happy ... '

3. 'I don't want to be lonely ... and time is running out.'

   The fear of being 'left on the shelf' to lead a lonely life can make a person accept or make an offer of marriage in order to cancel out this fear.

4. 'I feel sexually frustrated.'

   Marriage as a solution to sexual frustration is often the unacknowledged reason behind the initial proposal. These strong sexual feelings are frequently disguised, so that the person says, 'I'm in love', rather than, 'That person can satisfy my sexual needs.'

5. 'I want to solve my financial problems.'

   Money can be the real motivation behind many marriages: either the prospective partner is already wealthy, or will inherit money, or has the career potential to earn a great deal. Alternatively, the person is looking for a partner who will manage money efficiently and even make true that great lie 'two can live as cheaply as one'.

6. 'Marriage will help me escape!'

   The person wishing to be married sees it as an escape from something uncomfortable, unpleasant or unendurable. The situation to be escaped can range from the irritations of sharing a flat with others to the distress of abuse or violence in the family home.

7. 'I'm having a baby!'

   A forced marriage because of pregnancy is becoming more rare as social pressures on unmarried parents decrease. However, pregnancy can be deliberately engineered (sometimes unconsciously) in order to have a child of one's own, or as a desperate attempt to save a relationship.

8. 'Sharing a serious problem has brought us together.'

   There are two possibilities here: the two people have the same problem, for example a mutual family problem, or they share some emotional shortcoming; or the two people face a certain problem together, such as the grief they both feel at the death of a friend.

   In some cases, *once the problem is resolved* the basis for this kind of marriage disappears!

9. 'I'm so bored — there's nothing to do, nothing to look forward to ... '

   For this person, life is essentially dull and boring, but the excitement of a wedding, the setting up of a house — that will give some meaning and purpose to life, won't it?

   Since the person is looking for something outside himself/herself, something to entertain and divert, it is unlikely that marriage on this basis will be of much help. The problem lies in the personality of the bored person, and cannot be solved by the band-aid of marriage.

10. 'There's one thing I really love about him/her!'

    This situation leads to the single-factor marriage, where *one* thing only about the other person is the source of attraction. It may be sexual compatibility, it may be that the other person is a great tennis player, loves music the way you do, is a fantastic dancer, or is (or has the potential to be) a famous person.

It may, in fact, involve the overall impression the potential partner gives to others, so that a person thinks: 'I'm proud to be seen with him/her.'

11. 'All my friends are getting married ...'

When it seems that all the members of a group are getting married, setting up house, planning for a future together ... then there is an anxiety not to be left behind, not to be left out of interests and activities that all these other people now share.

12. 'Wow! I won't let that person get away!'

Put simply, the reason behind this marriage is to land a 'good catch'. While the chance is there, grab it, because it may not come this way again. As counsellors we have often seen men who married because she was 'so beautiful I could not let her go', even though many danger signals of incompatibility were showing. In the same way, women often report, 'I married him because he was so handsome' or 'he was such a fantastic athlete.'

13. 'Isn't it time you got married, dear?'

Family pressure to marry can be considerable, and can lead a person to marry in order to escape the constant anxiety of justifying why he/she is not married.

Family pressure can also have a negative effect: the family frowns upon a particular union, with the quite unintentional effect of driving the couple into each other's arms.

14. 'I've known him/her all my life ... I suppose I might as well ...'

This is the attraction of the familiar, the boy or girl 'next door'. The two drift into marriage because of proximity and because nothing better has come along.

15. 'I must have a husband!' 'I must have a wife!'

The reason for marriage in this case is necessity. For example, a person seeking high political office knows that to be married gives an impression of stability and the authority to make statements on matters affecting the family. If your career or social life demand a spouse, you are likely to make great efforts to find a suitable one.

16. 'I can change him/her after we marry.'

Here the selected mate is seen as pliable, and able to be moulded into that 'perfect spouse' after the knot is tied. Alternatively, the potential mate is most acceptable, except for some glaring fault, which the person confidently (but mistakenly) expects to alter after marriage.

17. 'I feel better when I'm married.'

This applied to the divorced or widowed person who has become *accustomed* to the married state and who believes he/she cannot be complete as a person without a partner.

Dora is marrying Gavin because he's just completing his studies as a doctor, is good looking and her mother keeps saying, 'Don't let him get away, dear! You'll never get another chance like this!'

Gavin is marrying Dora because she will be the perfect wife for his career — she's attractive, vivacious and socially adept.

How do you rate their chance of success in marriage?

Positive Reasons for Marriage:

There are many positive and optimistic reasons for deciding to marry:

1. 'In the fullest sense of the word, I love him/her.'

    A developed and well-grounded love includes respecting, valuing and enjoying the company of the person you love. You see him/her as an equal, complete and separate person, with whom you can share the deepest intimacies.

2. 'We have the material to build a lasting relationship.'

    The foundations upon which a permanent relationship can be constructed include some or all of the following:
    • common values: manners, behaviours, lifestyle
    • common interests
    • common goals, both short and long-term
    • agreement or acceptance of each other's spiritual beliefs
    • agreement or acceptance regarding political views, whether similar or different
    • agreement on having/bringing up children
    • similar energy levels, so you can share activities and interests

3. 'I feel secure enough to be honest with you and I'm sure we can resolve any major conflicts that may occur.'

    In a secure and loving relationship, honesty is possible because there is no threat that such truthfulness will lead to a break in the partnership. This is not to say that conflict will not occur, but there is a firm belief between the two people that major issues and conflicts can be resolved to mutual satisfaction.

4. 'I have a realistic, positive self-image, and this helps me to reinforce my partner's view of himself/herself.'

    If you have a positive and well-based view of yourself and your abilities, you will be in a position to give your partner support for his or her self-image.

5. 'Sex?'

There should be no serious sexual turn-offs for either partner, such as lack of personal hygiene or unacceptable habits or behaviour. Some people like touching/being touched, others do not — it is important to be matched in this area.

If your partner is not sexually attractive to you now then after marriage this could create a decline in sexual interest. It is, of course, the sign of a strong relationship that any problems to do with sex can be freely discussed.

6. 'Children? We've discussed the whole subject.'

Amazingly, some people marry without ever having even decided together whether or not they intend to have children. It is not good enough to assume you know what your partner thinks on this subject — you should be able to discuss having a child or children, how many, the way they are to be brought up and what type of schooling you would like them to have.

If there is disagreement on this matter it could spell marital disaster. It is important that this issue be resolved before marriage. The subject is such a significant one that if partners cannot resolve it themselves it may be necessary to seek professional guidance.

7. 'My in-laws are okay.'

A source of great conflict can be the attitudes and values that in-laws have. It is a great help if your partner's parents and family share similar views to your own, or, if there is a difference, that the attitude is 'live and let live'.

8. 'Our careers are not in conflict.'

The rise in the number of women choosing to pursue a career means that the comfortable situation of the past, where it was expected that a wife would support her husband's career, if necessary moving home from one place to another to enhance his prospects and providing meals for business associates when required, has ended. Now in many marriages it is vital to discuss the direction and emphasis of *two* careers, so that joint decisions can be made.

9. 'We can support ourselves financially.'

One of the sources of greatest conflict in all types of partnership, but particularly in marriage, is money. It is vital to the well-being of the relationship that financial management be discussed and agreed upon.

10. 'We can deal with conflict.'

Conflict is *normal* when two people attempt to share life and space together. In a healthy relationship conflict is dealt with effectively. This does *not* mean that one person agrees with the other just to avoid a fight. It means that when the inevitable conflict occurs, the differences are brought to some sort of resolution. This is not a perfect world, so not all conflicts can be resolved completely, but they can be dealt with so that they don't cause lasting damage.

We strongly recommend that couples learn how to deal with conflict *before* marriage. Step Six provides detailed information on conflict resolution.

11. 'We know what's non-negotiable.'

There are some opinions, thoughts and attitudes that are non-negotiable — that is, the person will not be persuaded to change. Examples include the situation where one partner definitely wants to live in the country, or one believes wholeheartedly in 'health' foods, or one is committed to enrolling in a course of study. Couples planning marriage need to be sure about such 'non-negotiable' contracts.

12. 'My partner is my friend.'

Like any close friend, your partner should be someone you trust — a person whose company you enjoy, with whom you can share laughter or grief, to whom you can express your thoughts, emotions and ideas. More than this, however, is the capacity to share the deepest intimacies which gives marriage an added dimension.

PRE-MARRIAGE CHECKLIST

This checklist can be used to indicate potential sources of conflict in a partnership.

Help yourself make the right choice! Go through the checklist by yourself and circle your answers. Your partner should do the same. Then, together with your partner, compare your answers.

Ideally, each partner will answer YES to all questions, although Question (4) is intended to help you become aware of the way your family dealt with conflict. If your family had negative ways of dealing with conflict, you will need to resist the lessons you have learnt there, and change to a constructive means of conflict resolution.

NO answers from either partner identify *an area of potential conflict* where issues will need to be resolved between you.

1. Do you have common interests? (list them)   YES/NO

2. Do you share more values in common than not?   YES/NO

3. Have you determined that your fundamental values are not in con-

flict? (e.g. Sexual morality, relationship with family, home presentation, alcohol or drug use etc.)   YES/NO

4. Does your family of origin deal with conflict in a constructive way, so that conflicts are resolved?   YES/NO

5. Do you tend to be in harmony with respect to your energy levels?
                                                                   YES/NO

6. Do each of you see your relationship as one to which you are willing to commit yourself wholeheartedly?   YES/NO

7. Do you accept each other's spiritual beliefs?   YES/NO

8. Do you communicate openly and honestly with each other about any issues that arise between you?   YES/NO

9. Do you deal with your anger constructively so that rather than bottling it up, you are able to use communication skills to talk about it and resolve it?   YES/NO

10. Is your partner sexually attractive to you?   YES/NO

11. Are you able to discuss your sexual relationship or future sexual life with each other?   YES/NO

12. Have you mutually decided how to manage your finances?   YES/NO

13. Have you discussed and agreed upon your future goals such as lifestyle? Work patterns? Where to live? When/if to have children?
                                                                   YES/NO

14. Are you prepared to learn more about what marriage involves and how to make it work — both now and as the years go by?   YES/NO

15. Do you feel secure with this person?   YES/NO

TAKE CARE: If you are considering marriage, failure to examine each of the items on this checklist before you marry may lead to disaster. Don't just look before you leap — think deeply before you take the plunge!

REALLY RELATING IN MARRIAGE

Really relating in marriage requires that we have appropriate and accurate information and that we rise above the mass of misinformation which can have the power of a myth. Some of those myths are mentioned below along with the stages of marriage.

Notice that marriage is not a static 'settling down' wherein people live 'happily ever after'. Marriage is dynamic — always developing or deteriorating. This book will help you to destroy the myths and to build skills for going through all four stages of marriage.

MYTHS ABOUT LOVE AND MARRIAGE

Here are nine commonly held myths about love and marriage. Notice how often the word 'really' occurs, implying that somehow a false love has fooled you into believing it is 'true' love. This fascinating (and false) idea that there is one kind of special, complete and unique love that each person should suddenly recognise when he or she experiences it, will be examined in detail in Step Two.

- Because we're in love, we'll live happily ever after
- If we *really* love each other, marriage and happiness will automatically follow
- If he/she *really* loved me, he/she should understand me
- When you fall out of love your marriage has lost its meaning
- People *really* in love don't have difficulties
- People who have difficulties not only aren't *really* in love — they don't have a good marriage and aren't mature anyway
- I've fallen out of love — so it's time to move on
- We're not happy now ... so it couldn't *really* have been love in the first place
- If we can't help ourselves (sort out our marital problems), no-one else can.

THE FOUR STAGES OF MARRIAGE

A marriage usually experiences distinct stages as it grows and matures. Some marriages, however, will end before they can develop and some will stall in one stage or another.

Stage One: Courtship

This is the stage of 'falling in love', and it can be a thrilling and exhilarating experience. Under the influence of romantic love, each person puts forward the 'best' parts of self and at the same time idealises the other person, being blind to faults and problems that may exist.

Stage Two: Honeymoon

During this period of the marriage (not necessarily *on* the honeymoon!) the intoxicating effects of romantic love have begun to wear off, and each person is beginning, unwillingly, to see that their choice of marriage partner is *not* absolutely perfect in every way.

This early disillusionment may not be caused by anything serious. It may merely be the result of misconceptions about romantic love. It can also mean that the normal differences between people are starting to surface.

Stage Three: Conflict

Conflict occurs when each person begins to struggle for individuality and to have his or her own needs met. Disillusionment with the promises romantic love seemed to offer is then complete.

At this stage people often think that if only the other person would change, romantic love would reappear. They are mistaken.

This is the stage where one or other partner may think: 'It's all been a terrible mistake ... I shouldn't have married him/her.'

When people end their marriages it is almost always during this stage of conflict. The conflict may be in the form of open warfare, or seething hidden resentment.

Marriage should *not*, however, end here! Why? Because it is necessary to pass through this stage to reach Stage Four. This handbook will show you how to successfully negotiate Stage Three and reach the rewards of Stage Four.

We think the high failure rate of marriage is largely due to the belief that '*conflict spells the end*'. It does not! It is the hurdle over which almost all marriages must jump in order to reach the next stage and to achieve the goal of a 'good' marriage.

Stage Four: Resolution

In the stage of resolution conflicts are resolved by the use of communication skills and each individual has undergone great personal growth. The delights of a positive and secure union are now enjoyed.

Beware, however, of *appearing* to resolve conflict by *avoiding* it. Often 'resolution' is temporarily achieved by avoiding the potential conflict. This results in a stale marriage or the reappearance at a future time of buried issues, meaning that Stage Four has never been achieved — only simulated.

It is extremely important to understand that even if the original reason that made two people marry was not a 'good' one, the marriage itself can develop into a deep and rewarding relationship if the steps outlined in this book are followed.

Sheila and Kurt are a good example of starting off on the wrong foot. They had what friends called a 'stormy' marriage. People would shake their head and say, 'Well, what can you expect with two such strong personalities? It's obvious they'll have to separate before they tear each other apart.'

But, in spite of all these gloomy forecasts, Sheila and Kurt's marriage grew steadily better as they learned to recognise the hidden reasons behind their conflict. And as they discovered more about themselves and about each other, they found their relationship becoming correspondingly deeper and more rewarding. As Sheila said laughingly to Kurt, 'The early years of our marriage were obviously the storm before the calm!'

It is important to note that these stages of marriage are sequential and non-sequential. In the early part of a couple's relationship one stage comes after the other. As the relationship or marriage progresses, it is important to circle back to previous stages. For example, every couple needs to have what can be called 'second honeymoons', fresh attempts at courting each other. Every day is an opportunity to renew the romance behaviour of the period when love was young. Committed relationships should not be taken for granted.

Couples who are experienced at resolving their conflicts with honest attempts at compromise can experience a satisfying warmth. So there is a circling back from resolved conflict to something like the early passion of a new and growing relationship.

Summary

In Step One we looked at Marriage and examined:

- why people marry
- the forces that have changed marriage in our modern world
- the reasons behind many marriages
- a pre-marriage checklist
- myths about love and marriage
- the four stages of marriage

Step Two

What is this thing called love?

Romantic love is powerful — it galvanises, activates, engrosses the imagination, seizes the heart, fascinates the mind, captures the soul, consumes the body. A person 'in love' is gripped by intense feelings and devoured by deep passions and desires. Life is exciting, meaningful and significant. The person loved is ideal, perfect and, in essence, the answer to a prayer or dream — the one who will bring happiness and fulfilment.

People 'in love' feel that they are special, that their love somehow lifts them out of the ordinary, mundane world, into a world of experiences that are extraordinary, thrilling and spellbinding.

People who have 'fallen out of love' usually actively seek to fall in love again: to experience once more the all-consuming emotions that held them in a tension of longing and desire.

People who have never been 'in love' often feel cheated: how is it that they have not experienced this wonderful state that seems to be so necessary? Is there something wrong with them, or is it just that the right person hasn't come along?

Although some people will deny that they believe the experience of 'true' romantic love is necessary, it is still part of the mythology that most of us unconsciously accept. We do want to feel that we are living with someone who is irresistible, someone we just can't possibly do without, someone we have to be with more than anyone else in the world.

So the question becomes: why is romantic love such a powerful force and energy in our society? Why is it the mainspring of so much of popular entertainment? Why do songs, magazine stories, novels, movies and television programs enshrine romantic love as the *peak* experience in life?

It is likely that you will feel that you are missing something if you have not experienced this form of love. Indeed, our society accepts it as an expected experience: you should, says our culture, at some time in your life have been 'in love'.

People, therefore, push themselves to create this feeling. 'I need to be in love' they say to themselves, and they look around for someone with whom they can fall in love.

And the age factor also comes into operation: 'I'm getting older and my friends seems to have fallen in love and married, but so far I haven't ... now this person looks promising ... maybe I can fall in love too ...'

Our culture suggests that being in love is a necessary condition for marriage and if you don't have this experience of overwhelming romantic love, either you are not ready for marriage or this is not the perfect person whom you should marry.

Because this need to experience romantic love is so powerful, it can lead people to create an illusion or fantasy to satisfy it: they become in love with being 'in love'.

Where Did the Idea of Romantic Love Come From?

Surprisingly, the idea of romantic love as a driving force in human relationships has not always existed. It is only comparatively recently that society accepted that intense romantic love was a necessary part of the selection process for a marriage partner. Before then, marriage was a contract based on more practical issues, such as property and power, and having a family. In this world, love as we understand it was of no relevance. Obviously it was pleasant if affection existed in a union, but it was regarded as being less important than it is today.

The origins of romantic love lie in the concept of 'courtly love' which developed during the twelfth century, particularly in France in the court of Eleanor of Aquitaine. The society of that time was, in many respects, cruel and brutal. Life was a constant struggle to survive and it was only in the courts of the nobles and royal families that there was time and opportunity to develop the mythology of romantic love. There was also a religious element in this, as the concept of romantic love created an awareness of the spirituality of the self and of another person.

The troubadours, who wandered from place to place telling stories and singing songs, spread the idea of love for an ideal, perfect woman — a love that was intense, but never satisfied by sexual intercourse. The love they sang about was the stuff of myths; it was above the brutality and cruelty of the world of that time; it symbolised a perfect union of emotions, with the lover and the loved one forever bound in ties of passionate love, but in a love that would never be satisfied; it transcended the physical because the loved one was always unattainable.

These ideas of love continued through the centuries, being reflected in songs, stories and plays, and later, as the mass of people began to read and write, in novels. Even so, it is only in the last two hundred years that the idea of 'falling in love' has gained the power it now enjoys.

Today, a flood of popular escapist entertainment has taken the concept of romantic love and made it seem essential to life — a relentless tide of books, magazines, pop songs, movies and television programs reinforce the idea that falling in love is the norm for an individual in society: it is something to be actively sought, something desirable, necessary and 'right'.

Why Do We Have to Analyse Romantic Love?

Whether we accept it or not, romantic love has an enormous influence upon most of us, an influence we do not really understand. Because of this, it has the power to cause great unhappiness and damage in our personal relationships.

The emotion of love is a very complex human experience, one which is different for every individual and therefore difficult to explain or describe to another person.

To add to the confusion, 'love' is used to describe a whole range of different feelings; 'I love chocolate icecream'; 'I love driving fast'; 'I love tennis'; 'I love him'; 'I'm in love with her'.

Relationships are affected by the lack of agreement between partners as to what 'love' means. Most people use the word loosely and this can be the cause of an enormous amount of dissatisfaction and unhappiness. Indeed, this absence of understanding is one of the greatest sources of marital conflict and divorce. If you haven't clarified exactly what you mean when you say 'love', then how can you understand what your partner means by the word?

What Can Be Said to Define 'Love'?

LOVE is used to describe a whole collection of mental and physical reactions, many of them arising from the unconscious mind.

There you are, looking across a crowded room, and suddenly, it's him/her!

You are excited, captivated, enthralled! Your breathing quickens, your heart pounds, perhaps you feel the unmistakable stirrings of sexual desire.

In a moment, you are convinced, 'This is it! I feel so good, this must be love!'

This is not a time of rational thought; it is a time of electrifying, engrossing emotion. But, unfortunately, it is the very time you need to examine what you feel, and why.

Not only do you need to know what being 'in love' and 'loving' some-one else actually means, you also need to know why romantic love is such a powerful force in our society, with the potential to cause both great happiness and deep despair.

WHY IS ROMANTIC LOVE SO POWERFUL?

Although we live in a technological age, when it is widely believed that science can achieve near miracles, we ourselves are still human beings and the unconscious, irrational side of us rules much — some say most — of our behaviour.

A person's mind can be compared to an iceberg: a small portion — the rational, logical, conscious mind — is above the surface, and can be looked at and examined. But below, hidden from view, is by far the largest portion of the mind — the unconscious.

Just as the *Titanic* came to disaster when she struck the concealed part of an iceberg, so we can suffer disaster when our hidden unconscious exerts control over the way we see the world, the way we act and the way we behave in our relationships with others. We are often quite unaware of the influence this powerful, mysterious unconscious has on our lives.

And it is the forces *behind* romantic love that coalesce to give it its extraordinary power.

What Are These Hidden Forces?

The need to pair:

'It's only natural ...'

The need to pair is an innate drive, an instinct so powerful that it appears in all living things. It ensures the survival of the species — in this case, humankind.

The need to bond:

'I want someone to be always there.'

The desire for companionship, closeness and intimacy with another person is a powerful force and drives us to attach ourselves to someone else and be close, both physically and emotionally. It can, however, drive people to make bad choices in marriage.

Emotionally, the need to bond has its basis is childhood. As children, we want, and need, to be close to our parents, both for protection and emotional growth. This need is so pronounced that any abandonment by a parent creates enormous anxiety in a child. Thus the fear of being solitary and isolated drives us to find someone to cancel out this fear of aloneness.

The need for intimacy:

'I want to be loved absolutely and completely for myself.'

Being close to someone else is not enough: we also need to be intimate with that person on all levels — to know and be known. To really 'know' another person on all levels, physical, intellectual and spiritual, leads not only to understanding of that person and the realisation of the uniqueness of the individual, but also to self-knowledge. To know someone else intimately is also to know yourself.

Our experience in counselling has shown us that the need to be really understood by someone else, preferably a marriage partner, is a keenly felt need. Sadly, few people achieve it. This book will show you how.

The need to be whole and complete:

'The right person will help me be complete and whole.'

Within us there is a natural and instinctive desire to integrate ourselves, to be whole and complete. Many people look for someone else to make them feel a whole person, not only in themselves, but in society. They want to be a two-person unit — to join their 'other half', to merge or unite so that together they form a whole.

Many religions and beliefs incorporate this idea of halves uniting to make a whole. Examples are the concepts of female and male energy, and the Chinese theory of the forces of yin and yang.

Be warned: as an underlying, usually unconscious reason for 'falling in love' it is a trap.

The expectation of being in love:

'It was like lightning! Suddenly, I was struck by love!'

We expect, at some time in our lives, to experience being 'in love'. Popular literature, songs and the mass media all bombard us with the message that love is important, that being in love is a state to be actively desired, that 'love makes the world go round'.

If we do not fall in love, we are likely to feel as if something is wrong, that somehow we have failed to live up to what society expects of us, that a whole dimension in our experience is missing ... so we go looking for it!

TAKE CARE: You can be fooled into marrying someone incompatible because you feel strongly 'in love' and this clouds your judgement.

The need to be in love:

'I must fall in love so I can prove that this is the right person for me.'

Generally speaking, our society has rejected the part that parents used to play in selecting partners for their children. Since there is no longer a rational approach to the business of selecting a wife or husband, the problem arises: How can I tell if this is the right person?

The answer our culture has found to this problem is to say that you can verify your selection by deciding if you are 'in love' with that person. If you are, then your choice is correct.

This solution immediately causes another problem: how can you tell that you are really 'in love'? What if it is just an infatuation? *Love is blind*!

The need to create illusions:

'This is the one who will make all the difference to my life.'

Because we are often committed to 'love' rather than to a real person, we idealise the object of our love. We look for our 'knight in shining armour' or our 'goddess on a pedestal'.

Imagination can be one of the most powerful forces in the world. We fall in love with our own ideas. We love the person we want to fall in love with. We project a fantasy on to an individual, ignoring the flaws, and see-ing, hearing and thinking only what we *want* to see, hear and think.

Here is an example from our counselling experience:

> Thomas has a warm relationship with Katherine. They seem suited to each other and they enjoy each other's company. Thomas, however, is not content. He has in his mind a sure image of the perfect woman for him. This is how he 'knows' that Katherine isn't 'right' — she isn't tall and she doesn't have long blonde hair.
>
> Thomas has decided to terminate his relationship with Katherine because he is sure that particular tall blonde woman is out there, somewhere, waiting for him.

In Thomas's case, the power of his imagination is such that he is willing to abandon a rewarding relationship to pursue his idea of romantic love. Eventually Thomas will find a tall, long-haired blonde woman and he will project on to her what he believes a tall blonde should be. Then, having created the right person, he will proceed to 'fall in love' with her, even though the qualities he has given her to make her a perfect partner for him are illusions. But illusions don't last ... the real person does.

TAKE CARE: Don't create an imaginary 'perfect' person and then try to find someone to fit the image ... you'll almost certainly be heading for dis-aster.

The need for self-esteem:

'I must be worthwhile, since a perfect person loves me!'

There is nothing so wonderful for our self-esteem as romantic love. When you have someone who loves you completely it is difficult not to have your self-esteem inflated. This person paying such flattering atten-tion to you boosts your confidence as you see yourself reflected in his or her adoring eyes.

TAKE CARE: Romantic love leads to a pseudo self-esteem, because it is based on the uncritical opinion of another person. Also, when romantic love fades, as it will, your self-esteem might well deflate.

The attraction of elusivity:

'I can't stop thinking about you — I wish you were mine.'

It is well understood by writers of romantic fiction that one factor that heightens tension and desire in relationships is elusivity. If the loved one is elusive (that is, hard or impossible to possess, or is at a geographical distance) then the longing for that person will be enhanced. The lover's imagination is devoted to delicious pictures of what it would be like to spend every waking — and sleeping — moment with the beloved person. Of course, this time is idealised, so romantic love will be given a severe jolt once reality impinges.

This means that in many cases, when elusivity vanishes, romantic love begins to fade — often very rapidly.

Addiction:

'I just can't get enough of you ...'

Under the power of romantic love, some people show all the indications of addiction and take this as a sure sign: 'I really *must* be in love! I cannot live without him/her!'

Such people show the following symptoms:

- they have an intense craving for the other person, a feeling so intense that withdrawal can make them absolutely desperate
- they get a 'high' out of being in love — it excites, delights and lifts them out of the ordinary world into a different one which is somehow more beautiful and welcoming
- they become dependent on the person for their happiness and inner peace

Some people become so addicted to the experience that they will go from relationship to relationship, in each case moving on once romantic love has waned.

Sexual desire:

'My heart flutters and my stomach churns and I feel keen desire ... so this must be love!'

Many people underestimate the sheer power of biological drives, because, in some way, acknowledging such a strong 'primitive' impulse for sex is unacceptable. Sexual drive causes many people to misinterpret their experiences, so that they think they are in love, even though the object of their desire may be quite incompatible. The problem is that many of us find it difficult to admit that it is sexual desire that is the driving force behind the need to couple, so it is romanticised into being love.

Moreover, if the sexual drive remains unsatisfied, the tension is heightened and the feelings are interpreted as being not just 'in love', but 'hopelessly in love.'

TAKE CARE: It is distressingly easy to mistake sexual passion for genuine love.

In our modern age, pre-marital sex is much more common and this waters down, over time, the passion lovers have for one another because sexual tensions are relieved. Also, elusiveness is gone.

Even so, the myth of romantic love (passion) as a reason for marriage still influences many people, and as they experience it slipping away, they decide to end their relationship because they believe they no longer 'love' one another.

TAKE CARE: Marriages should not be based on passion, but on two people knowing each other. Romantic love is not a necessary experience for the formation of a good marriage.

The Advantages of Romantic Love

- historically, romantic love changed the way people looked at relationships, bringing into a harsh and crude world ideas of personal worth, spirituality, and awareness of the importance of the feminine side of an individual's nature
- romantic love's elevation of women from a very low place in the scheme of things provided the foundations for the concept of equality between men and women
- romantic love leads us to value and appreciate someone else, rather than just exploiting them to gratify our own needs and desires
- romantic love provides wonderful feelings of significance, of joy, of delight in living
- romantic love can be the basis of a deeper and ultimately more satisfying love
- romantic love is *fun*!

The Disadvantages of Romantic Love:

- much of romantic love is based on illusions, so reality can destroy it
- when romantic love fails, we suffer the deepest disappointment: 'Love let me down!'
- romantic love can lead us to choose partners who are not necessarily suitable or compatible

We have heard countless clients, deceived by their feelings, say: 'I thought I was in love', or 'Perhaps I wasn't *really* in love'.

TAKE CARE: If you are contemplating marriage, be sure you are *both* marrying for the *right reasons*.

And even if you decide you married for the wrong reasons, or that you were deceived by the 'in love' mythology, there is no need to suppose you cannot now build a good marriage that has lasting love.

In the following steps we will be showing you how a strong marriage can be built from the start, or out of a crumbling one, as new and strong foundations are laid to support your relationship.

Summary

In Step Two we have looked at Romantic Love:

- the origins of the concept of Romantic Love
- why it is vital to understand the mythology of Romantic Love
- the powerful forces that drive Romantic Love
- Romantic Love's advantages and disadvantages

Step Three

What can I do about myself to be happy in marriage?

THE IMPORTANCE OF A WELL-DEVELOPED SELF

When most people set out to find a marriage partner, they usually focus on the qualities they want in the person they would like to marry. They seldom say to themselves: 'Have I developed my *self* enough to create a rewarding relationship?'

By the word 'self', we mean the whole and special person, the unique individual that is *you*. Your core. The self is that sense of I-ness, quite distinct from all other people. It allows you to say: 'I know that I am.'

The quality of a relationship depends upon the quality of those involved in it. For people to have well-developed relationships, they must be well-developed themselves. A mature marriage cannot be enjoyed by immature people, nor can unhappy people create a happy relationship.

Towards the end of this step, we are going to introduce you to four styles or types of marriage. The first three of these do not require you to develop a strong sense of your *self* — you do not need to know much of the real you.

The last style, which we call the H-type marriage, requires considerable personal development, awareness and skill to build. You will need to have a knowledge of the real you. In fact, the rest of this book is aimed at helping you to develop more of the *real* self and the H-type marriage.

Successful relationships need a successful you — a you who is a well developed self. We can only be as good in a relationship as we are in ourselves. For example, Richard is unhappy with himself. He enters into a relationship with Louise, who is a relatively happy and secure person. Richard, almost automatically, begins to make the relationship an unhappy one because the negative feelings he has deep within himself leak out into his partnership with Louise and poison it. At some level, Richard is hoping that by going into a relationship with someone like Louise, who possesses what he *doesn't,* namely security and happiness, somehow those things will become his too. Louise is supposed to transform Richard's world, make him complete, whole and content. Of course, this is an impossible task, since Richard's problem is *Richard.* The success of his relationship with Louise rests not on one of them, but on both of them, as individuals.

Many people (perhaps most) marry or form permanent relationships when they still have a lot of growing, learning and maturing to do. Marriage thus can provide an exciting opportunity: the challenge of developing each person's true and unique self.

TAKE CARE: A person with a poor sense of self often attempts to change the *other* person. Rarely does it occur to most people that *each person* needs to develop his/her true and genuine self.

In our experience of counselling we have found that marriage difficulties are related to the difficulties both partners are experiencing as individuals. To put it another way: two broken people cannot create a whole relationship. Nor can one broken person and one whole person create a whole relationship. However, two whole people can make a whole relationship. And, more importantly, two people acknowledging their need to develop can grow together, and learn to really relate.

You, as an individual, cannot make your partner whole. What you can do is become more aware of your true self. You can develop the real, solid, basic and genuine person that you are. This is what it means to 'grow'. Then you bring to the relationship a knowledge and understanding about yourself that is of the greatest value in building a lasting and satisfying partnership.

This can be done, before and after marriage, when two people realise they still have growing to do and that it is a great advantage to grow in tandem.

It is true to say that *all* people can continue to grow all their lives. There is never a point when we can say, 'Now, at last, I'm there! I'm fully grown!'

WHAT MAKES US THE WAY WE ARE NOW?

If the self is to be developed in order to enjoy a good marriage, then first we have to see how we became the way we are now. What made each of us ourselves and no one else? What determined the way we behave, what we say and what we think, how we react and how we feel?

There are three components operating together:

1. Our own unique nature:

We are all so different in so many ways — how we look, how we think, how we move and stand, how we respond to life. In each person there is a special and separate self, but along the way this self is often programmed to conform to the expectations, needs and approval of other people. And in this process of adapting, we can lose our awareness of who we really are — our unique self.

2. The models and programming from our family of origin and from society:

As we grow up we absorb lessons in behaviour and ways of dealing with situations. We may come from a family where open conflict was always avoided, so that tension and anger were papered over. Conversely, our family may have encouraged the open expression of conflict to the point where physical violence or even the extremes of child abuse could occur. In the same way, we might come from a family where problems were openly discussed — or driven underground; where we were warmly encouraged, or coldly discouraged; where we were rewarded for truthfulness, or taught to lie.

Every one of us has absorbed countless messages (both spoken and unspoken) throughout our childhoods, messages about how to behave, what opinions to hold, what to think (or not to think), what attitudes to have towards sex, love, relationships. In short, we have been given years of lessons during the most formative period of our existence and these examples and models of behaviour can now literally rule our lives.

3. Our individual strategy for coping:

We all have a survival program we have developed for ourselves. This survival program is based on decisions we have made about how to cope with the people around us. It is designed to deal with the anxieties we experience in our life situation and, although created when we are very young, persists throughout life. We carry this program into marriage, work, social occasions — everywhere.

Why do we do this? Our aim is to reduce the threat of living, to protect ourselves from the fears and anxieties that otherwise might overwhelm us.

However, for many people, a problem arises in adulthood in that the program developed to *reduce threat in a child* is now no longer appropriate: it no longer works. In fact, every one of the thousands of people we have counselled for relationship difficulties reflects the incompatibility of his/her programming to the present life situations.

A clear example of how the strategies that work to reduce anxiety during childhood no longer work in adulthood is provided by the 'I don't belong' program.

The feeling of 'not belonging' or being 'outside' the family can arise for many reasons. For example, the person might have felt that he or she was shorter than the rest of the family, looked different, was adopted, had been 'pushed out' by the birth of a new baby — there are dozens of reasons for this feeling of not belonging to occur.

Sometimes the feeling of not belonging can come from outside the family ... Elise felt apart and different from the children in her neighbourhood. This sense of alienation was carried over into her school life, where she isolated herself from the other students. Later, in her adult life, she continued the pattern, failing to form friendships.

Programs for coping can be developed by the child as a response to family experiences, school experiences (where the influence of both teachers and the peer group can be considerable), as well as many other experiences in growing.

These strategies for dealing with situations are developed in childhood when the person has limited understanding of what is actually going on and limited knowledge of the options and alternatives that are available.

Typically, the person does not talk over the problem with anyone, but keeps the thoughts locked away. Strategies developed to cope include withdrawing or distancing ('I won't be hurt if I don't get too close') or daydreaming/fantasising about the future when the family can be left behind and somewhere can be found where he/she can truly 'belong'.

What happens in adulthood? The person is locked into the program. 'I don't belong here either' becomes a self-fulfilling prophecy as the person continues to follow the program that helped reduce anxieties in childhood.

A person such as Elise will always believe, at some deep level, that she 'doesn't belong' and in her marriage will be driven by the anxiety that goes with this belief to behave in many destructive ways. She may, for example, be looking for constant reassurance that she *does* belong — she may 'cling' to her husband, or alternatively, distance herself from him and be a cold aloof wife. Either way, the marriage will suffer as Elise lives out her self-fulfilling prophecy, so that eventually she will be able to say: 'I knew it all along ... I don't belong.'

What steps could Elise take? If she was to 'rewrite' her program and see life in a different way, then she could overcome her deep feelings of not belonging. She may need professional help to accomplish this.

ROOTS: YOUR FAMILY OF ORIGIN

An important influence on our thinking has been the work of the American psychiatrist Murray Bowen, who spent over thirty years investigating the influence of the family on the emotional system of the individual.

While you might not be aware of it at any conscious level, your emotional self is greatly influenced by the generations of your family that have gone before you.

This influence particularly affects how we react to stress and anxiety-producing situations, and a search into the past often brings great help to people wanting to develop themselves or to those in marital difficulties.

SPECIAL NOTE: For those people who are adopted, and thus have not been raised in their natural family of origin, it is the *adopted* family that programs your emotional triggers. Although inherited characteristics do play a part in personality development, for the purpose of working on yourself and your marriage, focus on your adoptive family of origin — the family in which you were brought up.

You cannot escape your roots. They are the source of powerful forces which determine how you deal with life. For most of us, families are the single, most powerful influence on our development into a SELF — a person.

Families are not only complex, they are different from each other, so your family experience is unique. However, there are two things that all families have in common: forces that push for togetherness and opposing forces which lead to individuality — your own sense of unique self. We will now look at these forces.

Let's Be One Big Happy Family!

When two people marry, and especially when a family is produced, there is almost always a 'togetherness' drive, so that members of the family try to think and feel the same, have common values and interests, and want the same things.

These 'similarity' forces try to break down the differences between the two adult people and also any perceived differences between family members. The family makes decisions, not the individual. Everything is for the good of the family, not any individual member.

What's more, emotions tend to 'glue' families together, and with emotional involvement comes the 'sticking together' in the face of outside threat or opposition. The very first emotional 'glue' we experience is almost always our bonding with our mothers, and this becomes a powerful force in our development. Our response to our fathers is usually less intense because, at least in the early stages, dependency upon males seems less important. This is aided by the fact that in our society a father's role is generally more detached and remote during early childhood.

Hold On — But I Want To Be Me!

Because the family is driven by forces that seek to undermine individuality, the urge to be different is often seen by the family as an attack on unity.

The drive for individuality is often resisted both in marriage and in families. It is seen as a threat and therefore it causes anxiety. It is as though the family is saying:

'If you want to be different, to be an individual, then you are deliberately saying you're separate, apart, distant ... you're going away from the family, you're cutting off emotionally ... and we've got to stop you doing this to us.'

It is very important to recognise that in the context of marriage and the family, the drive of a person to become a separate self is often an anxiety raiser. And when anxiety is raised the forces of the family go into action in an attempt to force conformity.

However, developing a strong sense of yourself, as distinct from others, is essential when others attempt to make you think, feel and be like them.

Your family experiences are unique to you, because your upbringing is, in subtle as well as obvious ways, different from other people's. Sometimes you will find yourself over-reacting in a stress situation; for some reason that you haven't identified, a 'trigger' is pulled and you react in a programmed way. The reaction may be aggression, or refusing to speak, or withdrawing to sulk — any one of a hundred ways of behaving.

Without realising it, you are playing out a pattern of emotional reacting which developed due to the way the members of your family of origin related to each other. Perhaps you had an extremely critical father who was impossible to please, so that when you sense criticism, you lash out. Or possibly you had a father and mother who never talked, so you become anxious and uncomfortable when you think people aren't communicating with you.

Ask yourself: 'What triggers an emotional response in me?' Different families have different triggers. Stand back and watch yourself react, all the time remembering that your family experiences have programmed you to react in situations of stress or anxiety in certain ways.

Here is an example of childhood programming carrying over into adult life:

> Bridget's childhood was filled with anxiety and fear caused by the constant violent conflict between her parents. Her father regularly came home drunk and when challenged by Bridget's mother, would maintain he hadn't had anything to drink at all. A fierce argument would almost inevitably follow, often ending in violence. Bridget

endured this for fifteen years until her father eventually became seriously ill from his drinking, joined Alcoholics Anonymous and became a reformed alcoholic.

Now, years later in Bridget's married life, the experiences of her childhood are still influencing her — she has a programmed response. If Bridget's husband is delayed at the office she is filled with anxiety — is he drinking? If he comes home with the slightest hint of alcohol on his breath rage sweeps through her ... 'He'll be just like my father!'

Bridget's emotional over-reaction is caused by fear that the situation that distressed her so much as a child is going to be repeated. She acts as if it's going to happen all over again, even though logic should show her that her husband is not her father, and there's no reason to suppose he is potentially an alcoholic.

Because emotional reactions are 'triggered' by past experiences and feelings, people are usually not conscious of why they react the way they do. It is likely that Bridget, for example, does not connect her present behaviour with her past history.

YOUR INDIVIDUALISED PROGRAMME FOR SURVIVAL OR COPING

Accompanying the efforts of the family to program you in a particular way, there are also your own individual decisions and coping strategies which enable you to handle the basic anxieties of living.

Even as a very small child, each person develops personal strategies for survival, and these include working out how to function in the least anxiety-producing manner. These survival programs are your answer to the problem of being small and helpless in a large and frightening world. Let's look first at our basic, instinctual fears, remembering that anxiety is essentially a low level of raw fear.

The Role of Our Instinctual Fears

There are two basic fears common to all people:

1. *Fear of abandonment.* This originated in us when we were babies, when to be totally abandoned would have meant death. As adults, this is more commonly experienced as *fear of rejection.*

2. *Fear of not being valued/accepted.* Our self-esteem, the way we value ourselves, begins to develop in babyhood, when we get the sense of being valued, or not valued, by our primary care-givers. To not be valued by others is to not value ourselves, and there is within us all a basic anxiety underlying that. We need and seek to be

valued/accepted by others — and feel anxious if we sense an absence of our acceptance by others.

All of us, as children, developed ways — behaviours — to alleviate these two instinctual anxieties.

Dealing with Fear of Rejection

When some people feel threatened — when they find themselves thinking: 'He/she is not loving (or liking) me ...' or 'He/she is disagreeing with me ...' or 'He/she wants to leave me ...' — they instinctively want to get closer, be held, be reassured, so as to reduce the anxiety these thoughts produce. This type of person seeks 'enmeshment' (being 'as one' with another). As a child, such a person would probably have sought mother's apron strings, or tried in many other ways to be close, possibly using tears to gain comfort from another.

Some people have the opposite reaction to this fear of rejection: they alleviate their anxiety by distancing themselves. They might play 'no speaks', lock themselves in a room, go out, or even leave the relationship altogether. As a child such a person would probably have gone out to play, keeping distant from the individual perceived as rejecting him/her, or, in the social setting, moved on from the 'rejecting' friend.

Some people will actually go to the extreme of leaving their families and cutting off all ties with them in order to feel safe from this harrowing *fear of rejection*. It is very likely, however, that they are not consciously aware of *why* they take this course of action.

Dealing with Lack of/Loss of Acceptance

There are two ways people try to help themselves feel accepted and valued. The first is by being strong, independent and responsible: 'I don't really need anyone ...', 'I do it best ...', and 'My way is best ...' The second is by being weak, dependent, irresponsible: 'I need others to take care of me and then I feel valued ...'

The 'be strong' way of gaining approval can be seen in the child who helps Mother and Father, assists in the family, becomes a leader at school or in clubs, and is fiercely independent: 'I can do it myself!'

The 'be weak' can be seen in the child who decides it feels good to be helped, to be dependent — even to be irresponsible — because then other people have to come to the rescue. This makes the child feel accepted, valued and loved.

These strategies for dealing with fear of rejection or lack of acceptance are *ways of reducing anxiety*.

Develop an awareness about your self by asking: What do I do? How do I reduce my anxieties?

Everyone uses these strategies to some extent, as they are instinctual, but be warned — *in the extreme they are potential dynamite to a relationship and to personal growth.*

Why? Because these strategies obstruct the development of your REAL SELF; instead, a PSEUDO SELF grows.

This pseudo or pretend self is the self created by an individual in order to feel secure and to reduce anxiety about being alone, about abandonment, and about not being loved.

THE PSEUDO SELF

The child learns very early in life to do everything possible to feel secure. The actions and attitudes taken are, of course, influenced by the child's personality and family experiences. The pseudo self then starts to thrive as self-protective strategies are learnt. Some childhood decisions are:

- I will push away the hurtful world and distance myself from those who can hurt me. That way, I don't risk rejection. (be distant)
- I like to be with my family — then I feel safe (be close)
- I will be very responsible so that I will clearly demonstrate to everyone that I am a person worth loving. Because I am so obviously an effective and good person, people will have to accept and love me.

This strategy is very often adopted by the eldest child in a family. The person is operating on this hidden agenda: 'I need to be needed ... then I feel loved.' (be strong)

- I will totally conform to everything my parents wish. I don't want to be 'me', I want to be the person they want me to be, and then they must love and accept me. (be weak)

Because the behaviours adopted are meant to make the person feel more secure or less anxious, they become part of the pseudo 'pretend' self. Unfortunately, the survival techniques we learn to rely on create a programmed response which effectively disguises the real self underneath.

The Characteristics of the Pseudo Self

This mask that we present to the world has been given many names, including the conforming self, the phoney self, the pretend self, the false self, the socially agreeable self, the persona.

Here are some behaviours of the pseudo self (note that *any* of these can be indications of operating out of the pseudo self):

- the pseudo self agrees with others in order to be liked and to reduce anxiety about disapproval
- the pseudo self thinks: 'What will other people think?'

- the pseudo self is non-assertive in all or some situations (see Step Four)
- the pseudo self is insecure about personal thoughts, feelings, wants and needs
- the pseudo self looks for love to bolster his/her ego
- the pseudo self looks to other people for what to think
- the pseudo self is indecisive, due to the fear of making decisions other people may not like
- the pseudo self takes compliments poorly: 'I'm not really worthy of that compliment'
- the pseudo self avoids conflict whenever possible
- the pseudo self can also react to others in an aggressive way, appearing to be confident, with a facade of toughness — however, underneath, the person is very anxious, or even frightened.
- the pseudo self is dependent on others and does not often enjoy his/her own company. Jealousy is often a problem
- the pseudo self can be very critical ('Critical Parent') and also extremely anxious to get along with other people ('Adapted Child'). Note: these two 'ego states' (Critical Parent and Adapted Child) are covered in detail in Step 8.

When people operate out of the pseudo self there might seem to be some very positive aspects to these behaviours. They enable survival in a world that seems very big and overwhelming to a child (and to many 'adults' as well!). They act as a 'social lubricant' to make it easier to get on with other people and they provide a basis for social and community life: patterns of acceptable behaviour to make life 'work'. Civilisation is based on this!

However, when people live out of the pseudo self they pay a huge price — the price is that they do not know who they really are. They do not know the REAL SELF. They do not grow.

Those of us who have a clear recognition of our real selves are quite aware of using some aspects of pseudo self in our dealings with other people. However, those of us who do not have this clear distinction can falsely believe that the pseudo self *is* the real self.

It is very important to realise that personal growth involves shedding pseudo self behaviours, attitudes and values, and developing your own true, real self. This is the key to marital happiness.

THE REAL SELF

The real self can also be called the solid self, the basic self, the genuine self and the unique self. Whatever, the goal of the real and unique self is individuality.

The Characteristics of the Real Self

- the real self is satisfied with self-approval
- the real self is in charge of his/her own thoughts, and knows the difference between thoughts and feelings
- the real self has confidence in his/her own convictions and beliefs
- the real self refuses to compromise basic values just to be accepted by others
- the real self does not say: 'What will other people think?' but rather, 'What do I think?'
- the real self agrees with others when appropriate, but *not* to gain approval
- the real self accepts that conflict in a relationship is inevitable and deals with it constructively
- the real self is able to freely give compliments to others without expecting a payoff and also can accept compliments in return.
- the real self is decisive and able to live with the decisions made
- the real self has integrity and so is honest and true with innermost values
- the real self is confident and assertive (see Step Four).

Developing the Real Self

In you there is a natural self — the real unique self you were meant to be. The key is to learn *who you really are* and not to be content with *who you were trained to be*. But before you launch into a journey of self-discovery, consider the following.

It can take some time to diminish your reliance on pseudo self and so increase real self, and you will always need some of your pseudo self to conform to the expectations and rules of civilised society. For example, being sociable at a dinner party when you would much rather be asleep!

In a relationship, your partner's development of real self may not keep pace with yours. Also, as you discover your individuality, you may find that conflict in your life is increasing. You should look upon this as a part of change and growth.

The following fourteen steps to develop your real self might seem daunting at first, but they form the path to an exciting exploration of your true self, a lifelong journey that will enhance your appreciation of your unique individuality.

1. Assess the influence upon you of your family of origin (see Step Seven). Work on establishing positive and mature relationships with as many members of your family as possible. Unfinished business (past hurts, resentments and other emotional wounds) needs to be dealt with by talking things out with, or writing a letter to, those fam-

ily members involved in these issues. Sometimes professional help needs to be sought.

2. Develop self-awareness (in Step Four you will learn how to do this).

3. Develop self-acceptance (of yourself, as you *are* and *can be*).

4. Develop your self-esteem (the skills you learn from this book will help you do this).

5. Develop self-integrity (be honest with yourself about yourself; be honest with others).

6. Concentrate upon self-development: communication skills, career path, hobbies, sport etc.

7. Develop self-understanding: ask for constructive feedback; assess yourself objectively; enlarge your knowledge of human nature.

8. Develop self-reliance: don't rely on others to take care of you — be prepared to stand on your own two feet.

9. Develop assertiveness skills (see Step Four).

10. Develop self-altruism: do something for someone else without any thought of gratitude or personal reward.

11. Deal with self-deception: be brutally frank with yourself.

12. Deal with self-programming: try to determine the programs you have learned to use to deal with the world.

13. Deal with unfinished business: the issues of the past that can haunt you — grief, sadness, feelings of rejection, unresolved anger — all the inner conflicts that still have the power to hurt. Some people need professional expertise to help uncover this unfinished business and work through it. Unfinished business can exist in countless ways and manifest itself in countless ways — generally, however, it is indicated by life dissatisfaction, turmoil or inner disquiet.

14. Develop the spiritual side of your nature: that part of us that is concerned with the meaning and significance of life.

Carl Jung, the famous psychiatrist/philosopher, said: 'The self is our life's goal for it is the completest expression of that fateful combination we call individuality.'

THE FOUR TYPES OF MARRIAGE AND WHY DEVELOPING YOUR REAL SELF IS VITAL FOR MARITAL HAPPINESS

There is a tendency for people to marry others who have the same amount of 'self' development and self-esteem. This is a delightful tendency if the two people in a relationship have fully realised genuine/real selves; it is a potentially serious problem if they do not.

There are four possible types of marriages, based on the level of 'self' development. When speaking about people or marriage we are forced to generalise because it is difficult to make statements without using stereotypes.

When we place marriages in types, we are describing the predominant behaviour patterns and characteristics of a particular type of relationship. There are no 'pure' types, but it is possible to look at nearly all marriages and say what the general characteristics are.

This does not take into account that there are hidden aspects in a partnership — that the person, for example, who appears to be submissive (as in a lean-to marriage) might well have dominance in areas unseen by an observer.

Frequently, however, we have people say to us: 'I am in a typical A-type (or other) marriage.' It seems people tend to recognise the predominant characteristics of their interactions within a relationship.

1. The 'A-frame' marriage:

In this marriage (see Figure 3.1), both partners have their pseudo selves dominant, and they bring to marriage the same dependencies, the same desperate desires for love and approval, and the same unrealistic reactions to criticism or praise. Although they may not be aware of it, they look to the other person to provide them with relief from anxiety and insecurity. They often over-react emotionally in conflict situations or under stress.

The A-frame marriage is characterised by:

- dependency of each partner on the other
- partners do not self-disclose: they do not let the other delve deeply. For example, there may be anger, but no search to discover what lies *behind* the anger
- the relationship can have much conflict because there is a desire to have the other person fulfil deep (and unmet) needs. Coercion and manipulation are common

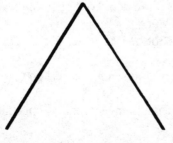
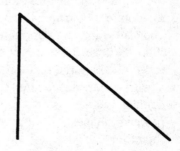

Figure 3.1   Figure 3.2

- anxiety levels are high when one partner distances himself/herself from the other
- when romantic love begins to wane, pressure is often put on the other partner to fill in the emptiness
- open conflict levels are often emotionally powerful
- there is usually little self-awareness beyond the obvious — partners operate at a level of emotional reactivity
- a struggle for power is common, usually with strong emotional pressure
- A-frame people often want to do most things together with the other partner, and feel unloved if the partner wants to do some things alone

2. The 'lean-to' marriage:

After marriage, when couples vie for control of the relationship, a 'lean-to' partnership may develop (see Figure 3.2). One partner seems more in control and dominant; the other becomes compliant. The 'leaning' partner is persuaded that conflict will be avoided by agreement: 'Anything for peace', 'I'll do whatever you say ...'

What happens? The dominant partner feels stronger, more in control: the 'leaning' partner is de-selfed and becomes a nonentity, a non-self who may burn with unspoken dissatisfaction at the arrangement.

The dominant partner, however, is really deceiving himself/herself by depending on pseudo self. His/her real self has very little opportunity to grow and develop as there is no adequate challenge to mature.

The lean-to marriage is characterised by:

- one person is more dominant and in overt control of the partnership
- one person submits to the other to avoid conflict
- the overtly dominant partner is given no challenge to encourage development of self. The overtly submissive partner gives up development of the real self
- the submissive partner gathers resentments
- the submissive partner often bursts out with actions unsuspected by the dominant partner. Resentment is often acted out by finding someone else who will understand and accept
- there is little opportunity for new options to grow out of conflict experienced in the relationship
- a lean-to marriage is often the preferred answer to a person who is a conflict-avoider
- power struggles are suppressed by the submission of one partner to the other

3. The 'parallel-type' marriage:

In this marriage (see Figure 3.3), the two people have little or no communication from the real self. This means that they distance themselves from each other, leading, in many respects, entirely separate lives. Their relationship is often stale and they have very little emotional contact.

This kind of marriage allows two people to operate out of the pseudo self and they usually know little about the other's real self.

The parallel marriage is characterised by:

- each person is quite self-contained and dependency levels are low. Partners can often live in quite separate worlds.
- some people find this arrangement satisfying enough, since there is little conflict or emotional pressure (and not much depth!)
- in many such marriages there may be times of feeling close and friendly, but in some cases there is a need of much space and time apart
- partners are often good companions, but depth of self-awareness and self-disclosure of the real self is minimal
- each person often lives a great deal out of pseudo self
- this type of marriage often develops when both partners are conflict-avoiders
- level of physical intimacy is low. Frequency of sex is low — sometimes non-existent
- each partner is often able to pursue a career, interests, hobbies, friendships etc. without the other's involvement
- whilst the parallel-type relationship is peaceful most of the time, it is also subject to marital boredom or staleness
- this arrangement is vulnerable to one or both partners seeking emotional/physical satisfaction elsewhere
- a power struggle is usually denied or quietly avoided, being replaced by an unspoken agreement not to fight

Figure 3.3   Figure 3.4

The three kinds of marriage described above are all based on heavy pseudo self behaviour. Intimacy levels are low because partners are not sharing their real selves. The goal of these three types of marriage is security at the expense of individuality and intimacy.

4. The 'H-marriage':

The H-marriage (see Figure 3.4) is the growing ideal in Western society. *In this marriage each person has the opportunity to be his or her real self.* It is, in practice, a real *partnership* where each person is free to develop both as a person, and as an equal half of a relationship. Structurally the H relationship is stronger than any other, and it is made to weather the storms of life.

The H-type marriage is characterised by:

- both people are able to be independent, confident, and have high self-esteem
- both partners are in pursuit of self-understanding, self-development and the discovery of the real self
- both seek to develop a mature love marriage (as outlined in Steps Nine and Ten)
- both are involved in the three Rs of marriage: Responsibility, Real Self and Romance (these are discussed in detail during the course of this book)
- both want to know each other's deeper thoughts and feelings
- both self-disclose from their awareness wheel (see Step Four)
- conflict exists, but skills are sought to deal honestly and assertively with the differences
- sexual intimacy is often rich and varied with time devoted to this area
- emotional depth is present and desired
- time is made to be together
- both are interested in the development of their full potential in all areas
- the partnership is marked by equality and high respect for each other

The H framework in a relationship allows partners to give and receive love in an atmosphere of mutual trust. Intimacy levels are high ... mature love develops to a deep level, and a lasting and joyful marriage results. *but it is absolutely essential that you develop your real self to achieve this goal.*

WHY DO SO FEW OF US DEVELOP THE H-TYPE MARRIAGE?

Since the H-type of marriage obviously offers the most rewarding kind of relationship, why doesn't everyone choose to go that route? After all, we don't want to be unhappy. We don't want to have such limited marriages as offered by the first three types. Nearly all of our students choose the H-type when faced with the options.

Nevertheless, most people are predominantly in an A-frame, a lean-to or a parallel-type marriage. To understand this self-limiting behaviour, we have to look again at what happens to us in the developing years of childhood and adolescence. The answer goes way back to our family of origin, our roots, and our own strategies for coping with life's anxieties. Also involved are self-defence mechanisms.

Family of Origin and Survival Strategies

All marriages involve three parts:

1. The husband and his unique nature, his family of origin experiences and his survival strategies to alleviate anxiety.
2. The wife and her unique nature, her family of origin experiences and her survival strategies to alleviate anxiety.
3. The 'system' created when these two interact.

These three conspire together to limit the development of an H-type marriage. Maria and Joshua illustrate how the limitations function.

They came to us for counselling after seven years of marriage, their relationship at the point of self-destruction.

Joshua's point of view The problem is Maria's bossiness, loss of interest in sex and total pre-occupation with the children.

Maria's point of view The problem is Joshua's absence most of the weekend playing sport, his abusive behaviour towards the children and his drinking.

When we looked at their roots (family of origin) and individualised programs for coping, we discovered the following:

Maria's program I'll be the best mother in the world. I'll run a perfect house. I'll be responsible, competent and independent.

Joshua's program As the man I'll be head of the house. A man needs his mates and his sport. Children need to be put in their place because 'father knows best'. I need to know I'm really appreciated.

It's easy to see how these programs are barriers to marital bliss! As Maria and Joshua live out their individual programs — their survival strategies to reduce anxiety — their relationship is disrupted and all but destroyed.

What solution can be found? Both Maria and Joshua need to rethink and re-program their ways of *being* in their relationship if it is to succeed.

And should they fail to re-program? If Maria and Joshua split up and look elsewhere for the 'ideal' partner, they will each take their programs along with them as baggage for the next relationship ... and the problems will emerge again.

Another example is given by Michael and Kate. They came to us because of his extreme jealousy. When we looked at their roots and individualised programs for coping, we discovered the following:

Michael's program: I feel inadequate as a man. I am an inadequate sexual person. I cannot trust people's sexual desires. I must control my wife to be sure she does not cheat on me.

Kate's program: The most important thing in life is honesty, integrity and truthfulness.

So what happens? Michael is endlessly suspicious. He begins to distrust Kate. He is absolutely *sure* she must be sexually attracted to another man, and worse, that she is looking for an opportunity to do something about it. He tries to control her movements so as to deny her the chance to be unfaithful to him.

How does Kate react? She has the highest moral integrity, so to be distrusted, without any evidence at all, creates powerful feelings of resentment and anger. Usually a calm, effective person, she becomes distraught and deliberately distances herself emotionally from the source of her discomfort, Michael.

What effect does this have on Michael? His suspicions are confirmed. Kate *must* be contemplating an affair with another man.

A snowball effect occurs: Michael is more suspicious, Kate is more distant — this makes Michael absolutely sure he's right and his certainty drives Kate to push him even further away.

Such problems as these are shared by many people. Neither Maria and Joshua, nor Kate and Michael, were aware of their individual programming, nor of what was going on in his/her real self.

Self-Defence Mechanisms: What Stops Us Knowing Our Real Selves

Since awareness of real self is the key to growth and an H-type marriage, what is stopping us from exploring this genuine inner core? What prevents us from finding our true selves? The answer is that we use what are known as 'self-defence mechanisms' — ways of defending our inner selves against anxiety and tension. These protective mechanisms are used particularly as a way of preventing change, since many of us feel quite overwhelmed and threatened by the unfamiliar. They are also used to protect against possible rejection, abandonment or loss of self-esteem, as already described.

We are not really aware when we are using a self-defence mechanism, because they operate from our unconscious mind to help us see our world the way we want to see it.

Here are some of the defence mechanisms most commonly used:

Rationalising:

The person manufactures an excuse or reason for a loss or failure. It is not the true reason, but it is a convincing one.

Many people in marriage, for example, say, 'I don't need to change ... I'm quite all right as I am' or 'If we can't help ourselves then what's the point of going to a Marriage Counsellor?' By such rationalising, these people avoid the threat of change or of having to look clearly at themselves.

Repressing:

The person pushes painful or threatening memories, thoughts or emotions out of his/her mind. This is more than just refusing to think about something — the person blanks them out and forgets they ever existed. For example, a person who endured an incident of sexual abuse as a child may literally not remember anything about it ... the memory has been totally repressed (although it continues to exist, of course, in the unconscious mind).

Denying:

Using the defence mechanism of repressing, the person 'forgets' about something: when denying, the person does not see it as it is. Some situation or incident is just too disturbing and painful to accept, so the person says, 'It isn't so.' What is happening is that the person is changing his/her perception of reality because to accept it would be too much to bear.

Isobel came to counselling broken-hearted because her husband had left her. 'It was such a good marriage,' she said. Further disclosure revealed that she and her husband had not shared the same bedroom for fifteen years, they had not gone out together, did not talk and for the past eight months he had not even lived in the same house.

Isobel was definitely practising denial!

Displacing:

The person copes with his/her feelings of anxiety or anger by directing them elsewhere. For example, a shy, non-assertive man whose boss has yelled at him may bottle up the anger and resentment he feels until he gets home. There he gets rid of his hostility and anger by screaming at one of his children.

He does not realise that the *real* source of his anger is his boss (and perhaps his inability to deal with the situation at work).

Sublimating:

The energy of impulses that the person finds disturbing, threatening or frightening is directed into something else, so that, for example, extreme aggression or sexual drives are channelled into a challenging sport or into creative endeavours such as music or painting. Such energy might also be sublimated into say, a challenging program of study, or working long hours at the office in order to reach the top of the corporate ladder.

Regressing:

The person is overwhelmed by stressful feelings and so goes back to behaviour that was used in childhood to help cope with deep anxieties. This may involve behaviour from very early childhood, such as thumb-sucking, hiding or temper tantrums.

When Elizabeth had her first baby she used to cry and beg her husband not to go to work. This regression to childlike behaviour was a plea: 'Don't leave me — I'm afraid.'

Compensating:

Here the person's anxiety is relieved by covering up a weakness or limitation and developing something else to divert attention. For example, a woman becomes the best 'homemaker' in the neighbourhood to compensate for deep feelings of inadequacy. Or a man compensates for his small stature by becoming a champion sportsman. Note that neither person 'knows' why they do these things.

Another example is a person who finds it very difficult to relate to other people and becomes an expert with computers ... an avenue that provides both a career and an excuse for avoiding stressful situations!

Reaction Formation:

This defence mechanism has a strange way of operating — it is used (remember, unconsciously) when one emotion is too threatening for the person to experience, so the *opposite* emotion takes its place at a conscious level.

Anna has told Jim she is leaving him and he experiences hate for her, because to feel love would be too painful. Patricia says she 'doesn't care' if her husband Peter goes to sea, because to 'care' would destroy her.

Identifying:

Identifying with something successful — a charity, a cause, an organisation or even a person — allows the person to see himself/herself as a winner and to avoid feelings of inadequacy. The thought is: 'I'm closely associated with something successful, so I'm successful too.'

Tony becomes totally involved with the football team — so much so that he neglects his wife and children. He 'needs' this to feel a worthwhile person.

People can select marriage partners by identifying too: Joan married her husband because he came from a well-known and highly respected family and she felt a worthwhile person once she belonged to his family.

Projecting:

This defence mechanism destroys many relationships. When people 'project' they attribute to others the faults and limitations that really belong to them. For example, a husband might criticise his wife for being critical — never realising that *he* is the critical one. A wife might accuse her partner of not being loving, when really *she* is unloving herself.

Undoing/Ritual:

Many people deal with guilt by 'undoing'. Michael travels overseas a lot, often staying away longer than necessary. Upon his return he lavishes gifts upon his wife and children. This way he feels less guilty.

Megan works back at her medical practice for long hours and often stops to play squash before going home. She is especially affectionate to her husband when she gets home. This helps her to feel better.

All people use defence mechanisms to some extent. If you want to understand yourself better and grow as a person, you can look inwards and ask yourself whether it is possible that a defence mechanism is protecting you.

For example, if you find yourself being critical of others for some behaviour, you might ask yourself: 'Could it be that I am the one who has that behaviour?' (*projection*).

Or you could, if you find yourself spending unrealistic hours at your job, hobby or sport, ask: 'am I trying to make up for some deficiency in myself?' (*compensation*).

When people discover who and what they *really* are — and try to understand and change that — personal growth is on the way!

THE UNSTOPPABLE DRIVE TO BE A GENUINE, REAL SELF

In counselling, we often see a marriage where one person begins to develop, much to the distress of the non-developing partner. As this type of change is extremely threatening to the non-developing person, he or she does everything possible to stop it. But rarely does this deterring effort succeed.

Often the change is related to one partner deciding to enrol in a university or college, train for a new career or even to embark on a course of therapy or counselling. He or she begins to *stand upright* as the real self develops. The partner who tries to stop this growth does so at his or her own risk!

THE COURAGE IT TAKES TO DEVELOP THE REAL SELF AND THE H-TYPE MARRIAGE

The great journey to discover and develop the real you, and to build an H-type relationship, demands courage, great patience and persistence. There's no room for easy gratification people in this league.

Along the way you will experience times of failure, discomfort, discouragement, loss of face, anxieties about change, and new beginnings. Your childhood programming will get in the way, your strategies for coping with basic anxieties will deter you, and your self-defence mechanisms will blind you. At times you will fail to see your contribution to marital tension.

And yet, you will also, happily, know more and more the joy of a real, intimate and highly evolved marriage. The happy, H-type experience is that if you *both* dedicate yourselves to this journey of the Mature Love Program — if you are real, and you are responsible — you will experience great joy in the process and for years to come.

Summary

In Step Three we have examined the Real Self behind the Pseudo Self:

- the vital importance of a well-developed Real Self
- three influences that make us the way we are
- the profound effects of our Family of Origin upon us
- the strategies people use in order to cope with life and reduce anxiety
- understanding the Pseudo Self
- how to discover the Real Self hidden under the Pseudo Self
- steps to becoming the person you really can be
- four different styles of marriage
- why so few develop the H-type marriage
- how individual programs can destroy marriage
- how self-defence mechanisms operate and how they can blind you
- the courage it takes to work at the H-type marriage

Step Four

Skills for really relating I

Each of us directly influences the way we interact with other people, and that means we have rather more control than we might imagine over the way people interact with us. The next two Steps (Four and Five) will help you to improve the quality of all your relationships and also clearly show you the way inadequate communication can prevent marriages growing in love and intimacy.

The basis of relating well to others is ASSERTIVE COMMUNICATION. This is the key that enables you to get to know and to develop your *real* self, and in the process to understand, at the deepest level, someone else.

Often assertive skills and communication skills are seen as two separate areas to be mastered, but they are dependent upon each other. It is a 'horse and carriage' situation — in order to communicate all that is in your real personality you must use assertiveness and communication skills together. Note that it is important to make the distinction between *talking* and *communicating*.

'He never listens to a word I say ...'

'She never stops talking, but afterwards I can't remember a thing she's said ...'

Many people who *talk* a lot are very poor communicators: some people who use words sparingly are good communicators.

Using the components of good communication outlined in this Step will provide you with the opportunity to build a deep understanding with another person. It will be very worthwhile for you to try to understand and learn these communication skills as they form a crucial step towards building a more rewarding relationship — the marriage you would like to have.

These are the skills you can learn:

- being assertive (not non-assertive or aggressive)
- speaking for self
- defining issues

- tuning into your self-awareness using the self-awareness wheel
- disclosing your self-awareness using the self-awareness wheel
- inviting disclosure from others
- checking out (for clarification, accuracy and to avoid making assumptions)
- sharing a meaning (for mutual understanding)
- using the appropriate style for the situation
- setting procedures (to discuss an issue)

THE THREE WAYS OF RELATING

There are three ways people relate to each other (see Figure 4.1):
- non-assertively
- aggressively
- assertively

The use of these ways of relating can vary from situation to situation. It would be rare for any person to operate exclusively in only one, but you will find that each person has a personal style that favours a particular mode.

Two of the ways of relating to others have the capacity to *destroy* relationships: one way has the potential to not only *build* relationships, but also to lead you to an understanding of yourself — an understanding that can illuminate how you interact with others, how you enhance your confidence and self-esteem and how you develop love in your life.

Relating in a Non-Assertive Way

'Oh, I don't mind what film we see ... I'll go along with everyone else.' (Thinks: I really *do* mind.)

'Borrow my car? Of course ... sorry, the tank isn't full ...' (Thinks: If I say 'no' he won't like me ... *and* I'll feel guilty ...)

'Yes, of course, you're quite correct ... couldn't argue with that ... I do agree ... yes ...' (Thinks: Actually, I disagree, but I couldn't say so.)

'No, I'm not annoyed ...' (Thinks: I don't want to tell you, but I'm *very* annoyed!)

The non-assertive way of operating in the world means that you do not express a large part of what is inside you. You *hide* your real thoughts, feelings and wants. You do not share the real you, the person who is concealed underneath your quiet, co-operative exterior.

Because you are non-assertive, you are often liked by a wide range of people, but this affection for you is largely superficial, since no one really understands you. You don't cause waves, you don't insist on getting your own way, and you always seem pleased to fit in with everyone else.

THREE WAYS TO COMMUNICATE

NON-ASSERTIVE	AGGRESSIVE	ASSERTIVE
Puts self last	Puts self first/Hurt others	Treats others as equals
Low self-esteem Low confidence Lack of self-respect	Low self-esteem Low (inner) confidence Respects no-one	High self-esteem High confidence Respect for self & others
• Limiting beliefs • Pay-offs/rewards • Harsh inner critic	• Verbal Four • Non-verbal types of • Passive aggressive • Displaced behaviour	Express honestly • Thoughts • Feelings • Wants
'Gunny Sack' fills with unfinished business	'Gunny Sack' empties in a hurtful way	'Gunny Sack' empties constructively

Figure 4.1: The three ways people relate to each other

At first glance, this sounds like the ideal person, doesn't it? A restful companion, a good citizen, someone who doesn't cause unpleasant conflict and hurt other people.

This first glance is wrong. Non-assertive behaviour, on the surface so mild and unthreatening, is actually extremely destructive. To cope with the world in a non-assertive way is actually a trap, and if you cannot escape from it, you are condemned to suffer unhappiness and problems in your relationships.

What Makes a Person Non-assertive?

1. Self-limiting beliefs

I'm not as good as other people ...'

Each one of us has self-limiting beliefs about ourselves and our relationship to other people. From quite an early age we begin to compare ourselves to others: Who is the best? Who is the favourite? Who is the most loved? successful? rich?

Some children begin to form a belief system that constantly reinforces the idea that they are inferior to most, if not all, other people. They cannot play sport as well, they are not liked as much, they not as intelligent ... in short, these people begin to believe they are second-rate in every way.

These feelings of inferiority are accentuated in adolescence when peer group pressure becomes extremely strong, and the need to conform to a standard of success and popularity becomes overwhelmingly important.

By adulthood, the belief of personal inferiority is firmly established. Such a person may be frightened to query a doctor or a person in authority — 'Who am I to say anything?' — or may be in awe of wealth and position.

Other such beliefs are: Attractive people are 'better' than plain people; educated people are 'better' than uneducated people; rich people are 'better' than poor people; extroverts are 'better' than introverts' senior personnel are 'better' than junior staff; parents are 'better' than children.

All of these beliefs are myths — no one is 'better' than anyone else when it comes to the right to be a real person. And a belief system is only a series of thoughts ... these thoughts can be changed! Think about and write down all the self-limiting beliefs you have about yourself. Be aware of what makes you tick!

2. Payoffs:

There are many rewards or payoffs for being non-assertive. Each apparent payoff, however, has a darker side. Here are some payoffs:

- to avoid conflict/to keep the peace

For years Mary hasn't told her partner, Ron, what she really thinks, feels and wants. 'I just hate fuss,' she says. Friends admire the marriage because on the surface it seems so harmonious, but underneath Mary's calm exterior volcanic pressures are building, as hidden desires, resentments and hurts fester.

TAKE CARE: People who go through life trying to avoid conflict will usually create far more conflict than they set out to avoid in the first place. This conflict may emerge in subsequent generations — in the children (and their children) of non-assertive parents.

- to be liked

As we all do, Peter wants to be liked. In a way, he is saying to himself, 'People will be nice to me if I don't cause trouble ... they will like me because I'm pleasant and easy to get on with.' Of course, in his heart, Peter is convinced that he isn't really *worth* liking, but since no one can get under the surface of his personality, this fact is safely hidden.

TAKE CARE: The quality of *all* relationships will remain essentially superficial if there is a barrier to the real personality underneath the 'nice' exterior.

- to avoid both blame and responsibility

Neil's friends say to him, 'It's your turn to choose the video we'll watch tonight. Is there one you particularly want to see?'

Neil smiles. 'Oh, you know me ... I'll go along with whatever you want to choose ... I really don't mind what it is.'

By avoiding the responsibility of choosing the video, Neil has also avoided any blame if it should turn out to be a disappointment to the group. In a similar way, a non-assertive person can avoid the responsibility for a whole range of decisions, some of them very important ones.

TAKE CARE: Constantly avoiding responsibility and blame creates two problems. First, the person can nurse burning resentment when the decisions he or she has avoided are made by other people and such choices are not really what the person wanted. Second, this constant refusal to take responsibility for one's own actions can only undermine self-respect and confidence.

There are other payoffs for non-assertive behaviour. These include avoiding guilt feelings, being able to play the role of a martyr, avoiding the *fear* of rejection and loss of affection, believing that other people will not be 'hurt', and creating dependency on others for security.

These payoffs exist in the mind of the non-assertive person, although they are usually not recognised until that person starts to understand himself/herself.

Ask yourself: 'If I'm not speaking my mind, and saying to people what I want to say, I'm getting something out of this behaviour ... what is it?' Try to identify and write down *your* payoffs.

3. Harsh inner critic:

Many of us have a harsh inner critic from whom we cannot escape. This voice inside us says things like:

'You know you're not good at that!'

'Why bother trying, you always fail!'

'Don't speak up ... you've got nothing to say!'

'Why would anyone pay any attention to you, anyway?'

TAKE CARE: The harsh inner critic will almost always be harder on you than anyone outside and this destructive criticism will curl up your edges, stop you from daring, destroy your self-image and effectively prevent you from communicating on any honest level with other people.

Write down the dialogue *your* harsh inner critic uses to give you a hard time.

In summary, there are three reasons for adopting a non-assertive way of operating in the world:

- a personal self-limiting belief system from childhood that says: 'I'm no good' or 'I'm not as good as ...' (clever as/attractive as/successful as ...)
- certain payoffs and advantages such as being 'liked' and avoidance of conflict
- a harsh inner critic that constantly criticises and undermines

What Are the Characteristics of a Non-assertive Person?

- puts self *last*
- lacks confidence
- has low self-esteem
- lacks self-respect

Carrying the Gunny Sack

Many people go through life carrying a heavy 'gunny sack', but no one carries a heavier one than a non-assertive person.

The use of the term 'gunny sack' originated during the First World War to describe the sack holding ammunition for gunners.

The large invisible gunny sack each of us lugs through life can contain ammunition too — all the things we wanted to say, but didn't, all the angers, resentments, hurts, grievances that we haven't talked about and resolved.

This ammunition in our gunny sack is always there, and it can cause us stress, both psychological and physical. Many complaints, such as stiff necks, sore backs, upset digestive systems, depression and lack of motivation can be caused by the unfinished issues that we cart along with us through life.

These hurts, resentments, things we should have said and didn't, may have been in our gunny sack for ten, twenty, thirty years, or just for one day. If they are not resolved, they can become dangerous ammunition which will affect both us and our relationships.

TAKE CARE: In the long run it is very stressful not to face angers and resentments openly. In the case of relationships, failure to resolve problems can be potential dynamite.

Ask yourself, 'How full is *my* gunny sack? What are the things I should have said but haven't? How long have these "items" been in my gunny sack?'

Non-assertive people, by their very failure to express their own self-awareness, must stagger under the weight of the accumulated contents of their gunny sacks. Often they get caught up in a cycle of non-assertive and aggressive behaviour, as finally their resentments boil over.

Such a person thinks: 'I'm just a doormat!' 'I'm always put last!' The tension this creates mounts until the person suddenly (and to others' great surprise) boils over into aggressive behaviour. The resentments, grievances, hurts are dealt with aggressively until the tension is released (at least, for the time being).

This behaviour often produces guilt and shame: 'I won't do that again!' 'I'm so embarrassed — I lost control.' He or she is more determined than ever to be 'nice', to be easy to get on with, to be liked. The result is a return to the non-assertive behaviour ... and so the cycle starts again.

Relating in an Aggressive Way

There are four types of aggressive behaviour:

1. Verbal aggression

'You should know better than that!'

'You never listen to what I say!'

'You make me absolutely furious ...!'

'What's wrong with you? You ought to realise that'll never work!'

'You always forget to ...'

'You make me feel so angry!'

The word 'you' appears over and over again:

'You' never park the car the right way.'

'*You*' always make a mess of things, don't you?'

'*You*' should stop wasting time and get on with it!'

Watch out for: 'you *should* ... you *ought* to ... you *never* ... you *always* ... you *make* me ...' *All* of these are aggressive ways of talking, and destroy relationships.

Aggressive behaviour does absolutely nothing to make the other person feel good, as it includes:

- criticism
- sarcasm
- blaming others
- ridicule
- accusation
- threats
- withholding
- discounting

    'You fool! Look what you've made me do!'

    'Oh, congratulations! (said sarcastically) You really made a success of that, didn't you?'

    'What would you know about it?'

TAKE CARE: Nothing incites aggression like aggression: if you want to make someone angry and aggressive, the most effective way is to be aggressive to that person.

2. Non-verbal aggression:

It is possible to be extremely aggressive without saying a word: you walk in the door, happy and enthusiastic. 'Hello!' you say cheerfully, but you are greeted by a cold, closed face, and the person makes no spoken response at all. How do you feel now? Or your partner (or you) play the 'no speak' game. Some people give the 'silent treatment' as standard punishment for days on end. By refusing to speak or respond, you make the other person feel uncomfortable, uncertain or hurt.

Non-verbal aggression can also include physical violence, or, on a more subtle level, a range of facial expressions and body language that in some way puts other people down and devalues them.

TAKE CARE: Aggressive behaviour hurts other people, and therefore leads to conflict, resentment and a store of ill-will towards the aggressive person.

3. Passive aggression:

In many ways, passive aggression is the most insidious and the most serious. Many people do much of their interacting with others in this way. It is the sort of communication that is 'supposed' to be innocent, but is really vicious in its intent. What's more, it feeds on itself, so that each act of passive aggression can lead to another.

In the following example it is easy to see how the disguised aggression grows and grows:

Andrew gets up from the television and makes himself a cup of coffee, neglecting to ask Felicity if she wants one too.

Felicity is furious, but she doesn't say so.

The next morning, Felicity gets breakfast for herself, but none for Andrew.

Andrew is very angry and knows she is 'getting at' him, but he doesn't say so.

Andrew deliberately comes home late from work and doesn't ring to say he's delayed.

Felicity is angry, hurt and disappointed, but she doesn't say so.

The next day is Saturday, and they usually play tennis together; however Felicity, without a word, goes out in the morning, and so isn't there to play at the required time.

... and so Andrew and Felicity go on ...

Or take the example of Sylvia. She 'gets at' Phillip by throwing out the newspaper before he has read it. She also insists on turning the radio up loud, even though she knows this irritates him.

Why do people do these things? After all, most people know that this behaviour does not *help* a relationship. They do it to achieve a sense of power. In reality, people who do this are non-assertive and feel inferior. This sort of behaviour, in a perverse (and destructive) way, gives them a sense of being in control.

TAKE CARE: Passive aggression is a damaging way of getting power — it is dishonest and destructive communication that leads to misery and alienation.

4. Displaced aggression:

This occurs when the feelings of tension you have cannot be expressed at the time or with the source of the feelings. For example, a person in authority makes you feel angry and resentful, but you can't take it out on *that* person safely, so you wait until you find someone you *can* attack and then relieve your feelings.

The innocent victim of your aggression has done nothing to deserve the full weight of your anger, but you manage to inflate some small irritation or annoyance into a full scale conflict, just so that you can relieve the frustration and tension caused by somebody else altogether.

Violent crime is often the result of displaced aggression. In marriage, many people use their partners as the recipient of anger which really belongs somewhere else.

TAKE CARE: The unfairness of the treatment the victim of displaced aggression receives, plus the disproportionate amount of punishment for what is usually a small fault or failing, leads to extreme resentment. Aggression is bad enough, but unfair or inexplicable aggression is worse!

What Are the Characteristics of an Aggressive Person?

Surprisingly, except for the first characteristic, the others match those of a non-assertive person:

- puts self *first*
- lacks confidence
- has low self-esteem
- lacks self-respect and respect for others

Aggressive people, however they appear to others, are basically lacking in confidence, have a poor image of themselves and fail to respect others because they cannot, in their hearts, respect themselves. In many ways they are driven by fear, but whereas in predominantly non-assertive personalities this is shown by an unwillingness to become involved, in aggressive people it appears as: 'attack is the best form of defence'.

In almost all instances, aggressive people are *really* non-assertive: their failure to say what needs to be said (to gunny sack) results in aggressive release of tension and a false feeling of power.

Relating in an Assertive Way

At last! Here is the way that respects both your own rights and the rights of others — that says: 'I am a person who has equal rights with you to say what I think, feel and want. As a person, I am neither inferior, nor superior, to you.'

When you are assertive you have a full awareness of your thoughts, feelings and wants, so that you can speak for yourself (no one else!) honestly and appropriately in any situation.

The key to assertion is respect. You respect yourself *and* you respect the rights of other people.

What Can Assertive Behaviour Do for You?

Assertive behaviour enables you to:

- develop your confidence
- stand up for yourself without anxiety preventing you from expressing your real thoughts, feelings and wants

- express all feelings honestly
- respect and exercise your personal rights as well as respect the personal rights of others
- build your self-esteem and sense of real self
- build a strong marriage relationship

When you develop assertive ways of behaving, you begin to build your self-confidence and your self-image. You act as an encourager to yourself and to other people, and you become a winner in life.

How Do You Behave When You Are Being Assertive?

- You speak for yourself, no one else

  You use the words 'I, me, mine, my' so you do *not* say: '*You* upset me!'

  but: '*I* feel upset when you ...'

  You do *not* say: '*You* shouldn't do that! It's wrong!'

  but: 'I think it's wrong to do that.'
- you make comfortable eye contact
- you have confident body posture
- you make appropriate gestures that show warmth, openness and confidence
- you don't give confusing messages — your body language and your words match
- the tone of your voice and the volume you speak at are appropriate
- you *listen* to what other people have to say

Clear, unambiguous communication is achieved if you match your spoken language with your body language. If there is a clash, then you are giving confusing messages to the person listening to you.

SCENE ONE

Dan leans towards Melissa, his hand on her shoulders as he looks deep into her eyes. On his face is an expression of great affection. He speaks slowly, his voice soft and full of passion.

Dan: Of course I love you, Melissa.

Melissa: (pleased) Oh, *really,* Dan?

SCENE TWO

Dan stands with his body turned at an angle to Melissa. His hands are on his hips and he gazes out the window. He smothers a yawn and speaks quite loudly and rapidly, with very little tone in his voice.

Dan: Of course I love you, Melissa.

Melissa: (not convinced) Oh, really, Dan?

Of course these are extremes but in the second example Melissa will be confused and not know whether to believe the spoken word or not.

Assertive people are *congruent* — they do not send contradictory messages. They can communicate effectively in a positive and confident manner.

SPEAKING FOR SELF

This communication skill is essential if you are to be an assertive communicator. It involves being responsible for your *self*, owning *your* self-awareness.

Speak for yourself — no one else.

'I am responsible for myself, therefore I use the word "I" to express:

- how I feel
- what I want
- what I think
- what I see, hear, smell, taste, touch
- what I experience in my body (pain, ache, itch, tiredness etc.)
- what I have done, am doing and will do in the future.'

Many people fall into the habit of saying 'you' when talking about themselves, as in:

'You always lose the car keys when you're running late.'

'You know how it is — you try to please everybody and you end up pleasing nobody.'

But this is not speaking for self — it is using the word 'you' instead of 'I'. What needs to be said is:

'I always lose the car keys when I'm running late.'

'I know how it is — I try to please everybody and I end up pleasing nobody.'

If you concentrate upon the skills of assertive communication, being careful to use the words 'I, me, my, mine' (and avoiding the dangerous word 'you'), then speaking for yourself becomes easy. And it has such advantages: it shows respect, both for yourself and for the other person; it shows self-confidence; it shows a positive self-image; it doesn't threaten or badger the other person.

NOTE: People often ask us, 'Isn't it self-centred and brash to do this? I was taught not to use the word "I".'

Our answer to this question is: 'It is the most important way to be *in touch with self* — to *own* what we say.' Naturally it needs to be used appropriately and without an aggressive emphasis. So practise and perfect it.

The use of 'I' messages encourages you to clearly and accurately state what *you* are feeling, thinking and wanting, in an honest and straightforward way.

It also helps you to build a sense of your own identity and increase your self-esteem. We have heard many people report to us, after learning this skill in our Assertive Communication classes, that they have an exciting sense of 'who they are', as well as new-found confidence.

HOW IS ASSERTIVE BEHAVIOUR DIFFERENT FROM NON-ASSERTIVE AND AGGRESSIVE BEHAVIOUR?

Non-assertive: 'No, George, of course I'm not angry.' (Really is.)
Aggressive: 'George, you *make me* so angry!'
Assertive: 'George I want you to know that I feel angry at what you said.' (Speaks for self.)

Assertive behaviour is different from the other two patterns of communication because an assertive person:

- puts self on an *equal* footing with everyone else
- has confidence
- has high self-esteem
- has respect for self and for others

Both non-assertive and aggressive people are locked into a pattern of behaviour. They have no *choice* but to continue the mode of communication they have become used to when dealing with other people. Assertive communicators *do* have a choice, because they have control over their behaviour. They can choose to assert themselves, or not. They can choose to reveal their true thoughts and feelings, or not.

This ability promotes a sense of personal power or influence and self-respect and confidence is strengthened as a result.

Do assertive people carry gunny sacks? Yes, they do, but they make sure they keep them empty! Perhaps some resentment, for example, rests within for a day or so, but the assertive person talks about it with the person concerned at the first opportunity, thus removing it from the gunny sack. Assertive people control their communication — their communication doesn't control them!

Ask yourself: 'Am I non-assertive, aggressive or assertive? In what situations? Do my behaviours vary depending on where I am? Am I, for example, assertive at work, non-assertive at home? Am I aggressive with my partner and non-assertive at work?'

Think about yourself carefully — know yourself. *Only then* can you make changes. (Figures 4.2, 4.3 and 4.4 show how these different ways of being affect marriage.)

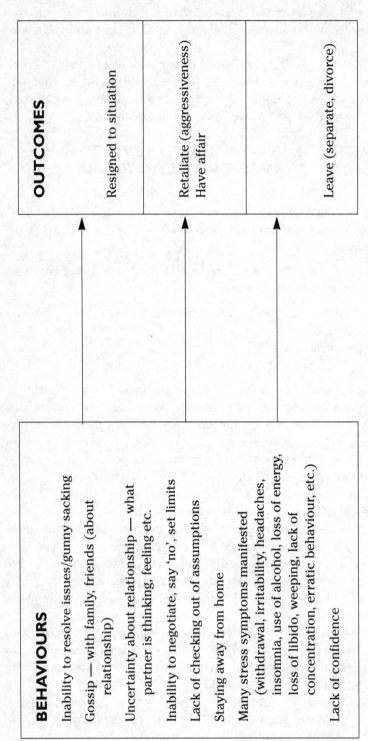

BEHAVIOURS

Inability to resolve issues/gunny sacking

Gossip — with family, friends (about relationship)

Uncertainty about relationship — what partner is thinking, feeling etc.

Inability to negotiate, say 'no', set limits

Lack of checking out of assumptions

Staying away from home

Many stress symptoms manifested (withdrawal, irritability, headaches, insomnia, use of alcohol, loss of energy, loss of libido, weeping, lack of concentration, erratic behaviour, etc.)

Lack of confidence

OUTCOMES

Resigned to situation

Retaliate (aggressiveness)
Have affair

Leave (separate, divorce)

Figure 4.2: Non-assertive behaviour in marriage (Lose/lose)

BEHAVIOURS

Verbal (sarcasm, criticism, threats, blame, reprisals, abuse, orders, discounting, demands...)

'YOU' talk

Non-verbal (body language % of communication — also tone of voice)

Passive ('sabotage', go slow, lack of co-operation etc)

Displaced (onto partner, other people or objects in various situations)

OUTCOMES

Triggers either aggressive or non-assertive behaviour in partner

Breeds resentment/loss of respect

Creates stress

Creates distancing/Divorce

Creates FEAR (therefore issues are not resolved)

Destroys Love

Figure 4.3: Aggressive behaviour in marriage (Lose/lose)

BEHAVIOURS

Good self-awareness
Issues identified and resolved
Treat partner with respect
Positive, confident manner
Speak for self — assume responsibility for self

Effective communication with partner

Ability to say 'NO'

Ability to set limits
Ability to plan
Ability to give positive and negative feedback
Ability to work towards goals/objectives
Ability to resolve conflict
Ability to deal with anger constructively
Ability to encourage partner
Ability to work on Mature Love programme

OUTCOMES

Builds respect for self and others

Creates 'fear free' environment

Builds self-esteem in self & partner

Goals/objectives met

Issues resolved therefore improved relationship

Reduction of stress (in self and partner)

Marriage satisfaction — Mature Love is built

Figure 4.4: Assertive behaviour in marriage (Win/win)

The Value of Assertive Communication

1. Self-respect

By standing up for ourselves and letting ourselves be known to others, we gain self-respect *and* we gain the respect of others.

2. Self-image

Self-respect and the respect of others reinforces a positive self-image and, because we have a secure image of ourselves, our confidence increases.

3. Personal relationships

Personal relationships become more satisfying because we are sharing with others our honest feelings and reactions, and, in turn, we are accepting from them their thoughts, wants and feelings.

4. Achievement of goals

Assertive behaviour encourages you to know yourself, to accept yourself and to understand how and why you do things. At the same time, it makes you much more sensitive to other people and their drives and motivations. This deeper understanding provides you with the opportunity to *act*, rather than to avoid situations, or to meet them with aggression. Therefore, the achievement of your personal goals becomes more likely, since you are developing the insight and interpersonal skills to tackle them.

5. Building a sound marriage

Assertive communication is the *most important* building block of a good marriage, because it puts you in touch with your real self. It enables you to put awareness into words and communicate with your partner in a way that respects both yourself and himself/herself. In this way, intimacy and trust are able to grow because communication is open and honest. Assertive communication also provides the tools with which to resolve the inevitable issues that arise in any relationship.

Start to express assertively what you think, feel and want. Use 'I' language. Understand what makes this hard for you. Keep a journal listing your successes.

NOTE: Truly assertive people can be assertive with *all* people, in *all* situations, and are able to express comfortably *all* their thoughts, wants and feelings. The following sections will show you how to do this by using specific communication skills.

DEALING WITH ISSUES AND PROBLEMS

During the years of our counselling we have come across couples who have asked for guidance before marriage in the belief that they could 'iron out' any problem areas early. In this way they thought there would then be no issues for conflict in the relationship once marriage had occurred.

We have had to tell such couples that life is full of issues, that life is not static. It is simply unrealistic to expect to anticipate the problems and issues that will arise in the future. Instead, what these couples should do is *learn the skills* that will help them resolve the areas of conflict as they naturally occur.

Even a healthy H-type marriage will inevitably encounter issues that need to be resolved. It may sound strange, but the ability to be an assertive communicator and deal with issues — even conflict — is a sure way to build a good marriage.

Many of us fail to be good communicators. Why?

Some people literally don't know what to say. Although inside they have feelings, thoughts and wants, either they have no idea how to express these things or, they are so out of touch with their inner selves, that they truthfully don't *know* what they feel, think and want.

Most people can express *some* of their inner responses, but these are often limited.

Note that people frequently confuse 'feel' and 'think'. You will hear someone say: 'I feel that's a good idea', instead of the more accurate: 'I think that's a good idea'. Feelings are emotions: thoughts are not. Don't confuse the two.

Many people build brick walls between themselves and others: whole edifices of assumptions, fears, misapprehensions and misunderstandings. These walls effectively block real understanding and cause frustration and unhappiness to both partners.

How do you break down a 'brick wall'? Or even better, how do you stop a brick wall being built in the first place?

You need to be able to gather your full awareness about issues in your life and then communicate this to your partner in an open and respectful way.

What is an 'Issue'?

An issue can be personal (for example, giving up smoking, getting fit, finding a job) or relational. Couples have issues, families have issues, friends have issues, and so on.

An issue is the occurrence of differences between people resulting in disharmony. These differences must be resolved for harmony to exist. If they are not resolved, then the issue becomes a *problem.*

Fortunately, using communication skills, issues can be resolved ... and problems can be solved.

The benefits of resolving issues are many: for example, there is no risk

Figure 4.5: Many people build brick walls between each
other by not communicating

of gunny-sacking; each partner maintains self-respect as well as respect
for the other by talking things through constructively; and in doing this
intimacy is created as partners get to know each other better.

Issues can be many and varied. Examples are the household budget,
matters surrounding children, in-laws, friends, food, recreation, home
chores etc. Issues can also include personal behaviours, such as eating
loudly, interrupting, laziness, lack of co-operation, no affirmations of
affection, touching that is unpleasant, poor communication, ignoring the
other person, etc. Issues concerning personal behaviour usually create
the greatest discomfort and are often the most difficult to resolve.

To resolve an issue you need to be able to get in touch with, and then
communicate your own awareness about this issue.

(We give credit to the Minnesota Couples Communication Programme
for the communications framework used in this book.)

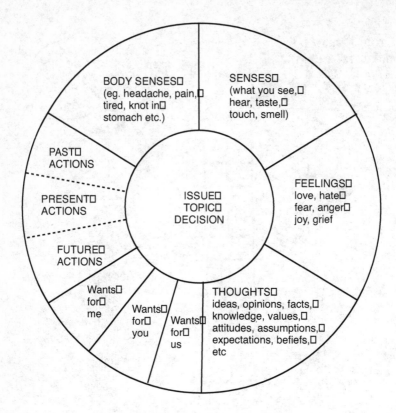

Figure 4.6: Self-awareness wheel

THE AWARENESS WHEEL

The Self-Awareness Wheel (see Figure 4.6) provides a way for you to get in touch with how you *really* respond to an issue, topic or area in which you must make a decision. Imagine you have a conflict situation that you find extremely upsetting or annoying. With respect to *this issue only,* you decide to use the awareness wheel to help you understand exactly what is going on inside you. Going around the wheel, you ask yourself:

1. Senses

The messages my senses are receiving: What do I see, hear, taste, touch, smell?

2. Feelings

The emotions I have: What range of feelings do I have? Love? Hate? Anger? Fear? Grief? Joy? (Many hundreds of feeling words relate to these six basic emotions.)

We believe that each of these emotions is positive, in that an emotionally healthy person will be able to be in touch with each emotion when appropriate. It is our experience that some people believe they should not feel anger and hate (dislike), even fear and sadness, because these emotions are negative — they are 'weak' or 'not nice'. Many children are brought up to believe that the expression of anger (or even the *feeling* of it) is, in some way, a bad thing. Our view is that it is desirable to be in touch with the emotion and thus be able to deal with it constructively — usually by way of communication skills.

Anger is often the emotion that you may find it hardest to express. Anger can, in fact, be disguised as something else. For example, many women who feel hurt or upset about a situation are not aware of being angry; many men, on the other hand, feel angry when really this emotion is masking their feelings of sadness. In most cases this is the result of cultural conditioning, whereby girls are taught not to be angry, and boys are taught not to be upset (cry). To be a *real* person is to be accurately in touch with the deep emotional experiences appropriate to the situation.

Strange as it may seem, many people find it hard to express love, caring and gratitude. An assertive communicator can say 'I love you'.

3. Thoughts

The thoughts I have: What are my ideas, opinions, values, attitudes, assumptions, expectations, beliefs? What is my knowledge?

4. Wants

My wants: What exactly do I want? Are there things I *don't want*? What do I want for you? What do I want for both of us? (Wants can be the springboard for future change or action: if you *want* something there are often *actions* you can take.)

5. Actions

This segment has three parts. Regarding the issue or topic:

(a) what action did I take in the past?

(b) what action am I taking now?

(c) what action will I take in the future?

6. Body sensations

How do I feel in my body: Do I have a headache? Am I tired? Aching? Do I have a knot in my stomach? A tight throat?

When you use the awareness wheel as we shall be teaching you to do, you will find that tuning in to these six steps will almost magically clarify *where you are, what your real response is* and *what you want to happen*.

Here's how using the spokes of an awareness wheel can help break down walls and resolve conflicts. First, you need to know how to use the wheel ...

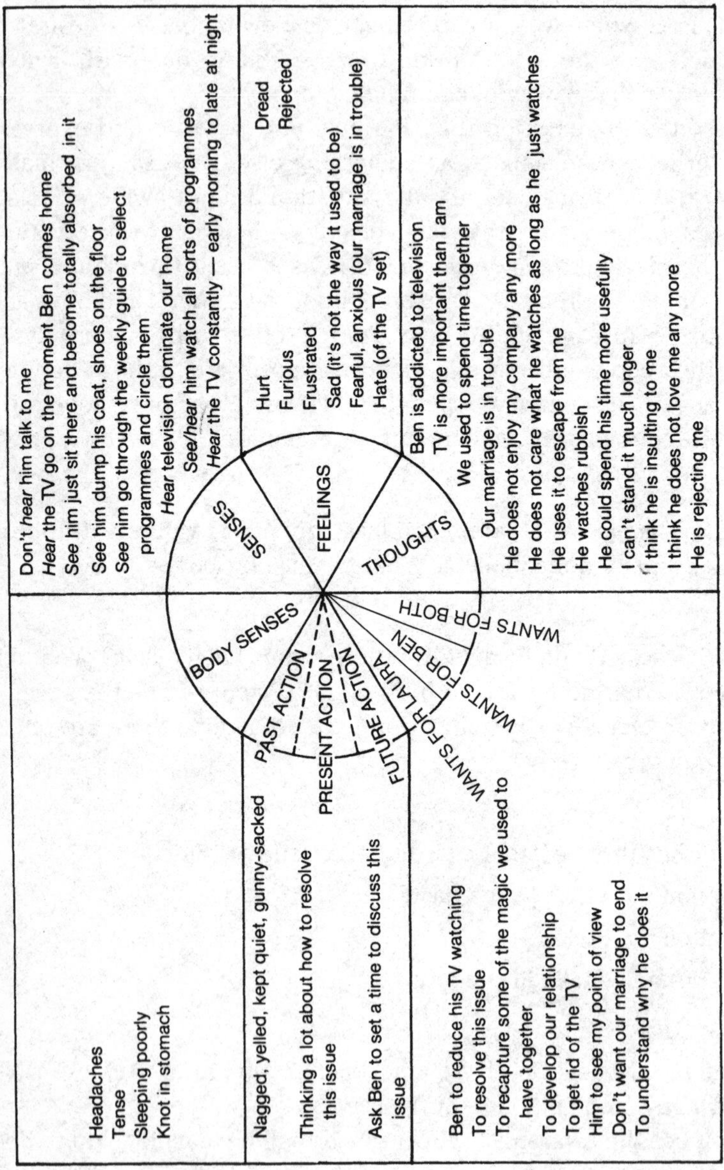

Figure 4.7: Laura's issue — Ben's television-watching habits

Doing the Self-Awareness Wheel:

- Take a piece of paper and draw an awareness wheel — *your* awareness wheel
- fill in all six areas with *your* awareness about an issue you have. All parts of the awareness wheel must be in use for an issue or conflict to be resolved
- refer to Laura's issue as a guide (see Figure 4.7)

NOTE: Although the wheel diagram is divided into six equal parts, this does not mean that Laura's awareness is similarly divided into six equal areas. According to the situation or topic, so one or more parts will have greater emphasis.

Using an awareness wheel effectively takes practice but it is easy to learn, and being in touch with your awareness is the only way to help your partner understand you.

We suggest you practise using your wheel for many different issues. You will need to be very familiar with this skill if you are to become a good communicator. You should *always* use your self-awareness wheel for issues you wish to discuss. Being able to confidently do this is the basis for *all* your communication with your partner.

On page 88 the use of Laura's Awareness Wheel is demonstrated with her partner, Ben.

Some helpful hints:

- always take time to prepare your wheel when you wish to discuss a particular issue
- check whether you have *fully* got in touch with yourself
- with respect to your feelings, check your awareness against each of the six basic emotions (love, hate, anger, fear, grief, joy), to make sure you are *fully* aware of yourself

Summary

In Step Four we have examined How People Relate to Each Other:

- the three ways of relating: non-assertively, aggressively and, most usefully and positively, *assertively*
- the negative aspects of non-assertive behaviour and how gunny-sacking can poison both self and relationships
- the negative aspects of aggressive behaviour
- speaking for self
- identifying issues
- the self-awareness wheel and how to use it

Step Five

Skills for really relating II

PUTTING THE SELF-AWARENESS WHEEL TO WORK

By using the self-awareness wheel detailed in Step Four, you can be in touch with your total, personal response to any issue you may have. Regarding this one particular issue, you can be aware of your emotions, your thoughts, your wants (or don't wants), your physical sensations, your sensory data, and be in touch with the past and present actions you have/are taking. You will then be able to plan a future course of action.

Equipped to speak clearly for *yourself* (no one else!) and armed with the confidence that comes from being aware of exactly where you stand, you will now be able to DISCLOSE to the other person your personal awareness of the issue at hand.

But remember, when you 'do your homework' and prepare your awareness wheel, *take your time!* Perhaps even days will pass before you are confident you have thought through your complete self-awareness thoroughly.

SETTING PROCEDURES

Laura (see Figure 4.7) has worked on her awareness wheel *before* she attempts to talk the issue through with Ben. She can now take one of two approaches in planning her talk with him. She could just say to Ben later that day, 'There's something I want to share with you — something in my gunny sack — so is it all right with you if I talk about it now?', or, she could *set procedures*. To use this set of skills she:

1. Tells Ben what her *issue* is.
2. Says she would like to be alone with him (no one else to be present) to talk about it.
3. Arranges with Ben a *time* to do this (that day, the next day ... whenever is appropriate and convenient).

4. Says *how long* she would like (say, forty-five minutes).

5. Arranges with Ben *where* they can sit and talk (the area should be comfortable and quiet).

6. Assumes they will both have the energy for the discussion (that is, neither will be too tired).

7. Agrees to *stop* (and resume at a newly planned time) if emotionality gets in the way, or fatigue takes over, or one of the children wakes up etc.

Setting procedure skills are therefore, in summary:

* define the ISSUE
* say WHO should be there (*only* the people whose issue it is)
* TIME (when?)
* LENGTH OF TIME (how long?)
* PLACE (where?)
* ENERGY LEVELS (too tired? sleepy?)
* STOPPING CLAUSE (arrange if necessary)

This set of skills is *most important*. Use them whenever you have an issue to resolve. We so often have heard couples say: 'We always end up fighting' or 'She won't talk about it' — and upon enquiry found that the attempt to discuss the issue has been late at night, or in the middle of the kitchen while a meal is being prepared. The timing *and* venue are very important ... they must be right!

Check through this routine of setting procedures and use it next time you want to resolve an issue.

When Laura and Ben get together to discuss their issue, they will each disclose their *own* awareness wheel with reference to this particular issue. They will, of course, have different points of view. One way to understand the different perspectives people have is to look at the 'ball in the paddock'.

WHY DON'T WE SEE THINGS IN THE SAME WAY?

People see things from their *own* perspective (no one else's!) yet they seem to think everyone shares their point of view.

Imagine a ball — a very, very large plastic ball which is half blue and half white. This extraordinarily large ball is in a paddock and positioned on each side of the paddock are four people (named A, B, C and D) who have been brought there blindfolded (see Figure 5.1).

Their blindfolds are removed, they are each given radio equipment for communication, since the ball is so large they can neither see nor hear each other, and they are then given this instruction:

'You are to work out with the others what it is you are looking at. You are to do this by standing still, observing closely and then communicating with each other until you all agree.'

Person A announces: 'It's obvious. It's a very large white plastic ball.'

Person C is puzzled by this: 'Yes, it is a large plastic ball ... but it's *blue*.'

Person B, thinking how unobservant the first two speakers are, says: 'Okay, it's a large ball which is plastic, but it's not white *or* blue — actually it's white on the left and blue on the right!'

Person D sighs in exasperation: 'You're all wrong — surely it's obvious! The ball is certainly plastic, but it's blue on the left and white on the right!'

What has happened here? To us, with the whole view, it is quite obvious. Each person is both right *and* wrong, because each has some of the truth, but not all of it.

This is what happens so often when people try to resolve issues! Each person believes he/she is *right* and the other is *wrong*.

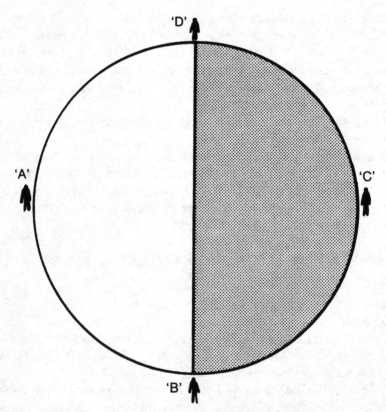

Figure 5.1: Ball in the paddock (or how people see the
issues from their *own* perspective)

RULE: Each person, because of his/her own unique brain function, personality, and history, will see things differently.

How can our imaginary people in the paddock resolve the issue of what they see? There are two possible methods:

Each person could move to the other three positions in turn. They would then be able to say: 'Now it's clear why we had differences ... depending on where we stand, we see the ball differently.'

The matter/issue would then be resolved — it is a very large, blue *and* white, plastic ball.

Alternatively, they could remain where they are and use communication skills to tell each other what they see, and, keeping calm and rational, eventually deduce the truth about the ball.

The ball in the paddock is a very useful illustration of what happens when people try to resolve issues. Although the first strategy can sometimes help people understand each other, usually it is impossible to totally exchange roles, so the second strategy is the most effective one.

RULE: Use communication skills to share your own individual awareness about an issue. Allow your partner to do the same. Always respect individual points of view — remember the ball in the paddock.

Of course, it is still quite possible that you will not agree with each other. Does that mean you cannot resolve the issue? No — it means you will have to: be *calm, consider, communicate* and *compromise*, until you are both able to agree with the outcome.

INVITING DISCLOSURE OF YOUR PARTNER'S SELF-AWARENESS

Your use of the self-awareness wheel technique has given you insight into where you stand, so you can put into words your range of responses ... but what about the other person?

It will help if the other person is highly skilled in communication, but if there is no awareness of the techniques involved, *you* have the skills to draw out personal responses that will usually lead to effective communication.

Of course, some people will *still resist* open discussion, and this needs to be understood more clearly. Can you discover reasons for this reluctance to disclose?

Techniques to Encourage Disclosure So Another Person will Open Up to You (Inviting Disclosure):

Ask a question:

There are two ways to use questions to invite or encourage disclosure.

A *closed question* is one which is constructed so that it has a restricted answer, often consisting of 'yes' or 'no'. The answer you get is limited, but can be very useful. Examples of closed questions are:

'Have you thought about the question?'

'Are you going to the beach or the mountains?'

Open questions, on the other hand, provide more information because the answer is open-ended, and requires more thought to construct. Examples of open-ended questions are:

'What did you do on your holiday?'

'How do you feel about what happened?'

'What did you do last night?'

Make a statement:

Some people feel badgered by a series of questions, particularly if the word 'why' is used over and over again. For this reason it is wise to vary the way you obtain information by altering questions to statements. Examples of statements that invite disclosure are:

'I'd like to hear about your holiday.'

'I'm interested to know the cause of your accident.'

'Tell me how I've disappointed you.'

Use a prompt:

Used sparingly, this can help the other person communicate more clearly. Notice in the following example that Paul is not jumping in to finish Pat's sentence, but is prompting her to give more information:

Pat: 'I don't like scenes, and when Lucy ... she was upset ... well, I didn't know what to ... I didn't feel ...'

Paul: 'Comfortable?'

Accent a word or words:

This is another technique that must be used carefully, but it can be valuable in highlighting the key word or words the other person has used:

Amanda: 'I didn't like to say anything when the others were here, and I suppose you didn't realise what you were doing, but last night your attitude made me really cross.'

Philip: 'Really cross?'

Amanda: 'Yes, really cross because ...'

Generally, the most valuable tools to invite disclosure are the open question and the statement, because each of these encourages a fuller response from the other person.

What Makes It Difficult for a Person to Express Her/His Real Self?

Many things can make it difficult for people to open up and communicate about themselves: for example, tiredness, a headache, distractions such as other people coming into the room, the aggressive attitude one person takes. The effect each of these factors may have, of course, varies from person to person.

The physical environment:

Attempting to communicate when the television is blaring in the corner, or when the lighting is too bright, or too dim, or when it is too hot, or too cold, can be difficult. Some people are not particularly concerned by noise or lighting or discomfort, while others are. It is essential that *both* people feel comfortable and are not distracted by outside things when they want to sit and share themselves in communication — especially if they are wanting to discuss an issue in their lives.

Personal space:

Each of us has a feeling for 'personal space' — the invisible cocoon of air around us. Many people become uncomfortable if someone comes too close and invades this area, and their emotional response can be to feel the other person is too familiar, or is insensitive, or is threatening.

Some people try communicating from too great a distance. For example, if you are trying to discuss something, and the other person is across the room, you may interpret this as lack of interest or refusal to become involved.

When you are wanting to open up, be sure that each one of you is comfortable with your proximity to each other.

Eye contact:

Many people find it difficult to open up their thoughts and feel comfortable when the other person avoids eye contact. Rightly or wrongly, refusal to look someone in the eye is variously interpreted as lack of interest, untruthfulness, shiftiness, untrustworthiness or unreliability. This is *not* to say that you should unwaveringly fix the other person with a steady stare — this behaviour can be even more disconcerting than refusing to meet their eyes!

Time:

Time is crucial for communication: it is important first, to have adequate time for discussion, and second, to choose a time that is appropriate, when you will not be interrupted and are not too tired or distracted.

We have counselled many couples who never got to really discuss an issue because they always tried to do it *at the wrong time* — when dinner was cooking, before leaving for work, when climbing into bed.

Interruptions:

It is extremely difficult to achieve effective communication if there are constant interruptions, such as the telephone ringing, children asking for attention, or the radio or television blaring. To allow these interruptions implies lack of respect for the other person and/or lack of interest in achieving understanding on the subject under discussion. (It is important to be assertive and eliminate interruptions.)

Lack of trust:

It is almost impossible to communicate freely unless you have mutual trust. Trust is built in many ways, including respect for privacy and confidentiality. Also, if we allow each other to speak for ourselves honestly, then the foundations of trust will be laid.

Fear:

Communication is hindered by the fears that many people have. Here are some of them:

- fear of criticism
- fear of sarcasm
- fear of being ridiculed
- fear of reprisals
- fear of being discounted
- fear of not being heard or understood
- fear of opening up in case it will later be used against you
- fear of rejection

This last fear, that of rejection, is a particularly potent one, which we discussed in Step Three.

Other hindrances:

There are many other reasons why people can be inhibited when it comes to open self-disclosure. Here are some of them:

- distractions
- lack of privacy
- fatigue
- drunkenness

- not being allowed to speak for self
- aggressiveness
- negative body language (for example, the person turns away)
- facial expressions (for example, a frown or scowl)
- other person never self-discloses
- lack of interest shown (for example, no response)
- lack of attention (for example, person's attention is on something else)

If you can identify what, for you, makes it hard, then you have gained further understanding of yourself. Perhaps you could find a way to let your partner know this about you?

It is very important for *you* to know what makes it hard for you to open up and communicate about yourself. If you *know* what makes it hard, then you can *do* something about it.

It is also important for you to know what inhibits your partner. That way both of you can maximise positive outcomes of your interaction.

We have counselled many cases where one partner consistently denies that any problem exists in the relationship, so blocking the self-disclosure of the other partner. Alfred and Lyn, for example, illustrate the destructive effects of refusing to acknowledge that any issue should be discussed:

> Alfred is a high-powered professional, successful and hard-working. He has made it a habit for many years to bring work home from the office, eat dinner with Lyn, then retire to his study to work until after midnight.
>
> Whenever Lyn attempts to self-disclose about an issue that is troubling her, Alfred says: 'Lyn, you're just an unhappy person. Now, if you were a happy person and would just relax, everything would be all right.'
>
> Alfred is discounting Lyn's thoughts, feelings and wants — indeed, he is denying that there even is a problem.
>
> But if Lyn has a problem, then *so does Alfred*.

TAKE CARE: In a relationship, if one person has an issue, then both have the issue to resolve.

Lyn's behaviour is assertive: she has learned how to raise an issue for discussion — but she has a partner who denies, discounts or trivialises her disclosures.

What happens? Lyn learns not to even try to self-disclose. She 'gunny-sacks' her anger and resentment. Lyn and Alfred essentially lead separate lives and the time is likely to come when Lyn says: 'Our marriage isn't working ... I don't love you ... I want a divorce.'

Alfred will be shocked: things have gone on for years without any problem that he has noticed, so what's wrong with her?

The real issue in this marriage is not, of course, the fact that Alfred brings work home and stays in his study very late every night: the real issue is his behaviour when Lyn attempts to self-disclose. To repeat a vital point: *it takes two to resolve issues.*

Make up two lists for yourself; one of what helps you to disclose intimately to your partner, and the other of what makes disclosure difficult for you. These lists will help you get to know yourself better; and if you know yourself better, you will be able to share this knowledge with your partner, so he/she will get to *know you.* All this creates intimacy and understanding and can bring about change in the way you communicate with each other.

But take care, sometimes people over-disclose — they say too much. You need to understand how self-disclosure affects a relationship. The next section explains this.

Over-Disclosure

The graph in Figure 5.2 is a way of showing how the extent to which a person opens up and self-discloses earns for that person little or much love, intimacy and friendship.

Person A is closed, does not reveal much of self and so is not known to his/her partner — consequently little love, intimacy or friendship ever develops.

Person B has been able to open up and disclose over time much of

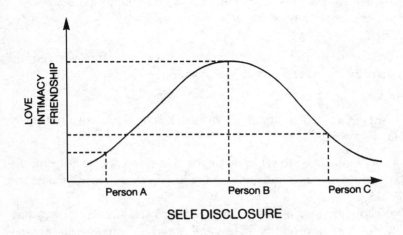

Figure 5.2: The effects of self-disclosure

his/her *real* self. The rewards are obvious: maximum love, friendship and intimacy.

Person C, however, has unwisely over-disclosed, telling his/her partner things best left unsaid. Examples are:

'I don't think you are as good a lover as my first husband/wife ...'

'I keep dreaming about being with my secretary ...'

'Whenever I go to visit your family I'm so glad I came from another sort of family ...'

'When I look at the cellulite on your legs, I ...'

'When I look at your pot belly, I ...'

'I didn't really want to marry you in the first place ...'

All of these are examples of what should *not* be said. They are utterances that destroy a relationship — even if it has passed through a period of maximum love, intimacy, friendship. We sometimes call these 'atomic bomb disclosures', because the fallout can last for years.

RULE: Every person has a right to keep some things to himself/herself and, in fact, should!

There are other types of over-disclosure which can destroy relationships. Sometimes people tell their partners about the things they have done, all the time operating with the hidden agenda of hurting the other person.

This is not the way to build a relationship — all it does is build a brick wall between two people.

A final important point about disclosure: the time factor. Have you ever sat next to someone on a bus who favoured you with his/her life story in fifteen minutes? Or have you ever met someone at a party who then and there disclosed to you some awful truth about his/her life? Did you want to get away — to avoid that person? Probably, yes!

These cases are examples of too much, too soon.

RULE: Love, intimacy, friendship need *time* to grow.

CHECKING OUT

Checking out is used for clarification, accuracy and to avoid making assumptions. This is a very important communication skill to be used when you want more information so as to be sure you understand a verbal or non-verbal message clearly — to be sure that you've *got it right*!

'Did you say we'll meet at six o'clock?'

'Are you angry with me?'

Checking out is absolutely necessary if two people are to understand and build their relationship, especially because of ASSUMPTIONS we all make.

One person can *assume* that he/she *knows* what is meant by the spoken or unspoken communication from the other, but it isn't always so. Most people do not realise that there is a real danger in neglecting to check out their assumptions.

SCENARIO ONE

> Barney has hardly spoken to June all evening. She assumes she has done something to annoy him. She broods over the unfairness of his treatment. He hasn't even bothered to tell her what she is supposed to have done wrong — he's just given her the silent treatment. June is burning with resentment and looking for a chance to snap at Barney to release her anger.

SCENARIO TWO

> Barney has hardly spoken to June all evening. She says to him:
>
> 'You haven't spoken to me much tonight. Have I done something to annoy you?'
>
> Barney replies: 'Oh, I'm sorry — I didn't mean to ignore you, it's just that I'm very tired tonight.'

OR

> Barney replies: 'Yes, you have, and I'd like to tell you what it is.'

In the second example June and Barney have communicated clearly because June used the valuable technique of checking out instead of just assuming she knew the reason for Barney's behaviour.

TAKE CARE: It is easy to misread signals, and assume you understand quite clearly what someone is saying, or to draw conclusions. In fact, it is a real trap to believe that you interpret all messages (verbal and non-verbal) accurately. This bad communication practice can only lead to misunderstanding and confusion, and eventually to frustration and despair.

RULE: Always check out your assumptions.

SHARING A MEANING

Of all the skills used in the flow of messages between people, the one that most promotes clear understanding is 'sharing a meaning'.

This is a skill that helps you both to understand a message the same way — it is a skill for *mutual understanding*.

Sharing a meaning involves two people agreeing to spend time together using some special communication skills, until they are satisfied they both understand the meaning of a message the same way (see Figure 5.3).

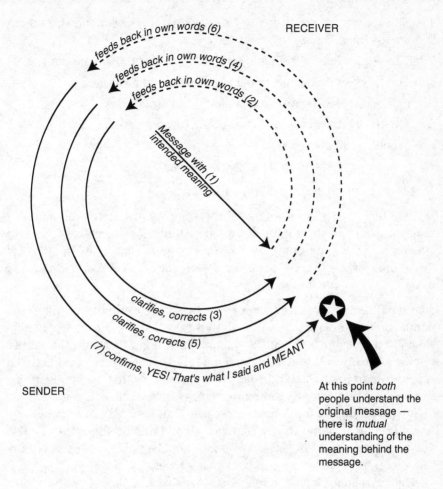

Figure 5.3: Sharing a meaning (for mutual understanding)

Steps to Take to Share a Meaning:

1. Something is said by one person (the sender of the message) the meaning of which needs to be *really* understood by the other person (the receiver of the message).

2. Either the sender and/or the receiver have an awareness that the message is *so important* that it needs to be clearly understood by both parties.

3. Either the sender or receiver ask to share a meaning:

    Receiver: 'I'd like to say back to you what you said so I'm sure I understand.'

    Sender: 'I'd like you to share with me what you think I said.'

4. The receiver then, in his/her own words says what he/she understands the message to have been.

5. The sender listens, then corrects and/or clarifies as necessary.

6. The receiver then repeats back the corrected message.

7. If necessary, the sender again clarifies/corrects.

8. The receiver again repeats back the corrected message.

   ... and so on, *until*

9. 'Yes!' says the sender, 'That's what I meant!'

At this point there is mutual understanding.

NOTE: The receiver *does not* interpret — he/she just states the message as it was given, no short cuts, no added material. If the receiver wishes to interpret, this should come *after* the message is shared. Note also that this is not just 'reflecting back' what was said. It is understanding the *meaning* behind the message.

Sharing a meaning involves *two* people working together until they have mutual understanding. It's as though they say: 'Let's work together to help each other to achieve this goal', or, looking at it another way, the sender thinks: 'I'll really help you to understand me,' while the receiver thinks: 'I'll really try hard to understand you.' This skill ensures that the receiver really hears and understands the sender's message and its meaning.

If the message is too long, the receiver can feed it back in small sections. Do not be afraid to say, 'I'm sorry, I still don't understand. I'd like you to tell me again.' Be assertive, and remember, it's not a competition! The receiver may need to feed back many times.

The interchange between sender and receiver should not be stilted, but rather an easy flow using all the communication skills. It is important, however, that the sender is clear about the original message and sticks to it.

Practise this skill with your partner. If you are without a partner, ask a family member or friend to have fun learning this skill with you. It can be both interesting and amusing to record yourselves and listen to your attempts to share a meaning.

Sharing a meaning has a vital role to play in the creation of a sound and rewarding relationship. Why? Because the sharing of a meaning is essential to clear, effective communication and when you share a meaning with your partner you have mutual understanding.

As well as building understanding of self and the other person, sharing a meaning builds self-esteem, trust and intimacy, and it helps to bypass dangerous passages of confusion, doubt and inter-personal distance. As an added bonus, it develops listening skills.

Sharing a meaning can, at first, seem simple. Do not be deceived — it is a very sophisticated skill and it takes practice to *truly* understand the meaning behind someone else's message.

We believe this may be the most important communication skill of all as far as the building of intimacy and real understanding between two people is concerned. There is a certain magic in experiencing someone taking the time and effort to *really understand you.*

STYLES OF COMMUNICATION

There are five communication 'styles', all of which have their place in communication, although only two are effective in resolving issues.

These five different styles of communication not only have different characteristics, but they also have different intentions or purposes.

Style One: Conversational Style

'... and then, she said to me ...'

'... the plumber just took one look at the water heater and frankly, he laughed ...'

'Mum rang ...'

We all use this style — life would be unbearable without it and it can be used in the initial stages to build a relationship. It has been described as oiling the wheels of society and it allows us to communicate, one with the other, on a pleasant, non-threatening level.

Behaviours associated with conversational style:

- reporting what's happened
- describing
- joking
- storytelling
- general chitchat and pleasantries

Characteristics of conversational style:

- it is sociable
- it is friendly
- it doesn't create tension — quite the opposite
- it is 'safe'

The intentions of conversational style:

There are a range of reasons, these are some of them.

- to be accepted and liked
- to put others at ease
- to fill in awkward silences
- to stay on safe topics

- to be self-protective
- to avoid conflict

Advantages of conversational style:

This style of communication is essential in helping a relationship grow. The climate for developing closeness is based on conversational style, as you share the events of the day, stories, anecdotes and comments with another person. It also has its place as a safe means of communication to keep the lines open during times of conflict. It is safe because there is no self-disclosure involved — discussion is about things 'out there'.

Disadvantages of conversational style:

Because it is essentially shallow, constant use of this style can block exploration of the depths of each other's personality. It can be used deliberately to stop any consideration of things that are personal, contentious or liable to cause discomfort. One of its great advantages, that is 'safe', is also an important disadvantage. It can be used to replace what might be called 'real' talk — the sharing of innermost thoughts, ideas, feelings, desires.

TAKE CARE: The price you pay in a relationship for sticking with conversational style and avoiding other styles of communication is huge, because you will never really get to know each other. You will never trust each other enough to share your real selves and develop an H-type marriage!

Some people are married for thirty, forty, even fifty years, but never know each other. Their life is filled with conversational talk — easy, safe, even fun ... but *not* growth producing.

Style Two: Light Control Style

'My advice is that you should put the breakfast cereal back in the right place ...'

'If I were you, I'd be ...'

'The best way to do that is to ...'

When we use light control style we are taking on a position of some authority. Our attitude is that we want in some way to control things, either because we think we know best or because this style of communication has become habitual.

Behaviours associated with light control style:

- advising
- teaching
- directing

- selling
- lecturing

Characteristics of light control style:

- it gives the impression of 'I know best'
- it creates some tension

The purpose of light control style:

The positive purpose is: 'I really want to help you.'

The negative purpose is: 'I should be in control because I know best.'

Advantages of light control style:

There are some situations in which the light control style is the most effective style of communication. These include lecturing/teaching, giving advice when the speaker is an expert in some field, and giving directions. It should be used only where appropriate.

Disadvantages of light control style:

Light control style can be a relationship destroyer, as it often appears when there is a power struggle between two people. It also can occur where pseudo self-esteem is being built, and the person is claiming 'I know everything' in order to bolster his or her self-image.

TAKE CARE: The use of light control style can be extremely damaging to a relationship because one person is taking a position of authority and superiority, thus implying that the other person is not an equal.

Claude always converses in light control style: he talks to his wife this way, he talks in the same manner to his children, his friends, his dentist, strangers, acquaintances, in fact everybody.

Claude delights in advising, directing and lecturing on any subject, whether or not he knows anything about it. He is an authority on an amazing range of subjects, including what his wife thinks, what motivates his children, and helpful advice for his friends in all fields of human endeavour!

Lately Claude has noticed a certain coolness in his marriage, his children seem to be avoiding him, and his friends and acquaintances are showing very little gratitude for the advice and instruction he is selflessly ready to give them.

Claude shakes his head: he'll just have to instruct everyone on the appropriate way to behave ... after all, he knows best — doesn't he?

Style Three: Heavy Control Style

'Get over here!'

'You fool, why did you do that?'

'You never co-operate, you never ever help me ...'

'I'm warning you ...'

Behaviours associated with heavy control style:

- blaming: 'It's your fault ...'
- accusing: 'Why did you do that?'
- threatening: 'Just you wait ... you'll pay for this!'
- demanding: 'Tell me now!' 'Get home early!'
- labelling, ridiculing: 'You fool! You're a joke!'
- distorting: 'Everybody thinks you ...'
- criticising: 'You're so clumsy and stupid!'
- complaining: 'You never help me ...'
- withholding: 'I'm not going to tell you' (or playing 'no speaks')
- disqualifying: 'What would you know? You're only ...'
- whining: 'Poor me ... you never say you love me ...'
- placating: 'Let's just forget that and be happy ...'
- criticising by inference: 'Just like your father ...'
- warning: 'Watch out for that car!' (NOTE: This is the only positive use of heavy control style)

Characteristics of heavy control style:

- it is aggressive
- it creates tension
- it contains many 'you' statements
- it indicates the speaker has low self-esteem

The intentions of heavy control style:

These can be summed up in the thoughts a person using heavy control style might have:

'That'll teach you to mess with me!'

'Come on, don't get emotional!'

'I'll create a fight so you'll let me know what's going on ...'

'I'll let you know who's really boss round here ...'

Advantages of heavy control style:

There are a few situations in which this style of communication might be appropriate, but they are very few. Commands given by an officer to soldiers, for example, need to be in heavy control style, as do instructions shouted to a crowd of trapped and panicking people in an emergency. In these situations, it is an advantage to clearly state with authority a course of action to be followed.

It is also possible that this style of communication might, with some people, force them to bring things out into the open. Hence, it is used as a tool (actually, a dangerous weapon!) to force the expression of some 'home truths'.

Disadvantages of heavy control style:

The disadvantages are self-evident. Because heavy control style is aggressive and shows no respect, it creates extremely negative feelings in the person subjected to it. It seems positively designed to hinder if not destroy, any chance of deeper understanding.

TAKE CARE: Heavy control style actively destroys relationships and has no place in building understanding. It should be consciously eliminated from your range of communication styles used in close relationships.

Styles Four and Five: Search Style/Straight Style

'I would like to know how you feel about ...'

'I feel uncomfortable because ...'

'My thoughts on this are ...'

Search style and straight style can be discussed together, because they are the two styles to be used when issues are being resolved. They provide the ideal way to communicate at a deep level because they are open and honest. They say: 'This is how it is for me, tell me how it is for you.'

The main difference between them is that search style does not involve the emotions, whereas straight style does. When used properly, neither style creates tension and the other person is treated with respect as an equal.

Behaviours associated with search style:

Search style is saying: 'Let's get together, and see what we both think.' It involves use of all the communication skills already mentioned *except* disclosure of feelings and body sensations.

In Figure 5.4 you see a focus on THOUGHTS. These are expressed *tentatively* ... two people search together — always tentatively. There is a complete absence of *feeling* or *body sensation* statements.

This style is used in all situations where issues need to be resolved or problems solved. It is important to keep *calm*.

Characteristics of search style:

- it explores
- it speculates

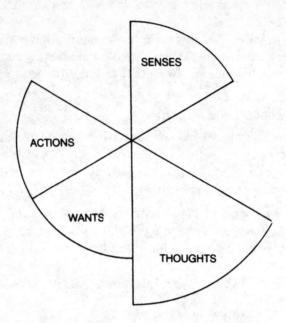

Figure 5.4: Awareness wheel for search style

Figure 5.5: Awareness wheel for straight style

- it reflects
- it uses 'I think ...' statements
- it is tentative (doesn't assume to have the answers)
- it does not create the tension of a win/lose situation

Straight style, although similar, is concerned with *opening up* and is different in that feelings (emotions) are communicated. The *core* of a person is disclosed — the innermost parts.

Straight style involves the use of all the communication skills and *all* of the awareness wheel. However, there is a particular emphasis on *feelings*.

Figure 5.5 shows how in straight style all areas of a person's awareness are disclosed. The key is that a person reveals his/her *innermost* self, so trust is needed to operate in this style. Trust is also *created* by the use of straight style.

Characteristics of straight style:

- it is honest and direct
- it is caring and accepting
- it helps to resolve tension
- it says 'This is the *real me*'
- it says 'This is how it is *for me* and I want you to know me'

TAKE CARE: If you usually use conversational style, light control style and even heavy control style in your personal relationships, you will never give yourself the opportunity to forge deep understanding between yourself and anyone else.

We cannot emphasise enough that you need to open up, communicate the *real* you in a positive way, in order to build and maintain your relationship *and* to build your real self.

CASE STUDY: Laura's issue with Ben

Laura and Ben's issue was mentioned previously. Laura has now prepared her awareness wheel and set procedures for the discussion (these procedures are shown on page 68–69) so that both she *and* Ben are ready to discuss the issue.

They set the time of 8.00 p.m. on Monday and have allowed forty-five minutes. The children are in bed and they are now sitting quietly in their living room. The television has been turned off. Each holds a piece of paper with his/her completed awareness wheel (see Figure 4.7).

You may be thinking to yourself, 'We would never do that!' or 'How tedious that all seems!'

One couple once said to us, after taking one hour to discuss and resolve an issue: 'Does it always take that long to resolve an issue?'

LAURA	**BEN**
1. Laura tells Ben everything she has written down in her awareness wheel for this issue except her WANTS and FUTURE ACTIONS.	
	2. Ben shares a meaning to make sure he has heard her accurately.
	3. Ben tells Laura everything he has written down in his Awareness Wheel for this issue except his WANTS and FUTURE ACTIONS.
4. Laura shares a meaning to make sure she has heard Ben accurately.	
5. Laura tells Ben what she WANTS (a) for Ben (b) for herself (c) for them both.	
	6. Ben shares a meaning.
	7. Ben tells Laura what he WANTS. (a) for Laura (b) for himself (c) for them both.
8. Laura shares a meaning. Areas of agreement/disagreement are acknowledged	
9. Laura tells Ben (a) what she is willing to do (b) what she is not willing to do.	
	10. Ben shares a meaning.
	11. Ben tells Laura (a) what he is willing to do (b) what he is not willing to do.
12. Laura shares a meaning.	
13. They both discuss, using search and straight style, until a compromise/agreement is reached — each must be prepared to give	
14. Laura says what she will/will not do in the future.	15. Ben says what he will/will not do in the future.

Figure 5.6: Steps They Will Take

We asked them how long they had been trying to resolve this particular issue, and they replied: 'Sixteen years!'

'Well,' we said, 'you've now taken one hour ... that's not long, is it?'

Laura and Ben are building their love, understanding *and* marriage by learning to communicate this way. They are prepared to work at their marriage, having come to the realisation that good marriages usually don't just 'happen'. Laura and Ben are getting in touch with their full awareness and sharing this with each other.,

This is not the situation with Jan and Craig!

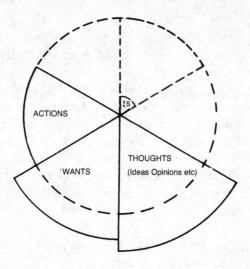

CRAIG'S USUAL (LIMITED) PATTERN OF
COMMUNICATION

Figure 5.7: Limited awareness

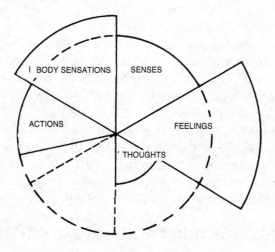

JAN'S USUAL (LIMITED) PATTERN OF
COMMUNICATION

CASE STUDY: Jan and Craig

This couple are a living example of: *limited awareness = limited people*. A look at Jan and Craig and how they communicate (when they do!) reveals the following:

Craig is not able to get in touch with his FEELINGS. Craig needs to develop emotional awareness in order to become a more complete person and a more proficient communicator. (Remember: good communication involves being in touch with *all* parts of self).

Jan has a different problem. She is very non-assertive and has difficulty getting in touch with her WANTS. Jan needs to be able to know what she wants and then communicate this to Craig. When Jan knows what she wants she will then be in a position to express her future actions (what she plans to *do*).

Now let's look at the patterns of communication Craig and Jan use. Figure 5.7 shows Craig's usual pattern:

Craig's THOUGHTS (especially his ideas and opinions) usually dominate his communication. He also states his WANTS decisively. ACTIONS he has taken, and plans to take, are expressed by him, and some of what he SENSES (usually what he has heard and seen). There is a complete absence in his communication of how he FEELS as well as his BODY SENSATIONS.

Craig clearly has limited communication skills to create intimacy and understanding in his marriage. He needs to develop an awareness of his emotional experiences (FEELINGS), BODY SENSATIONS and SENSES in order to communicate these and disclose his *full* awareness.

Figure 5.7 also shows Jan's usual pattern of communication.

As you can see, Jan is nearly always in touch with her FEELINGS and expresses them constantly. She also communicates a lot about her BODY SENSATIONS (mainly headaches, aches and pains). She keenly observes and expresses her SENSES (in particular, what she sees and hears) and some of her ACTIONS, past and present. Jan is not, however, able to communicate any WANTS or plans for future ACTION, and it is unusual for her to say what she THINKS.

Jan needs to work hard at developing assertive skills, saying what she THINKS and WANTS, and making decisions to plan to be involved in future ACTION. It is quite likely that, as she does this, she will not need to be so focused on her emotions and body sensations. Jan's present communication pattern does not help to build a strong marriage.

BLOCKING COMMUNICATION BY FAILING TO LISTEN

Communicating effectively means that you both speak *and* listen — and not at the same time!

Some people do not listen very effectively, although this is not because they are not interested in trying to — they want to listen, but have difficulty. Practising the skill of sharing a meaning will help you if this is a problem for you.

Other people do not hear for other reasons. Here are some internal blocks that prevent people from hearing, listening and understanding:

1. 'I already know what you're going to say ...'

This is based on familiarity: you are used to the pattern of conversation that the other person uses, and you also assume that his or her feelings and thoughts haven't changed, that they are the same as they were yesterday, and will stay that way in the future. This attitude is creating a barrier to communication, because, of course, people *do* change, so you must never assume that you could ever really be sure of what he or she is going to say, and what it will mean.

Always be curious as to what your partner might have to say.

2. 'I'll get my response ready ...'

The person speaking has just said something that might threaten you or your ideas in some way. Mentally, you immediately begin to line up the points you will use to defend yourself. Naturally, while you are occupied doing this, you are not able to listen to what the other person is saying.

3. 'I'm waiting to get my *point across ...'*

This shows very little interest in what the other person is saying. You are much more concerned with what *you* are going to say. As you wait for a gap so you can leap in to the conversation, the other person becomes aware of your self-centred failure to listen, which does nothing for his or her self-esteem.

4. 'Hurry up, I don't have much time ...'

How do you feel when someone interrupts you to say, 'Come on, get to the point!' or indicates by body language that he or she is impatient, bored or in a hurry? Most people feel defensive, irritated and resentful. None of these emotions will help to build deeper communication paths.

5. 'I'm not about to change my mind ...'

People are sensitive to the fact that their audience is not listening because of a 'closed mind' attitude. If your mind is already made up, you will tend to stop listening to a point of view that doesn't match with yours, and, unless you have an actor's skills, the person speaking will read the signs correctly and be discouraged or angry at your failure to listen.

6. 'This is what you should do ...'

You don't need the person to finish speaking, because you already know what advice to give — and you do so. And does the speaker thank you? Quite possibly not because in your rush to give your valuable (to you) opinions and advice you have shown very little interest in his or her thoughts and feelings.

7. 'Basically, I have no interest in what you're saying ...'

This non-listening attitude makes effective communication impossible since it shows no real respect for the other person. Why should he or she pay *you* respect, if you are not willing to give it in return? By the spoken and unspoken messages you are giving, you are implying that, as far as you are concerned the speaker doesn't have the right to express his/her awareness to you.

8. 'What impression am I making here?'

If your concerns are your contribution to the conversation, your acceptance by the other person and the overall effect you are having, you will have very little chance of listening effectively, since your preoccupations will take up most of your attention.

TAKE CARE: All of the above hidden attitudes will not only stop you from hearing and really understanding what is being said to you, but will also 'teach' your partner not to bother talking to you at all!

CREATING A SENSE OF BEING UNDERSTOOD

In counselling couples, we have found the most common complaint is 'He/she doesn't understand me'. The conviction that the other person *really* understands you has to be established before you can achieve a deep and rewarding relationship. How is it accomplished?

Empathy

Empathy is the action of 'putting yourself in another's shoes' — of using your imaginative skills in an attempt to deeply understand another person's point of view and experiences. Not to be confused with sympathy (feeling sorrow for someone else), empathy implies an openness and a willingness to accept and respect someone else's unique self.

EXAMPLE: (to downcast partner) 'It must be miserable for you to be so disappointed.'

Acceptance

This does not mean you have to agree with all the other person's ideas, values and behaviours. What you are doing is *accepting the person* as having value as an individual.

Acceptance has two components:

(a) you are willing to forgive (fully accept) mistakes thus making it easier for the person, in turn, to forgive himself/herself

EXAMPLE: 'I know you are sorry for what you've done.'

(b) you are willing to accept that the other person has the right to feelings (including ones of hostility or hatred), thoughts, wants without judging the person and attempting to change these feelings, thoughts, wants.

EXAMPLE: 'I do understand that you're angry with me.'

Sharing a meaning

Listening carefully to the other person, then restating the content of the message you have received in order to be sure you've 'got it right'.

'Let me see if I understand you ...'

'The way I understand what you said is ...'

Making a response

When you do not respond to a communication message it can imply that you are ignoring the speaker's efforts because either he/she is not important, or the ideas expressed should be disregarded. People may feel unrecognised, worthless or empty if they receive no response when they try to communicate. They will often feel not understood.

When you respond to someone, you are showing concern for the relationship. Here are some possible responses.

If you agree with the communication:

'I agree ...'

'I've often felt that way ...'

'My thoughts are similar ...'

If you disagree with the communication:

'I understand your point of view, but I don't agree ...'

'I see you feel strongly about that, but I feel differently ...'

If you neither agree, nor disagree:

'That seems very important to you ...'

'Thanks for sharing that with me ...'

In this way, even if you disagree, you are showing respect for the other's right to hold his/her view.

Participation

Both people must have the opportunity to be heard, and to respond. Just as it takes 'two to tango', it takes two to build a deeper understanding.

Establishing the right to be heard

Each person is important to a relationship — you can't have one by your-self! Therefore each person has the right to share feelings, ideas, atti-tudes, wants, *whether or not the other person agrees with these things*. It fol-lows, therefore, that each person has the absolute right to be *listened* to when he or she speaks.

Silence

Silences and pauses can be part of communication. It is often tempting to fill in silence with sound to somehow 'keep the lines of communication open'. But silence can also give each person time to think — to consider what has already been said. It also implies trust and security: a relaxed and accepting atmosphere.

NOTE: Many couples say to us: 'We have so many issues, wherever do we begin?' Our answer to them is always: 'Start with the simplest one, then you are more likely to succeed. That way, your success will build future success.'

We hope that you, too, will build success in your marriage as you use these communication skills. They truly are the building blocks of a solid foundation for your happiness. Start now to practise one skill at a time. You will not become an excellent communicator overnight, it takes time, so be patient.

Summary

In Step Five we have examined Communication within a relationship:

* the skills of communication: self-disclosure, setting procedures, Ball in the Paddock, inviting another's disclosure, checking out, sharing a meaning
* hindrances to expressing the Real Self
* self disclosure graph — under disclosure/over disclosure
* the five styles of communication: Conversational, Light Control, Heavy Control, Search Style, Straight Style
* blocking communication by failing to listen
* what leads to a sense of being understood

Step Six

Is there a constructive way to resolve conflict?

THE DAMAGE CAUSED BY UNRESOLVED CONFLICT

Unresolved conflict is a cancer that eats at a relationship until it is weakened or destroyed. If it is so destructive, why leave it unresolved? Because conflict causes anxiety and feelings of insecurity, many of us will do anything to avoid it, to deny it exists, to repress it and hope it will go away. (Usually it won't.)

Here are some of the results that occur when conflict is unresolved.

Emotional distancing

People like agreement and harmony in a relationship because its presence carries a reassuring message which goes something like: 'Everything must be okay because my partner agrees with me. I know I'm not going to be left alone so I feel safe in the relationship.'

This is fine as long as things are going smoothly. But what does the person feel when conflict arises, as, of course, it must from time to time? The message may now be alarming: 'You don't agree with me, so I can't really trust you, can I? I'll push you away, because if you're close to me and you leave me, it will hurt a lot. If I keep my distance it won't be so bad.'

In effect, the person has *distanced* himself/herself emotionally, so that there is a buffer to offer some protection from the feelings of anxiety and insecurity that have the potential to cause so much pain.

It is important to realise that most of this is not really apparent to the person. He or she doesn't understand the dynamics of the situation, or why certain emotional reactions have occurred.

There is a positive side to *emotional distancing* — it makes you feel safe, at least in the short term. However, if the issues behind the conflict that caused this self-protective reaction are not settled, the gap between the two people grows and grows:

Emily has been programmed by her family background to keep the peace at all costs. She firmly believes that harmony and closeness go together and that open conflict indicates that the relationship is on the rocks. Her partner, Robert, on the other hand, doesn't mind arguments, because they 'clear the air'. At the first sign of open conflict, Emily, to protect herself from the anxiety conflict causes her, distances herself from Robert emotionally. She says to herself, 'Robert can't really hurt me, because I'll keep myself far enough away to be safe.'

Robert, sensing that she is moving away from him, demands to know what is going on. Why is she so cold? What have I done to deserve this? Emily is alarmed by this additional source of conflict. 'Nothing's the matter,' she says reassuringly, while she retreats further from Robert.

Robert is puzzled and hurt. Two can play this game, he thinks. 'If she doesn't care, neither do I!'

In the case of Emily and Robert, it is clear that her initial reaction of emotionally distancing herself from the person she felt had the power to hurt her and to destroy their relationship, has led to things going from bad to worse — and all because the conflict between them has been unresolved.

TAKE CARE: Emotional distancing is fine if you use it for a breathing space — a chance to assess the situation — but if you use emotional distancing as a habitual technique to avoid conflict you run the risk of widening the gap between yourself and your partner to the point where it is unbridgeable.

Death of feelings

Giving in, burying the issues, refusing to admit that conflict exists, avoiding arguments, repressing emotions — all these techniques give short-term relief from the fear and anxiety that conflict can cause many people. But this refusal to face areas of disagreement, this avoidance of the real issues, can have a catastrophic long-term effect.

Bethany has been married to Richard for several years. She came to counselling as a last resort. Her words are bitter: 'Richard's been winning for years. I always give in to avoid a fight. I never say what I want, because he won't listen anyway. He never gives an inch. Never! Now I know I made a mistake marrying him. My feelings are dead and I despise him.'

To avoid conflict, Bethany developed a pattern of giving in to Richard over any point where they might argue. As a result, she covered up her feelings of hurt and resentment, and left them to fester underneath the apparently harmonious surface of the marriage. But, of course, these feelings began to poison the relationship. Bethany began not to enjoy sex: it became, for her, a mechanical routine. Eventually she began to despise and hate Richard, and refused to have sexual relations at all.

We have seen many people bury their marriage by burying their differences. Every experienced marriage therapist is constantly faced with the permanent damage caused by this non-assertive approach. The 'gunnysack' is just too full to carry around any longer.

TAKE CARE: It is possible to deny, avoid and repress conflict for years ... but the issues won't go away, and those buried issues can eventually cause the death of feelings and the destruction of the relationship.

Triangling

Triangling occurs when one or both partners turn outside the relationship to find someone else to pull into the situation.

Interestingly, this third person does not have to be 'the other woman' or 'the other man', but can be a relative, even a child of the marriage.

Here are some triangles:

- The classic 'my wife doesn't understand me' triangle where the straying partner finds a third person who apparently *does* understand
- The 'back to mother' triangle, where one partner finds solace in telling mother all about the dreadful things he or she has to suffer
- The 'gossip with the children' triangle, where a husband or wife talks about the other partner behind his or her back to one of their children
- The 'best friend' triangle, where a close friend becomes a confidante and takes on the important role of 'someone who knows how I really feel'

Triangling is a temporary (and tempting!) solution to the conflict problems that are plaguing the relationship. Taking a lover may even be used to stabilise the marriage in the short term. However, this apparent stability cannot possibly last, since it provides an entirely false way of boosting the sense of self which has been lost by the person in the original relationship.

'At least I can find *someone* who cares for me!' says the person who has created the triangle, but in the process the important facts are ignored. No conflict has been resolved, no damaging situation has been overcome and no personal progress in growth of the 'real' self has been achieved.

People who turn to someone else as a solution risk entering another relationship with their still undeveloped self. The prescription is always, first work on your own self. Don't try to escape by getting sympathy elsewhere.

TAKE CARE: Triangling creates damage that can go far beyond the couple who created it in the first place — family units can be disrupted, the person pulled in as the third point of the triangle can be ruthlessly manipulated — and through it all the original conflict remains unresolved.

Game playing

Two damaging psychological games often arise from situations where conflict is not dealt with openly.

The 'Poor Me!' game:

> Here the person playing Poor Me actually has no interest in resolving the conflict — on the contrary, conflict is used to continue the game. 'Poor me, I'm treated so badly!' cries the person sadly, 'so you've all just got to feel so sorry for me! I'm a saint to put up with it, don't you agree?'

The 'I'm Better Than You!' game:

> This game is designed to prop up the ailing ego of the person. 'I'm better than you, partner!' says he or she, turning to a third person and asking anxiously, 'That's right, isn't it? I *am* better/more right/of more value than he/she is, aren't I?'

In both these games the feelings of alarm that conflict causes are deflected: in the 'Poor Me' game, the person has the reward of sympathy from others, the satisfaction of being a martyr and avoids facing potentially damaging marital problems; in the 'I'm Better Than You' game the pseudo self of the person is falsely inflated by ideas of superiority that have very little, or no, substance.

In both games the pseudo self is propped up, but the real self is left unchallenged. Once again a short-term solution takes the place of a more lasting one.

Self-fulfilling prophecies

Quite unknowingly and out of their unconscious minds, people will often act out self-fulfilling prophecies. Here is an example:

Scott has a deep-seated fear of rejection, so he avoids conflict with his partner Wendy. He thinks: 'I'll ultimately be rejected by her, I know I will, but I'll do my best to save the situation by never ever having an open fight, because that would really end everything.'

Conflicts between Wendy and Scott are not resolved, and eventually the relationship begins to sicken and die. 'There you are!' says Scott, 'I knew it all along ... I *knew* I was going to be rejected!'

TAKE CARE: If you think the worst, it will often come true, because unconsciously you are setting it up so it will be so. But this is a costly way of being proved right!

Using children as weapons in a war

There are many families where, say, the mother invests all her emotional eggs in one basket — the children. This behaviour ultimately can damage everyone in the family: the husband, the wife, and the children. For example:

> Alice and George do not confront the underlying conflict between them during the first years of their marriage. They develop a way of coping that is emotionally sterile, but, on the surface, agreeable. When the children arrive, Alice pours into them all the feelings she has denied in her relationship with George. They become everything to her and George increasingly is pushed to the edge of the family circle. Hurt and angry by the way he is treated, he withdraws further and further, becoming, in many ways, a recluse. Meanwhile, Alice has warmth, acceptance and love coming to her from the children, so she can safely ignore any needs George may have for understanding and affection.

So, at least Alice wins here, doesn't she? Not really, nobody does in the end. George is isolated, angry and emotionally crippled; Alice has built her self-respect and self-esteem upon false foundations (pseudo self) that will eventually crumble; and the children have been given a role model that, if they follow in their adult lives, will have the potential to destroy their chances of happiness in their relationships with other people.

POWER STRUGGLES — ACHIEVING PEACE, NOT WAR

A power struggle is not the same as two people having opposing views: it is inevitable that there must be some areas in which quite strong disagreement can occur. The difference with a power struggle is that instead of discussing the opposing views and coming to some mutually satisfactory solution (which may even be 'we agree to disagree') the two people involved become locked into a 'I want me to win and I want you to lose' situation.

A person who continually struggles to have it 'my way' within a relationship is effectively denying the other person the opportunity to grow, while, at the same time, stunting his or her own personal growth.

People in these situations are operating out of *emotionality* — the programmed emotional responses they have learned to use in the past. Unfortunately, these responses, which may take the form of extreme feelings, or, conversely, almost total withdrawal, are *over-reactions* and are not based on any calm, sensible thought. And people don't really understand *why* they are reacting this way — they just know it is their usual automatic response to a particular situation.

When there is a power struggle within a relationship, one person is trying to pull the other closer to make him or her conform. In some cases, the other person *appears* to agree, and therefore *seems* to be closer. In reality, this is not the case, as resentments and hurts are still there, even if disguised, so the unintended effect is to push the other person away.

The person attempting to take over is trying to weaken the other into taking a dependent position. This can be self-defeating, since dependent personalities are, in general, unexciting and uninteresting because they have learned to 'play it safe'. Therefore, the partnership is likely to be stale and boring. The rewards of discovering another person's real self will be denied to the 'stronger' partner, who values winning more than personal growth.

Why do power struggles arise if they are destructive to a relationship? Without realising it, the person struggling for power is operating out of an unconscious drive to reduce anxiety, which can be summed up as: 'Conflict makes me anxious. If the two of us agree, then I am assured of harmony in our marriage. If there is harmony, there's no reason for me to feel anxious.'

If these alarming feelings of anxiety cannot be dealt with by examining the conflict openly, using communication skills and mature understanding, then the person will try and *force* harmony by imposing it. 'Agree with me and everything will be all right!' Of course, everything will *not* be all right:

> Hannah and Ryan have been married for twenty-three years. They have three children, and two of these Ryan has literally driven from the home, although he would be the last to see it that way. His two eldest children, a son and a daughter, have learned to hate him because of his continual struggle to win, to be right, to have everyone in the family agree with him and do things his way. As soon as they were able, they escaped into the world, and will probably never return. Ryan will almost certainly drive his younger daughter away as well, because he is intolerable in his overpowering need to be the centre of the family, to have everyone submerge any individuality and acknowledge that he is always right.

> His marriage to Hannah has not fallen apart because his wife is a great placator — her way of dealing with his drive to be dominant at all costs is to appease him, always to agree for the sake of peace.

> Ryan tries to force everyone to agree with him because he feels more secure when they do, but the effect of this is actually to split his family apart. Hannah has opted out of any conflict by always placating Ryan, but the children, each with the normal drive to become an individual and not just a member of a family, find themselves in fierce battle with their father. Ryan wants to force them to comply with him in every way, but his children reject both his ideas and Ryan himself.

> Unfortunately, Ryan cannot see he is destroying the relationships within his family. The more opposition he receives the more insecure

he feels, and therefore the more desperately he seeks to impose his will.

People who are locked in power struggles are operating out of instinct and feeling which are the lowest levels of human functioning. They are so consumed by their struggle to win, that they cannot take into consideration other people's thoughts, wants and needs. They *must* win: their opposition *must* lose.

If relationships are played like a game, where one person must be the winner, and the other the loser, then conflict, whether open or hidden, must continue to eat away at the structure of the partnership.

Power struggles would be negated as a destructive force in relationships if each person were to say: 'I want us both to win. To bring that about, I'm going to listen carefully to your point of view and I want you to do the same for me. Then we have alternatives: we can agree; we can agree to differ; or we can come to a compromise.'

APPROACHING AN AREA OF CONFLICT CONSTRUCTIVELY

Typically, people try to resolve their conflicts either non-assertively, or aggressively (see Step Four). *These approaches never work*!

The communication skills discussed in Step Five are invaluable in conflict resolution, because it is by communicating clearly and unambiguously that you will lay the foundation for the solving of most problems in a relationship. Remember that unresolved conflicts will contaminate your relationship.

Ten Steps to Resolve Conflict

1. Define the issue

Clearly define *exactly* what it is that is the point of conflict. Make sure *both* agree that this is the issue to be discussed. If, during the process of discussion, you realise the issue is actually different from the one you *thought* you were to discuss, then you should start over again with a new self-awareness wheel.

2. Set procedures to be followed
- WHAT issue will you discuss?
- WHERE and WHEN will it be discussed?
  (a specific time and place must be agreed upon)
- WHO will be there?
  (it is essential only those involved be there, *no one else*)
- HOW LONG will the discussion last?
  (a time limit must be set: some people go on and on and never reach a conclusion)

3. Each person speaks for self

You have the right to speak for yourself, and no one else. Other people have the right to speak for themselves. No one has the right to speak for any other person.

4. Acceptance of another's statements

You don't have to agree with the other person, but you *do* have to accept the statements made as being *how* it is for the other person. Remember, everyone's inner world and past experience is vastly different from yours. Have a curiosity about your partner's unique, real self ... that's a sign of love!

5. Beware of assumptions

You think you know what the other person means and/or how they feel. You believe you understand the points he/she is making. But do you? Never assume — check out and clarify (see the skills discussed in Step Five).

6. Keep to the issue being discussed

It is surprising how often a discussion over one issue will move to another issue, often without the two people being aware that this has happened. *You will never resolve any issue* if you try to solve three, four, five, six or more issues at once. An awareness wheel is designed to hold only *one* issue at a time. And if your partner begins to diverge from the issue, bring the discussion back to the wheel.

7. Avoid emotionally charged language

In a relationship there are always trigger words that each person knows will get an almost instant emotional response from the other. You will cloud the situation with unnecessary emotion if you insist on using such words. Try to use language that is neutral: don't try to score points by upsetting the other person. Be calm!

8. Be able to stop

A good driver sees GIVE WAY or STOP signs, and wisely follows them. Agree to stop the discussion if one or both of you becomes emotional or irrational. You will solve nothing if you operate out of your feelings, and not your reason. It is quite simple to reschedule a fresh start.

If the time you have allocated to the discussion runs out, then renegotiate a time and place to continue it. Do *not* go on with the discussion if either person is tired or distracted or upset.

9. Give in order to get

Some people regard compromise as a sign of personal weakness. The ability to give a little, however, is the mark of a mature person. Compromise in a conflict situation can be a valuable way to preserve the self-respect of each person.

Look for opportunities to give instead of holding rigidly to your ideas. Successful negotiating feels good and creates love and trust. Coercion creates distrust and resentment.

There is no place in conflict resolution for win/lose situations: both partners must have a sense of 'winning' at some level, since it is only by a win/win situation that self-respect is preserved.

10. Try a new approach

When all else fails, look for a totally new approach. New ideas are needed, new approaches often work. Thomas Edison is reported to have tried thousands of different materials to invent the electric light bulb. He never gave up ... and he discovered the material that worked!

Remember, the imagination is one of the greatest powers on earth. And *think:* the marriage you save might be your own.

The Real Reason Behind Conflict

It is often extraordinarily difficult to pinpoint the *real* cause of conflict. The true reason may be hidden so well or disguised so effectively, that the partners firmly believe that the conflict is over money, or sex, or children, or any number of things — but in fact, it is over something else altogether.

From our years of counselling, here are some cases where the apparent reason for the conflict in the relationship was not the real reason:

Do the right thing

Samuel, as a child, was a 'good boy' — he had learned at an early age to ward off criticism from his strict parents by being careful not to antagonise them with 'bad' behaviour. His thinking was along these lines: 'I hate the feelings I get when I'm criticised. I'm going to make sure I do the right thing all the time, because, if I do, people won't be able to criticise me.'

When Samuel married Erin he continued this programmed behaviour. He believed that if he 'did the right thing' then Erin would love him and their relationship would be happy. But, of course, conflicts arose in the normal course of the marriage. Samuel was angry and confused. Why were there problems when he was doing his part? He thought: 'I'm doing all the right things, but it doesn't help. It must be Erin's fault — it can't be mine.'

Samuel was convinced that Erin's attitudes and behaviour were the source of the conflict in their relationship. His angry demands that she acknowledge his 'goodness' led her to become anxious and resentful.

The *real* source of the conflict was the false program for living that

Samuel had learned so many years before: 'If I am good I'll automatically be happy.'

We'll all be happy together

For both Jean and Terry it is a second marriage. From their first marriages Jean has two young sons, and Terry has two teenage daughters who live with his first wife. His daughters come to visit every second weekend.

Two years into this new marriage, Terry and Jean are in open conflict, much of it centred around their respective children. Jean is brimming with disappointment and anger. Terry just hasn't turned out to be the husband she expected him to be — it's all been a dreadful mistake. Terry has similar feelings about the partnership: how could Jean possibly have expected him to be more than he is?

Both believe that the problem lies in their choice of a partner — it's a case of twice unlucky for each of them.

The *real* source of their conflict is something else altogether. Although Jean never put this in words, and, in fact, is not in touch with her thoughts and feelings on this matter, she believed that once she married her two sons would have a good father, and so be wonderfully happy. In a similar way, *she* would be a good mother to Terry's daughters, and they would be wonderfully happy too.

Jean's expectations are quite unrealistic. The children from both families have found it a great deal harder to adjust to change than Jean took into account. She is disappointed and anxious that the children are not outstandingly happy, and, because she doesn't recognise that it is her false expectations that have led her to demand this happiness, she blames Terry for not providing it.

Don't leave me

Ian is jealous and sometimes violent. Every time he unreasonably thinks that his wife, Carol, might be going to leave him, he flies into an uncontrollable rage. Afterwards he is genuinely sorry for what he has done, and promises not to do it again. Of course, it is repeated, over and over. Every time he imagines Carol is making preparations to abandon him the same response occurs — jealous rage.

Ian believes the course of conflict in his marriage is Carol — she says she isn't going, but he believes, deep down, that she is. Carol says the conflict is caused by Ian's irrational and quite unjustified jealousy.

The *real* reason lies in Ian's upbringing. As a little boy of four years of age, his parents dumped him on distant relatives for some months while they travelled overseas. Ian was given no explanation and no warning. Suddenly he was dropped off with strangers who looked after him as a duty and therefore showed him little affection or attention.

In children, fear of abandonment causes extreme anxiety. Ian has continued this reaction into his adult life, so that when he has even the slightest expectation that someone he cares for is going to abandon him, he is consumed with anxious rage. He does not realise that this anxious rage is in fact caused by his fear of being left alone.

I'm programmed to believe ...

Nick's life experiences have taught him not to rely on anyone else. His mother always said, 'Stand on your own two feet!' and he believes she was right.

Judy's life experiences have taught her to always be very friendly, loving and helpful. If she behaves this way, then she will be happy because other people will be happy too.

When they marry, their programmed strategies become a source of serious conflict. Judy is programmed to do everything for Nick, and she does her best to do this, even though Nick doesn't seem to appreciate it as he should. The more Judy tries, the more Nick tries to distance himself from her, because he feels safest when he doesn't have to rely on anyone else. Judy redoubles her efforts to be happy by pleasing Nick. Nick is driven further and further away.

Judy feels alienated and upset: what is she doing wrong? She's following the rules that lead to a contented life, so why isn't the marriage working?

Nick is struggling to be independent because he 'knows' that is the way to feel most secure. He is angry with Judy because it is obvious she is trying to smother and weaken him with her attentions.

The *real* reason for their conflict lies in the forces that drive each one of them to live out personal 'programs' to lessen their feelings of anxiety.

Love me — love my family

Many families believe they have an important role to play in the marriages of their children and therefore become involved in marriage conflicts and the power struggles that their children are experiencing.

This can result in classic triangling, as discussed earlier in this chapter. For example, if the husband comes from a family which will play an important part in his marriage, and his wife does not, then he and his family will occupy two points of the triangle and the wife will be relegated to the third. His family might become involved because of a desire to solve any problems in the marriage, but the intervention will usually be seen by the wife as interference.

In these instances of in-law triangling there is no objectivity — *each person* is involved in his/her emotional over-reactions. People take sides, generations of tradition are appealed to, and all sorts of factors arise which sidetrack attention from the essential issues.

The *real* conflict in the relationship may be based on any number of things, but, whatever it is, it will be buried under the emotional issues of whether his parents are welcome or not and whether they should have any say in their son's marriage.

Triangling is always dangerous — you must resolve your issues yourself or with professional help.

Get closer

The problems associated with closeness and distance are related to individual personalities. Luke copes with difficult times in the relationship by becoming most distant: this lessens his feelings of insecurity. Nancy copes with difficult times by wanting to draw closer.

Neither understands that the way each behaves drives the other to heights of anxiety, and that these feelings make them fight with each other. Their marriage is a battleground, and it steadily grows worse, because Luke is pushed further and further away by Nancy's constant desire to be close. Nancy, on the other hand, feels extremely insecure because Luke is retreating, so she tries harder and harder to be closer ... and so on.

The *real* issue is their widely differing ways of coping with stress and anxiety. (See Step 3.)

I don't like your new life

Charles and Vanessa married in their early twenties and have had a reasonably happy marriage. Now, at thirty-five, Vanessa decides life should hold more for her. She enrols in university and embarks upon a course of personal growth. As she breaks new frontiers, meets new people, learns exciting new ideas and skills, Charles becomes increasingly upset. 'You'll have to give it up!' he orders. 'You never have time to run the household properly and you're neglecting me and the children.'

Vanessa doesn't want to relinquish her changed lifestyle, so she resists. Charles brings his parents, her parents, their friends — anyone he can enlist — into the argument in an attempt to force her to give up her studies.

Charles *says* the reason he is asking Vanessa to do this is for the quality of life of the family, and he may believe this. The *real* reason lies in Charles himself. He has low self-esteem and feelings of insecurity. Her actions in finding life outside their marriage threaten and frighten him. However, he does not face the true reason. He clings to the idea that Vanessa is deliberately destroying the family with her selfishness.

What is really happening is that *Charles* is destroying the relationship because of his basic insecurity and inadequacy, and the more he demands, the more Vanessa distances herself from him.

I blame you ...

This occurs when people try to find a scapegoat for the deficiencies of a marriage. For example:

Sally feels inferior because she knows she is not very well educated; Simon feels inferior because he knows that he is not a very expert or fulfilling lover. Both have a psychological need to find a scapegoat — something to blame — so they won't have to face their own inadequacies.

Simon says: 'It's because of Sally we have these problems and that's why I'm not happy.'

Sally says: 'It's because of Simon we have these problems and that's why I don't love him any more.'

Of course, Simon and Sally have *always been this way*. The fact that romantic love blinded them to each other's faults is ignored, as is the possibility that each of them deliberately presented the most attractive side to the other because of the fear that if the truth was shown, he or she might not be loved.

The conflict in their marriage has as its real basis the insecurities and inadequacies of each partner.

TAKE CARE: People in conflict must ask themselves. 'Is *this* conflict the real problem, or is it something else? Does it lie within me, within my history? Is it the interaction between us ... our expectations ... something else ...?'

The cause of conflict is often complex and hidden — don't assume you understand what causes it in your relationship. Spend some time looking for the way it operates and what hidden reasons there might be to explain it.

Some Reminders on Solving Conflict

- try to be calm and rational: separate what you feel from what you think
- always try to avoid aggressive behaviour: it causes anxiety and strong emotional reactions and thus makes the situation worse
- use an awareness wheel to clarify the situation
- be aware of the possibility that one or both of you is living out a programmed strategy learned in childhood
- develop your communication skills
- accept that the reasons for conflict may be complex and disguised

In our many years of practising marital therapy, we have seen thousands of couples allow marital conflict to destroy intimacy. These couples usually resort to one of the pseudo self marriages, or they divorce. These attempted 'solutions' to the problem of conflict actually deny personal growth and development of the real self. A great opportunity is missed!

We cannot over-emphasise how important it is to deal constructively with conflict. It is pointless to ignore warning signs and hope it will go away; it is just as pointless to say to yourself, 'It won't happen to me ...' It can, and perhaps will!

Seek professional help when intimacy and love are threatened and you can't solve the problem. And beware, denial of the problem can be the cause of marital death.

Summary

In Step Six we explored the Constructive Resolution of Conflict:

- the results of unresolved conflict: emotional distancing, the death of feelings, triangling, game playing, self-fulfilling prophecies, using children as weapons
- power struggles: how to achieve peace, not war
- constructive approaches to conflict
- the hidden reasons for conflict

Do I rule my emotions
or do they rule me?

I f we are going to really relate with others from our real self we must be in contact with the emotional part of ourselves. Unfortunately the emotions are often overwhelmed by powerful forces of anger, sadness, jealousy or fear. These emotions must therefore be mastered if we are to think clearly and use our emotions in a constructive manner.

Mastering your emotions does not mean that you deny that you can become angry or sad or jealous. What it does mean is that you accept that you are experiencing a strong emotion and you deal with what causes you to react this way. Understanding the often unsuspected things that trigger your emotions will give you mastery over them. This insight into the real reasons for your over-reaction to certain situations leads to the security of self-control as you develop a strong sense of your own self as an individual.

Emotional over-reactions can threaten relationships because they often create anxiety, disrespect, insecurity and despair. They often lead people to protect themselves by distancing, or by pretending everything is all right and feigning a closeness that really doesn't exist.

Anger and aggression can play an important role in the breakdown of a relationship: anger pushes the other person away; jealousy makes a partner want to escape; sadness and depression (both often disguised anger) drain the other partner emotionally and hence cause distancing.

The emotional outbursts that occur in relationships are often quite disproportionate to the fault (real or imagined). Outrage, powerful anger and violence indicate an emotional over-reaction that is rarely justified by what was done or said.

When dealing with marital conflict we used to teach people methods to fight fair and show them how to structure their anger in a safe way. But this approach did not isolate the *cause* of the conflict, it just treated the symptoms.

Triggers for Justified Anger	Sources of Unjustified Anger
Examples: Broken promises Betrayal Infidelity Disloyalty Violence Emotional Abuse Unfairness Dishonesty Disrespect	Family of origin (past history) Contracts Rules Crazymakers Anger as a weapon or cover-up Displacement of anger Tension release Communication triggers Unfinished business Jealousy Scapegoating Manipulation Burnout Depression Low Self-esteem Victim game General unhappiness Sleep deprivation Hypoglycaemia Alcohol or drug abuse

NOTE: ONLY A SMALL PER CENT OF ANGER DIRECTED AT PARTNER IS JUSTIFIED

Figure 7.1: Reasons for justified and unjustified anger

Today we use a far more constructive approach: we look for the reasons for the emotional over-reaction. Discovering *why* emotional responses are disproportionate in a particular situation gives an awareness that leads to self-control and also to appropriate emotional responses. See Figure 7.1.

After counselling thousands of cases of marital conflict, we now believe that less than ten per cent of emotional over-reaction is due to the problem presented. In fact, very few of the issues reported to us justified the amount of emotionality involved. This realisation turned our interest to what is behind these powerful emotional reactions.

REASONS BEHIND THESE STRONG EMOTIONAL REACTIONS

Experiences in Your Family of Origin

Most people have a family background and childhood experiences that contaminate their adult life. In times of stress and anxiety this past history can create so much emotional over-reaction that it is impossible to think clearly: it is as though the adult person is overwhelmed by the experiences of the fearful child he or she once was.

Two simple illustrations:

As a child, Jerry's mother always found fault with him and blamed him for 'being clumsy'. He felt powerless (as most children do) to do anything about this. Now, in his marriage, should his wife even so much as look at him if he spills something, he is consumed with rage and abuses her with violent language.

Maree's father had a large moustache. When she was a little girl, if her father was angry with her he didn't express it in words, but used to stare silently into her face until she was shamed, confused and frightened. Now, as an adult, she has an immediate emotional response to any man wearing a moustache. When her husband decided to grow a moustache, Maree reacted with an angry outburst (which of course, masked the *fear* she felt as a child with respect to her father).

The triggers that fire these over-reactions in the individual may, in themselves, be very slight, but the emotional outbursts can be extremely powerful and destructive to relationships.

Most people are unaware of the strong influence a family of origin can have upon adult behaviour:

Natalie came from a family where her mother used a powerful form of passive aggression: the silent treatment. As a child, Natalie learned to dread the sight of her mother's distant expression and tightly closed lips, which indicated her cold displeasure. This punishing silent treatment from her mother caused extreme tension in the family circle: neither the father nor the children knew how to deal with it, so feelings of impotence, fear and anxiety were created.

Now, when Natalie is faced in a relationship with a hint of a similar silent treatment or withdrawal, her immediate reflex reaction is fear: 'This is too much like home ... it was awful there ... I hate the way it makes me feel.'

She releases this extreme anxiety in the form of strong anger — a powerful and violent emotion that gives her the illusion of power, of being in control.

Very often the anger we feel comes from parts of us we don't know or understand, and because we are unaware of the source of our emotions, we cannot control them.

When you react to a situation with extreme emotion, always ask yourself: What does this remind me of?

When, in my childhood, was the first time I can remember feeling like this? Was it in any interaction with my parents, my brothers or sisters, my grandparents, my aunts ... anyone in my family? What was that past situation where I first felt the way I'm feeling now?

When we can understand our emotionality — 'where it came from' — we can then more easily diffuse it as it begins to make sense. Often, though, we will still have work to do to resolve this unfinished business. As you read on you will find ways to do this.

Building a genogram

A genogram is a pictorial display of your family of origin. If you want to explore sources of emotional over-reaction such as anger, fear, sadness, jealousy, anxiety of even hate, you can often discover them by drawing a genogram and thinking about the role of each person in your self development.

Our experience has been that you will nearly always see a connection between the past and the present. Each family history tells a story: a story of how people related to each other in the past. (*Note*: Adoptees should consider the adoptive family as their family of origin.)

Generation after generation hands on to the succeeding one whole patterns of behaviour and many habits are carried over from one generation to the next. You may today be using the same style of conflict resolution as was used in your family a hundred years ago. The family model of male/female relationships can also be repeated through the years.

What is the significance of this to you? The plain fact is that under stress you react emotionally according to what happened between you and significant others when you were a child. In other words, your family of origin has a profound effect upon your emotional behaviour, not only when you were young, but now, when you are an adult.

It is often extremely helpful in developing your real self to get in touch with members of your family of origin. Your pattern of interaction when under stress is not erased by distance, so even if these people are now far off, they will still be influencing you. The 'trigger points' are well established before you reach adulthood.

Here is a case to illustrate the powerful influences a family can have upon the behaviour and reactions of one of its members:

> Sue came to counselling because she had a disproportionate reaction to any criticism, however mild. The moment Sue sensed criticism or blame, whether real or imagined, she had an instant and powerful

emotional response. This constant and uncontrolled over-reaction was causing considerable problems with her husband and in her career, but Sue didn't understand *why* it was occurring, much less how to deal with it.

An abbreviated version of Sue's genogram is shown in Figure 7.2, showing her family back only to her paternal and maternal grandparents. Her husband's genogram is now shown, although it is valuable to examine both partners' families of origin. (*Note*: It is always helpful for partners to understand the influence the other's family of origin has had.)

Sue's extreme 'touchiness' to criticism becomes quite understandable when several crucial points are examined:

1.   Sue's father, John, was an only child, a man with a weak self-image, alcoholic and highly critical of Alice, his wife.

2.   Sue's mother, Alice, is the oldest of six children, but was surrounded by women all during her childhood. She had a poor idea of what men were like and selected John as a husband because he showed a strong need for someone to take care of him. Being the eldest in a large family, she knew how to lead and was a highly responsible person.

3.   John felt threatened by the strength of Alice and unconsciously attempted to take away her self-worth and make her more dependent.

4.   During Sue's growing-up years she feared the numerous arguments that occurred between her parents. These conflicts always started with John's criticism of Alice.

5.   Sue thus learned to 'twitch' whenever she sensed that her father (John) was being critical of her mother (Alice). The warning signs (her father's criticisms) generated *fear* because they spelt out to Sue the threat of marital and family breakdown.

6.   Sue is now thirty-five, but she still reacts to any suggestion of criticism in the same way as she did in her family situation years ago. Now, it is an over-reaction, triggered by those long gone past experiences.

7.   The fear she felt as a child is now covered up by *anger*. The fear step is left out as Sue, sensing criticism, jumps to (apparently irrational) anger in a split second.

The counselling Sue experienced was very valuable to her. For the first time, she clearly understood the reasons behind her extreme emotional reactivity to even a hint of criticism, and her eagerness to solve the problem for the sake of her career and marriage led to a successful resolution.

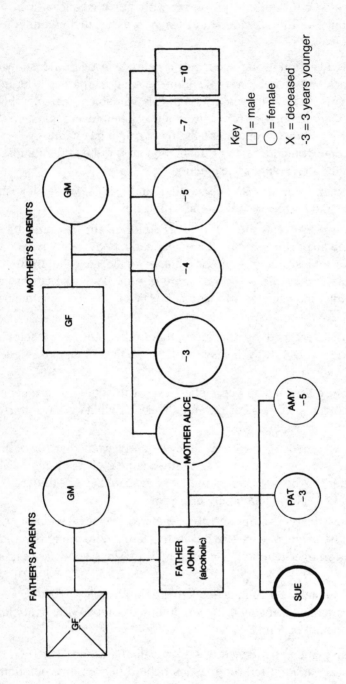

Key
□ = male
○ = female
X = deceased
-3 = 3 years younger

Figure 7.2: Sue's Genogram

Here is another example:

Sybil and Barney have been married for four years and problems of emotionality and conflict have emerged. Barney married Sybil with the (unspoken) understanding that she would support and help him to his chosen profession by doing all the household jobs, taking care of the children, being at home to answer the telephone and generally freeing him in the evenings and weekends to do his work.

Sybil is beginning to experience a lot of anger at this — after all, she married Barney to enjoy life *with* him — and he is rarely there! She raises this issue one evening, expressing her dissatisfaction with the situation.

The result? Barney suddenly explodes in violent anger: Sybil retaliates.

What is this conflict, this extreme expression of emotional reality about? What are its origins?

Sybil's childhood experience:

As the eldest of three, Sybil was well aware of her father's absence from home, either at work or to attend sporting commitments in the evenings and at weekends. Her mother spent the time without him, took the children out, did all the chores including the gardening, so it often seemed as though her mother was the only parent. Sybil resolved, as a child, that this would never happen to her — hence her reaction to her present predicament.

Barney's childhood experience:

When Barney was ten years old, his mother, who was often left in a similar situation to that of Sybil's mother, left his father, taking the children with her. His father was devastated. Now, when Sybil raises this matter as one with which she is not happy, his reaction of rage as an adult really covers up his feelings of extreme *fear* — 'What if she should leave me, the way my father was left?'

By understanding these family of origin histories, Sybil and Barney can talk it through with much better understanding of themselves and of each other. It will be possible to come up with a resolution to this issue; however, in order for both to *win,* there will need to be compromises on both sides: Barney and Sybil must make a real effort to spend quality time together.

We suggest *you* draw up *your* genogram and think about family patterns of communication and interaction and how you experienced these as a child. To help resolve past issues you may need to talk with members of your family and say how it was for you, or even write a letter setting out your impressions and thoughts. If the family members have died, it is still possible to 'work through' your emotionality by writing a letter as though they were alive (just to give yourself the opportunity to 'get it out') or by seeking professional expertise if you cannot work it through yourself.

'Contracts' and Emotional Over-reaction

People enter relationships with what could be called 'contracts'. Ideally, these contracts take the form of agreements between the two partners which are related to the doing (or not doing) of some definite thing. For example, some years ago a typical contract between marriage partners went as follows: The husband will support the family; the wife will stay at home and run the house.

In today's complex world, such simplicity of agreement is rarely possible. And the situation is further complicated by the fact that the contracts can take different forms: in the SPOKEN CONTRACT, the partners openly discuss the contract/agreement; in the UNSPOKEN CONTRACT, one or both the partners assume there is a contract or agreement, but it's never discussed; and in the UNCONSCIOUS CONTRACT, one or both the partners have a contract but are unaware that it exists.

Such contracts are designed to meet the deep wants and expectations of each individual, so that if they are not met, the result is anxiety and often anger. And because people make assumptions, taking it for granted that others share their particular needs and wants, contracts are a source of great conflict in relationships.

Spoken Contracts

Here are some common 'spoken' contracts:

- when we have $X we will look for a house to buy
- when I finish the course we'll move to another place
- we'll go skiing for our annual holidays
- we'll start a family in three years' time
- we'll visit both your family and my family once a month
- I'll cook and wash and you'll clean our home
- you can decide on home decorations
- I'll manage our finances
- we'll have a joint bank account

NOTE: Spoken contracts are talked about and agreed upon.

Unspoken contracts

Here are some common 'unspoken' contracts:

- I will develop my career — you will take care of the home ... once we're established, then we'll have time for each other
- I will love and cherish you, and then you will do the same for me
- I will be a good husband/wife and then you will always love me
- my career is really the most important thing in my life
- we must share every thought and experience together
- I will love you, and you will stop drinking
- our circle of friends will be *my* friends
- you will take all the responsibility and I will lean on you
- I'll not permit you to compete with me professionally
- I'll make sure you change the type of clothes you wear
- the care of the children will be mine alone: you will not interfere
- you will be honest and fair with our money
- I'll teach you the correct way to behave
- you will be the lover I've dreamed of all my life and I will love you deeply in return
- when we're financially established I'll have a baby
- I'll prepare health food meals so you'll lose weight

Frank and Emily marry, secure in the knowledge that they are in love, are suited to each other and can therefore look forward to a happy and rewarding partnership. Emily has an unspoken contract with Frank: she will wait until they are financially secure, then have a child. She sees no reason to discuss this — after all, it's normal for everyone to want children, isn't it?

Frank, however, has an entirely different unspoken contract in mind. He assumes that Emily agrees that they will establish themselves, then discuss having children. He tends to think that he'd rather not be a father, but is happy to leave the whole issue until some time in the future.

When the appropriate time (according to Emily) arrives, she announces she's pregnant. Frank is furious: Emily's broken the contract.

Emily is both astonished and angry at Frank's reaction: she didn't agree to discuss the issue, as far as she was concerned, there was no question as to whether they'd have children — that was the unspoken contract she'd had in mind when they married.

What has happened? Each person went into the marriage with a conscious (but unspoken) set of expectations of the relationship — 'contracts'. Neither saw the need to discuss the issue of children, since each assumed it was perfectly clear what the unverbalised agreement was. How wrong they were!

People enter relationships with plans, beliefs, expectations and fantasies. Some of these have been discussed openly, some remain unspoken, and some are hidden in the unconscious mind.

Unconscious contracts

Many contracts are never expressed in words because the person is unaware that a contract even exists in the unconscious mind.

The contracts that exist at this unconscious level may be quite unreasonable in the demands they make, and are often influenced by the life program the person carries from his or her family of origin. Here are some unconscious contracts:

- I'll give you sex if you give me comfort
- I will leave unless you become a good lover
- I'll allow you to dominate me — that way I feel protected
- I'll upset you occasionally because I like a good fight
- I am superior; you are inferior, therefore don't try to tell me what to do — ever!
- I'll do my thing and you'll do yours
- If you ever stop saying you love me I'll make sure you pay for it
- My possessions are mine and not to be touched by you

As we have said, these are unconscious contracts. Counselling often uncovers such unconscious contracts, in many cases to the astonishment of the couple, who have not realised contracts were operating in the marriage.

Contracts, spoken, unspoken and unconscious, are a source of great conflict and therefore deep emotion. Some contracts are just plain unrealistic, and can never be fulfilled; others fail because it is incorrectly assumed by one partner that the other understands the contract and agrees to it. To make things even more difficult, as a relationship develops, the contracts can change: the 'agreements' that exist in the romantic love stage will change in the familiarity of marriage, and the arrival of children will further affect them.

When Kirsten and Patrick first met and fell in love, they did everything together. Patrick was an enthusiast about sport, and Kirsten went along with him when he played golf, she feigned interest in motor racing and even took lessons in tennis to please him. In turn, he was willing to be paraded in front of her wide circle of friends and indulge in what was, to him, idle chitchat. Patrick's unspoken contract was: 'We will share our (mainly my) interests together.' Kirsten's unspoken contract was different: 'At the present time, during our courtship, I will be involved in your sports interests.'

Kirsten and Patrick marry. Quite soon, Kirsten changes her contract — now it is: 'My interest is really the home, so I won't continue to be involved in your sport.' Patrick's version of the contract hasn't changed. Patrick sees that Kirsten has lost her former interest in sharing his sport with him and he becomes angry: 'You always wanted to share things before we were married ... but now you couldn't be less interested!' He is furious because he believes that she has broken her side of the bargain.

Kirsten is correspondingly furious: 'What made you think I was going to spend the rest of my life following you around to sporting occasions, when I've now got something much more important to do?'

Such 'breaking' of contracts causes great emotional response. 'I've been betrayed' thinks one partner. The other is disappointed and angry: 'It was never discussed with me!' Rage and depression are common results, the outraged partner acting as though a real and legal contract has been unfairly broken. The emotional response is particularly high if one person firmly believes he or she has fulfilled one side of the bargain, and the other partner has not.

TAKE CARE: Examine your relationship for 'contracts' — have you assumed that there is an agreement between you over issues you have never openly discussed?

Never ever take it for granted that your partner has the same contract in mind ... check it out!

Rules and Strong Emotions

Every family has unspoken rules that govern behaviour and appropriate responses to certain situations. Every one-to-one relationship has similar unspoken rules.

Family rules are very rarely openly expressed, but each member knows they exist. These 'laws' are intended to control, and, as a child, they become known to you by the way the rule is repeated, over and over, until you unconsciously accept it. Here are some examples of unwritten laws/rules that are used to govern families:

- father always knows best
- don't ever lose your temper
- be careful not to let your real feelings show
- don't ever disagree
- don't ever take anyone seriously
- blame yourself if things go wrong
- the person who makes the most noise gets the most attention

- be nice and always do the right thing
- children come first

Each family has its own set of unexpressed, usually unconscious, but powerful rules. For example, if the family rule is 'Father knows best', but one of the children challenges this, the collective anger of the family can descend:

'Listen to your father! He knows what's best for you!'

'I'm your father — you should pay attention to me!'

The 'law' that the father is superior has been broken, and the father feels he is not being given the respect owed to him, so he becomes resentful and angry.

A common unwritten rule in many families is 'The children are the most important.' In such a family, if, say, the husband says to his wife: 'Let's leave the children with my mother and you and I have a holiday together,' the reaction he gets may be unexpectedly strong: 'Without our children? What can you be thinking of?' Alternatively, the reaction may not be strong — just a refusal to do what is suggested, with perhaps, an excuse: 'The children don't like being away from us.'

Although neither partner may understand the reason for her emotional reaction, the wife has become angry or anxious because a family rule has been violated. In this case, the personal growth of the wife would involve understanding what in her life history has contributed to this anxiety.

Rules in a one-to-one relationship can also be the cause of conflict, depression and even rage. The source of these strong emotions may not just be the rules themselves, but *who has the authority to make them*.

This struggle for the power to set the rules can result in what seems to be quite disproportionate emotional responses. For example, a partner may be quite ready to accept that the other has the 'right' to make a rule about which one of them is dominant in the relationship, but when the person *demands* the right to make this rule, the response suddenly becomes one of angry resentment. 'I was willing to agree until you demanded it!'

Any new relationship has a framework to follow:

- what rules will there be?
- who sets the rules?
- how will the rules be enforced?
- what happens if the rules are broken?

It must be emphasised that these rules or laws are not written down and are rarely even discussed. Their existence is shown by the patterns of behaviour that are repeated in a relationship. For example:

There is an unwritten rule in Pete and Joan's relationship that when opinions are given, he is to be listened to and she is to be humoured, but largely ignored. Every time that Pete gives his opinion, he expects Joan to listen respectfully. If she doesn't, he demands that she does. If necessary he will pause, or repeat himself, or make a sharp comment, all to make sure the rule is obeyed. When Joan speaks, however, Pete smiles indulgently, but doesn't really listen. At social gatherings he makes lightly critical remarks about Joan's opinions, and Joan, in turn, doesn't expect that her thoughts carry much weight. These patterns of behaviour are the norm — so the rule is clearly understood, although never written down or discussed.

Incidentally, this pattern of interaction is really an *issue* for Pete and Joan and needs to be resolved if the relationship is to grow into mature love (see Steps Four and Five).

Here are examples of some unexpressed rules occurring in relationships. Remember, people are usually not conscious that such rules are in operation. Note that each of them has the potential to cause explosive emotional responses if it is challenged:

- if you can't win — anything you do is wrong
- if you insist on talking about our relationship I refuse to co-operate
- before I listen to you I have to be sure you will be talking about an area in which I feel safe
- my opinion must not be challenged, except in a secret way known only to me
- I'm the mother of these children and I'll make all the decisions regarding their upbringing because I know best
- don't you dare insult my self-worth by disagreeing with me
- I'm the man and really the boss so don't disagree
- you're an emotional clod like all men so don't make-believe you have any feelings
- I won't forgive you until you have suffered to a measure which is known only to me and which you deserve according to my sense of justice

TAKE CARE: You live by these unwritten, unexpressed and usually unconscious rules at your peril. They are hidden enemies of a marriage. Understanding of self may bring them to consciousness so they can be dealt with, resulting in personal and relationship growth.

Extreme emotional responses, which may in times of stress even include physical violence, are largely *automatic*. The person who is anxious/angry/insecure/overly depressed needs to understand the reasons for these emotional responses.Remember, it is not the existence of the rules/laws themselves in relationships which is the problem — structure is necessary in all partnerships. Rather, it is the conflict which arises from: the type of rules and what they demand; the question of who sets each rule; and the fact that most rules are implicit, that is they are never discussed openly.

If the rules of your relationship are fair and reasonable and agreed to by both partners, then much of the possible source of trouble is removed. And rules that already exist and have the potential to cause conflict and anger can be replaced by counter-rules — new and better ones.

The key is to always remember that the breaking of relationship/family rules creates poorly understood emotional reactions ... and once you realise *why* you feel the way you do, you are well on the way to mastering those programmed responses.

Crazy-makers and Over-reactivity

Anger is produced by 'crazy-making' situations where it becomes impossible to think straight. You grow angry because the wires are crossed, it doesn't compute, you can't make sense of the situation.

Here are some classic crazy-making situations:

Will it never end?

A couple have poor communication skills. They discuss an issue that is causing them great conflict. The discussion goes around and around in circles. They talk endlessly about it. No solution is ever reached. Their computers (brains) become clogged with all sorts of contradictory messages and proposed solutions. All their problems are treated this way: talk, talk, talk. Nothing is ever *resolved.* The result: despair and anger.

The double bind

A father wants his son to be uninhibited and free — to express his personality without restriction. He also wants his son to be quiet at the dinner table. The result of these contradictory messages: confusion, upset, anger.

Here is another classic double bind:

Eric says to his wife, Jean, 'You're getting into a rut, dear ... can't you dress yourself up a bit more? I want to be proud of you, so why not buy something a little more attractive, a little more up-to-date?'

Jean is delighted to follow his request. She buys a striking new outfit for a friend's fortieth birthday party, and, when she arrives there, gains a great deal of favourable attention and comment.

Jean expects Eric to be pleased and proud. Instead, when they arrive home, he flies into a jealous rage. Why did she make such an exhibition of herself? Who was she trying to attract?

Jean is in the typical double-bind situation: if she follows Eric's wishes she's wrong; if she doesn't, she's wrong as well! The result? Anger, resentment and despair.

The double-bind is a powerful crazy-maker because people cannot win. If they do one thing they lose — if they do the opposite they lose.

Stop changing the subject

Two people in a relationship have problems that need to be discussed. One in particular is threatened by the idea of opening up and expressing real thoughts, wants and feelings. Every time an issue is brought up for discussion, he or she begins to continually change the subject, to raise irrelevant points, to avoid truthful self-disclosure. The result: disappointment, rage, despair.

'Yes, but ...'

People frequently respond to a communication from someone else with these words: 'Yes, but ...' The 'Yes' sounds like an agreement. It isn't! The person is actually saying 'No' because the word 'but' negates the positive meaning of yes. The person is actually saying 'On the contrary ...'

A lengthy series of 'Yes, but ...' responses can trigger an emotional reaction because the speaker is giving two contradictory messages simultaneously — Yes and No.

'Yes, but ...' can drive the calmest person into a frenzy of irritation, and unfortunately it is a very common spoken response in conversation.

People who use 'Yes, but ...' responses are usually not really wanting to hear or accept what the other person is saying. One reason for this is to ward off the anxiety of having to consider changing opinions or thoughts. This is a position of: no change = safety.

Anger as a Weapon

Anger can be used to manipulate other people. If one partner is afraid of strong emotions such as anger, then the other has a handy weapon to force submission. Being angry becomes an effective way to make the other person conform to the aggressive partner's ideas of 'correct' behaviour.

But the partner who tries to avoid conflict by collapsing, and so surrendering against his or her better judgement, will carry an increasing load of grudges and resentment, and may one day announce: 'I no longer love you. I don't want our relationship to continue. It's finished. Goodbye.'

The aggressive partner is likely to be astonished at this news. What can have gone wrong? Why, there were no arguments in the relationship, no conflict ... everything seemed to be going along quite smoothly ...

TAKE CARE: If you 'win' by using anger to coerce your partner into doing what you want, the price may be losing that person's affection and closeness.

Anger can produce fear, and fear is the greatest hindrance to intimacy.

Anger as a Cover-up

Anger can also be used to avoid the uncomfortable truth: we have feelings of anxiety/dislike/sadness, but we don't want to admit they exist because we fear they will *weaken* us, so we convert them into anger.

Why? Because anger gives a (false) feeling of being in charge — of strength and confidence. The anger is actually being used to prop up a vulnerable and anxious inner self, so it is, essentially, a cover-up — a way of *avoiding* rather than facing, reality.

For example, Rod is frightened that his wife Wanda will take away his independence with her over-protectiveness, but instead of being in touch with this fear, Rod becomes very angry and abusive when Wanda tries to do things for him.

Displacement of Anger

We often see situations in counselling where one person in a relationship *displaces* his or her anger on to the other. That is, the anger that actually belongs somewhere else, perhaps the workplace, is *not* expressed there, but brought home to be taken out on the (innocent) partner.

Here the feelings of tension and anger are taken from one place and put in another because the person finds it difficult to express his or her true feelings in the appropriate situation.

Some people have unresolved anger towards a parent and take it out on a spouse; some people are angry at a spouse and take it out on someone at work or on a child, or the dog, or a car door! Some people drive furiously and abuse other motorists when the anger really has to do with unresolved family issues.

So you see how the dissatisfaction with self is transferred to someone else. People who displace anger and tension are not in touch with their real selves: they are unable to stand back and assess the situation. Instead, the dissatisfaction is *displaced,* so that the anger is directed at a partner or someone else close, rather than the person or situation which triggered the emotion.

This displacement of anger is unfair, irrational and destructive to relationships, because it destroys trust and intimacy. Unjustified criticism of a partner leads to resentment and anger and occurs when the other person is afraid to look clearly at himself or herself.

Anger as a Tension Release

Some people learn that when they express anger or strong emotion they release their feelings of tension and end up feeling much more relaxed. For that reason, such people can become addicted to the expression of anger in rage or violence towards another person, because the relief is so great.

Anger as Scapegoating

After experiencing enormous tension for some time they find a way to *scapegoat* someone else: it can be done by husbands to wives, parents to children, supervisors to employees — anyone who can be put into an 'underdog' position.

Scapegoating is a universal phenomenon: it is found in the family, in the workplace, in schools. People find satisfaction in blaming someone else for the tension and anger they feel.

When you find a scapegoat to blame, in some way you pass your problem on to someone else as well as finding a convenient outlet for the tension and rage that fills you.

TAKE CARE: Often families locked in marital conflict will turn on one member and use him or her as a scapegoat for all the anger and tension that has been created in the family situation. This action not only disguises the real reasons for the conflict, but can also emotionally cripple the unfortunate person selected as a family scapegoat.

If we are filled with emotional energy such as rage, violence and jealousy, it can be helpful to release the tension with some kind of physical activity such as sport, running, gardening, even energetic housework. Some people even pound a mattress or a punching bag!

Anger as Manipulation

One way to get your way is to use anger with people who hate or wish to avoid anger. Many people will capitulate against their better judgement. Beware, however, as 'gunnysacking' often results in people who fear anger levelled at them. Feelings often die. Sudden decisions to end a relationship often brew for years and then cannot be changed as too much hurt has been done.

Anger from Burnout

There are increasing numbers of people so overworked and stressed that their state is called 'burnout'. They are functioning at a high level but with very little energy reserve. Control over their emotions has diminished and they are in urgent need of a program of recovery. It is a dangerous time because in so many ways the person seems normal and is functioning. Angry outbursts are, however, one sign of the condition.

Anger as a Sign of Sleep Deprivation

In recent years sleep researchers have highlighted the effects of snoring, sleep apnoea, and a lack of sleep. Once again one of the signs is angry outbursts and the inability to utilise normal controls.

Anger from General Unhappiness

People who are experiencing life as not going anywhere, boring, meaningless, painful may seek a way to dump on others. This can also stem from a playing out of the victim game. The 'poor me' game which Eric Berne highlighted is often manifested by picking on others.

Many people who present themselves for marriage therapy are vague in their complaints and it turns out that they are quite dissatisfied with their own lives.

Other Reasons for Anger

By now it is apparent that there can be many causes of anger: playing the victim game, depression, low self-esteem, hypoglycaemia, high-blood pressure and other health problems, grief, alcohol or drug abuse and so on. If you have experienced any of the above causes of anger, try dealing with the problem(s) instead of creating problems in your relationships.

Few people take care to understand that their anger can come from many possible sources. This single fact causes many to destroy their relationships rather than taking responsibility for their own inner distress. We have taken time on this critical area because herein lies the richest source of marriage failure.

WHEN ANGER IS JUSTIFIED

In the last section we dealt with many reasons for anger, but how about a situation where it is *justified*?

A small percentage of angry feelings are not only justified, but should be expressed freely. Bear in mind, however, that we are all extremely clever at finding reasons why we should feel badly done by and therefore be righteously angry. Be very careful that you are not fooling yourself into believing you are justified in the rage you feel.

If you are to express anger, *it must be expressed in an assertive way*. Here are some ground rules for expressing justified anger:

1. Determine if your anger is justified. Has the person broken a promise/commitment/contract? Have you been treated most unfairly? (Be honest with yourself: many pampered people find lots of things 'unfair'?) Has the person stolen from you? Cheated you? Destroyed your good name? Broken a promise? Genuinely mistreated you?

2. Do not attack in the heat of anger: calm down so that you will be able to express yourself clearly, fairly and assertively. This control will enable you to get your message across much more effectively than rage ever can.

3. Set procedures (see beginning of Step 5), or find an appropriate place to speak. Only the 'offender' should hear your expression of anger and if you find yourself looking for an audience, ask yourself why — perhaps you have hidden motives. In particular, the expression of deep anger in front of children should be avoided: children cannot be expected to fully understand the situation and they should never be used as pawns in an argument. Children learn much by positive expressions of anger.

4. Make out an awareness wheel, which will help you *identify exactly what you are angry about* (don't think it's obvious ... it may not be!)

5. Do not strike or hit anyone, break anything, or injure yourself. If you do any of these things you are *out of control* both of yourself and of events. (If you do have the need to do any of these things you should look at the reasons behind these violent emotions. You may need professional help to discover them.)

Justified anger should be expressed, not turned into resentment, which can fester for years, subtly poisoning a relationship.

Some people (usually women, because of childhood conditioning) say they never feel angry. We have seen many instances where a woman has had great advantage taken of her — yet she feels no anger. What she does say is that she feels *hurt* (and usually tears go with this). It is actually healthier to be in touch with your anger and deal with it constructively, rather than disguise it as hurt or disappointment.

JEALOUSY: AN EMOTION THAT DESTROYS

'I'm not jealous, I just love you so much.'

How many times have we heard words like that? Hundreds? Thousands? They are the words of a person for whom love involves excessive dependency. Many people in A-frame or lean-to type marriages have the experiences which we call jealousy.

Jealousy is an emotion which comes from the fearful part of the self. People with large amounts of pseudo self, who look to others for their self-worth, can be overwhelmed with jealous feelings.

At the first sign of threat to their dependent relationship, a tension can take over. It is the sign of fear of loss and can even be interpreted as love. What people call love is often body sensations to which the label 'love' has been applied. In reality it might be a physical/emotional syndrome which is actually anxiety or fear.

When people go to put labels on these psycho-physical sensations they often find the most socially acceptable one. Since people hate to admit jealousy they will conveniently call the surging up of powerful emotion 'love', 'caring', 'admiration' or some other socially acceptable word.

Jealous people may shift the blame by saying things like, 'I don't distrust *you*, it's those men/women you work with. I know they have their eyes on you!'

The fact is that jealousy is often a powerful inner force coming out of a person's insecure self. The force drives the partner to control, cling, hold on to what he/she fears losing. This fearful child part of the person might be so smothering that the object of affection wants to pull away to escape the dependency. The smothered partner might lose respect for the jealous person, seeing him or her as weak and helpless and not valuing his/her own self.

Remember, the more romantic part of love demands some elusiveness, not clinging dependency. Hence, jealousy kills anything romantic in the relationship. Any feeling of love must involve *freedom* and a partner feels trapped if the other is jealous. Take a person's freedom away and they feel resentment (not warmth, closeness, intimacy or love).

All of this explains why there is often so much emotional over-reaction in A-frame and lean-to type marriages. We might emphasise also that parallel type marriages are often a reaction to this pain of over-dependency. People can use a self-defence mechanism of denial or rationalisation and create a less dependent or less involved relationship simply to avoid the pain of jealousy. When someone says, 'I don't care anymore,' this can be a way of softening the hurt of rejection by using the defenses of Reaction Formation and denial.

What Can be Done to Conquer Jealous Feelings?

If you suffer from the very real torments of jealousy, then you need a prescription to help 'cure' you. The most suitable remedy is to create an H-type relationship. As you by now know, this is done by strengthening your real self. Naturally, this is not easy but, bit by bit, as you build your self-confidence, self-awareness, self-esteem, self-love — all those many parts of a mature self — fear will have less and less power over you.

The child in you which was hurt badly will still be there, of course.

Many of us have been reared in fearfully insecure environments. And there will still be twitches of jealousy — the triggers of fear can continue for a long time — but as you build the strengths involved in valuing your own self, more and more control over fear is created.

One secret is to face your fear honestly — don't deny it exists, don't rationalise and don't try to shift the blame. If you seek to excuse this soul-destroying force, you will never conquer the fear and anxiety — that fear of abandonment which comes from early childhood will go with you into old age. What a hell that can be to live with!

Another secret is to be honest with your partner about the fear. Don't label it 'love'. It's usually plain old-fashioned fear disguised in some other wrapping. By using the assertive communication skills of self-disclosure in a non-accusatory manner, you can defuse the power of the emotion. Say something like: 'I want you to know that I am jealous at times. I recognise this is a problem for me, so I am working at my problem. I trust you — it is me, not you. If you see me being jealous, forgive me. I'll conquer this fear eventually.'

It might sound a little bit 'corny' but the point is to find a way to be honest about the fact that you have a problem. Then, and only then, can you succeed in gaining a victory over jealousy.

Summary

In Step Seven we looked at Dealing with Strong Emotions:

- the influences Family of Origin has on strong emotional reactions
- constructing a personal genogram
- what causes emotional over-reactions: experiences in Family of Origin; 'contracts' and 'rules'; crazy-makers
- how unjustified anger can be used for ulterior purposes, and to avoid dealing with real issues
- expressing justified anger
- what causes jealousy and how to deal with it
- how anger can be used to avoid responsibility

Step Eight

How to build mature love and romance into your marriage

Romantic love is not the be all and end all of love: for many it is a starting point — for no one is it the end point. Why? Because that sort of 'love' passes — sometimes very fast, sometimes slowly — but it always ends.

What happens to people who want to go through many years of marriage together? How do they stay with each other and still love? During counselling we have frequently heard the statements: 'I love my partner, but I'm not in love,' or 'I don't love him/her because I'm not "in love".'

We have wrestled with this problem for fifty years: many experts have been read, thousands of clients have been closely listened to, and we, ourselves, have had to deal with our own changing experiences of love. Out of all this has emerged a way of understanding the problem of loving 'until death do us part'. Our most basic conclusions about love are these:

1. Everyone's definition of love is different

After all, it is a way of explaining what is a human experience. Love, as a 'thing', does not exist — what exists is a kind of experience which people define as love. This means that to understand what love is, we have to listen to each individual's explanation of what it is for him or her, not what we think it is.

When someone says 'I love you', don't think you know what is meant. A word like 'love' is only a convenient, shortcut label for a complex human experience. Ask the person to explain to you exactly what the experience of love means to him/her.

2. We need to understand each person's individual experience of love

Since everyone's experience of love is quite unique, we needed to find ways of understanding why it is so different for different people.

3. Romantic love needs to grow into mature love

The word 'mature' does not mean that such love is for old people: it means for us, 'balance'. It also means that we experience with many parts of our personality, something which can be summed up as 'love'. You will see later in this Step that romantic love is an expression of only one small part of our personality.

Why is this significant? Because it shows very clearly that the love most valued in our society — romantic love — is not very solid at all. It is fun, enjoyable, an enormous pleasure and can be addictive for that very reason, but it is not lasting. Because romantic love is only short-lived, it needs to grow into something more permanent, deeper, more intimate and more out of the real self.

4. Mature love is achievable

The MATURE LOVE PROGRAMME which we will describe for you later in this Step, is designed to show you the many ways that you can express and grow in love. It is not merely an insubstantial series of good ideas and hints that might help — it is a clear and precise program in which you can set specific goals and work towards achieving greater love in your relationship.

5. There is always potential for growth in love

The Mature Love Programme shows you where you are not mature and balanced — where you are needing to develop. In nearly all of us there are areas in which we are weak in our experiences of love. Now you can identify them and give yourself the opportunity to grow and grow in love.

All your life you can develop in expressions of love. The experience called 'love' can continue to become deeper, more all-encompassing, and more clearly recognised by you and your partner.

Such analysis of the love experience will lead you to see that many things which your partner does now and you presently take for granted are actually expressions of love. For example, when your partner is loyal and shows fidelity, you will see that this comes out of the CRITICAL PARENT part of self. You will recognise that your partner loves you in many ways which words cannot express — more ways than you are ordinarily aware of.

6. Developing Mature Love is not easy

The Mature Love Programme is not easy stuff. It is designed for people who want to think and work towards a more satisfying relationship. It may not be easy ... but the rewards are wonderful!

TRANSACTIONAL ANALYSIS: FOUNDATION FOR THE MATURE LOVE PROGRAMME

Before we give you details on how to develop your relationship towards mature love, it is important for you to understand the main ideas behind transactional analysis, as this is a necessary part of understanding the Mature Love Programme.

In the nineteen-sixties, Eric Berne published a bestseller called *Games People Play*. In this book he outlined a way in which interactions between people could be analysed. He identified three roles (or ego states): parent, adult and child as components of personality. (Figure 8.1.)

Dr Berne called the system transactional analysis (often shortened to TA), because he saw all our interactions with other people as consisting of a series of 'transactions', where one person would make contact and the other would respond out of one of the three ego states.

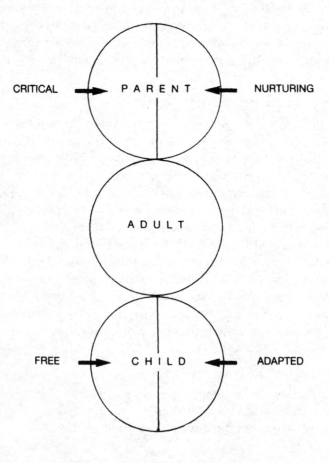

Figure 8.1: Egostates (the parts of your personality)

These ego states, that are embodied in our personality, manifest themselves in different ways in different situations and are reflected in our verbal and non-verbal communication. A clear understanding of the Parent, Adult and Child ego states and how to identify them in your own behaviour as well as in others, will help you to become aware of the dynamics of your relationship and how love is either built or destroyed. The interaction between two people is complicated: very often your behaviour will trigger certain feelings and behaviours in the other person that you don't intend, and which, in fact, can be quite puzzling. Just why did the person react that way? What did you say or do to provoke that response?

Here is a brief description of each ego state:

The parent ego state

The parent part of a person develops from all the parental messages experienced as a child. Two separate parent roles can be identified:

(a) Nurturing Parent: This behaviour is loving and protective — it is sympathetic, helpful and supportive to others (and nurturing to self as well, in thought and deed).

(b) Critical Parent: There are two functions that come out of this ego state: (i) criticism, fault finding, blaming, accusing, put downs, threatening, ridiculing and other aggressive behaviours; (ii) the valuable functions of setting limits, establishing values, reaching for noble ideals, being positive and assertive. (These two functions can be seen as negative and positive respectively.) The coercive, manipulative behaviour which is often seen in the Critical Parent is really an aggressive effort to enforce values, beliefs, customs and rules which could be taught or expressed in a non-aggressive manner.

Critical Parent behaviour can be directed towards others or towards self. Many people have low self-esteem because they are too critical of themselves.

The child ego state

There are two child roles which develop according to our individual life experiences:

(a) The Free Child: This is the delightful, spontaneous and fun-loving role we can all play, where we allow our feelings to take over and we relax into the freedom of enjoying our emotions. This state is associated with sexuality, with touching, with enjoying physical sensations, laughing, having fun, enjoying life, being creative.

The free child state can also allow us to show other emotions in an uninhibited way, so that we, for example, express fear, frustration quite openly.

(b) The Adapted Child: There are two distinct behaviours that come out of this ego state: (i) doing what is 'expected', being compliant, non-assertive, obedient, suiting the expectations of others. (ii) Sometimes the adapted child is aggressive and defiant in order to protect the sense of self which feels threatened by the rules and instructions received from people operating in parent or adult mode. This rebellion brings an automatic 'No!' as a response to any order or instruction. The rebellious part of the adapted child often appears strongly during adolescent years and is a vital step to adult development. When, however, this rebellion appears later, perhaps in the thirties or forties, it can lead to severe marital discord.

It is important to remember that when you are in the child part of your personality, you are coming from your *feelings*, not from your *reason.* You *respond,* rather than *think*.

The adult ego state

In the adult ego state you use your logic and reasoning powers: you examine facts and come to decisions that are based on reason rather than emotions (child state) or the 'rules' of life (parent state).

The adult role is for rational thought and decision making, but not much help where enjoyment, humour, passion and delight in life are concerned.

A person low on adult can often be said to 'lack common sense'. A person with excessive adult can have problems with feelings of love, warmth and passion — and might be boring or dull.

Important Points Concerning the Three Ego States:

• all of us have within us aspects of parent, child and adult ego states. Usually one or two dominate a personality.
• no one ego state is better/more important than any other
• a *balance* of parent-child-adult is a goal of maturity
• we can all choose which ego state is appropriate for any one situation and learn to recognise constructive and destructive responses

Recognising Different Ego States

It can be difficult to detect which particular ego state is in operation, either in yourself or in someone else. To add to the problem, people will often switch from one to another during the course of a conversation. Other people will disguise the ego state they are in so well that they appear to be, say, in an adult ego state, when actually they are in critical parent.

The clues which give away each operating style — parent, adult and child — are contained in body language, choice of words and tone of voice. If you listen carefully to what you say and how you say it, you will begin to understand the different behaviours.

Interesting though this all may be, of what relevance are the ego states and transactional analysis of long-term relationships?

The answer is that transactional analysis provides a way of looking at the unique qualities of your own personality and the personalities of those close to you. This provides you with awareness of your behaviour and the effect this has upon other people. More importantly, this will help you understand the Mature Love Programme.

What Happens When People Interact?

The way each of us is in our relating to other people has a profound effect on the way *they relate to us*. By understanding the different ego states that operate in each of us, we can begin to make some sense of what happens in relationships.

Here is an example:

Joan and Ted have been experiencing great difficulties in their marriage of only three months. To Ted, Joan seems to have undergone a personality change, saying things like:

'I asked you to buy some milk — why didn't you?'

'Get up, will you, it's late!'

'You're always leaving a mess in the bathroom!'

Joan never spoke this way before they were married. Worse still, every time she speaks this way Ted reacts violently and a fight follows.

What's happening? Joan's critical parent behaviour is 'pulling' from Ted rebellious child behaviour: she criticises, he 'twitches' and lurches into a rebellious response.

We think that critical parent behaviour (of the negative kind) may be the most damaging behaviour of all to a marriage. This is because it is 'parental' and pulls a 'child' out of the other person. This child response can be rebellious (aggressive) or it can be compliant (non-assertive).

What can be done to prevent this natural transaction occurring?

When Joan launches into her critical parent ego state, Ted could respond out of another ego state. For example, he could assume the adult ego state and say: 'I don't like it when you speak to me that way.'

Actually, Joan and Ted have an issue on their hands. They need to resolve it by using communication skills and sharing their awareness. Ted can make a REQUEST FOR CHANGE, that is, ask Joan to give her criticisms or complaints in an assertive way and/or request him to discuss whatever it may be as an issue.

Their problem really lies in their childhood histories, therefore, if each draws a genogram to help them think through the past, it is possible they will begin to understand why they behave in certain ways and this understanding will help defuse the situation.

If Ted and Joan cannot solve this problem of her coercive behaviour and his immediate emotional response, then they may need to seek professional help to avoid destroying their marriage.

NOTE: Issues must always be discussed with both parties in the adult ego state.

Constructing an Egogram

The ego states in Figure 8.1 gives us an idea of the relationship of the three roles — parent, adult and child — but they do not show how much energy an individual is devoting to each one.

This problem was addressed by Dr John Dusay in his book *Egograms* (Harper & Row 1977). The concept he developed of an 'egogram' is like a psychological fingerprint, providing a profile (using a bar graph) of the average amount of energy an individual invests in each ego state.

NOTE: Details for the construction and analysis of egograms are based on Dr John Dusay's book.

In Figure 8.2 an egogram is shown with equal amounts of energy in each ego state. You will notice that the five columns are labelled, from left to right as follows: CP (critical parent), NP (nurturing parent), A (adult), FC (free child) and AC (adapted child).

It is highly unlikely that anyone would have a perfectly balanced egogram like this — most people have distinct patterns of highs and lows on their bar graphs. In fact, equal distribution of energy in a person's egogram is not the goal at all. In our view, balance is being able to dis-

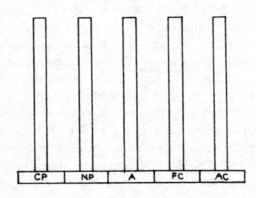

Figure 8.2

cover which ego states need more concentration of effort to achieve the best distribution of energy for the individual concerned.

Here are two examples of egograms.

The egogram in Figure 8.3 belongs to Bradley, a high-achieving, self-confessed 'workaholic'. Notice how little free child Bradley has in his make-up, and how much critical parent. This is a reflection of his lifestyle and overriding interest in business, and clearly shows how little fun and spontaneous emotion he enjoys.

The egogram in Figure 8.4 belongs to Celia, a person who has absolutely martyred herself for her family. Nothing is too much trouble for Celia, as long as it has to do with someone else ... *herself* she neglects. Her egogram shows this over-emphasis on nurturing parent and adapted child, but very little development of the aspects of critical parent and free child.

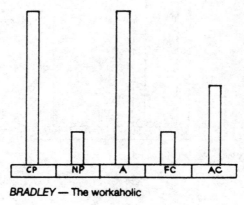

BRADLEY — The workaholic

Figure 8.3

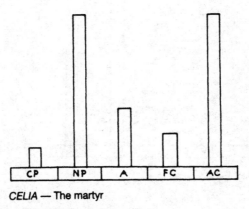

CELIA — The martyr

Figure 8.4

To give you practice in constructing an egogram, first choose a friend and draw one for him or her. Draw a high vertical column to represent the area you instinctively 'feel' is the dominant part of the person.

Then select the part of the personality that you sense is demonstrated the least. Draw a low column to represent it. The other columns can then be filled in, each at its comparative value to the highest and lowest.

Using your intuition this way is surprisingly accurate, because you unconsciously absorb a great deal of information about anyone you relate to, and you should therefore trust your hunches as far as the comparative heights of the egogram sections are concerned.

Here are another two sample egograms.

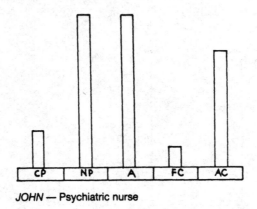

JOHN — Psychiatric nurse

Figure 8.5

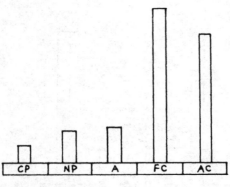

PHYLLIS — Risk-taker

Figure 8.6

In the egogram of Figure 8.5 we have John, who is a psychiatric nurse. His egogram shows a high regard for other people (high nurturing parent) as well as a low interest in his own need to relax and enjoy life (low free child). In addition, his need to be highly responsible places him high in the adult ego state.

Figure 8.6 shows the egogram of Phyllis, the risk-taker and excitement-seeker. Phyllis is always looking for that peak experience which will thrill and delight her. She experiments with drugs, and lives life in the 'fast lane'. Her personal egogram shows low critical parent (she ignores the rules of society), low nurturing parent (she doesn't look after anyone else, let alone herself), low adult (she never thinks about the consequences), but very high free child (all for pleasure).

Now examine the egogram you have constructed for your friend. Can you draw any conclusions about your friend's personality and behaviour and the egogram you have drawn? Do the areas where the person is particularly high, or particularly low in an ego state correspond with personality traits you have observed? Is there some suggestion of *why* and *how* your friend acts in certain situations?

The egogram for your friend was intended as a trial run: now you are at the interesting stage of constructing your *own* egogram.

When drawing your own egogram, don't illustrate what you'd like to be, or how you think other people see you — draw it as you feel you really are.

Remember, there is no 'perfect' or 'normal' egogram that everyone should strive to achieve. The aim is to have a healthy *balance* of the ego states, so that no one area dominates to the point where it completely overshadows the other ego states.

Analysing Your Own Egogram: Positive and Negative Aspects of Ego States

Be relaxed and honest when you draw your own egogram — no-one else need see it, and it is not a criticism or praise of your personality, but merely a tool to give you insight into your interactions with other people.

With your egogram beside you, read the following general comments on the positive and negative aspects of each ego state, so that you can gain a preliminary 'feel' for the relative balance of these states in your personality.

Critical Parent

The advantage of a good quantity of critical parent in your make-up is that it allows you to stand up for yourself, to say 'no' where appropriate, to prevent others from taking advantage of you and to use self-discipline.

The disadvantage of this ego state is that it encourages some people to criticise and bully others, creating fears and resentments that can undermine a relationship. It is important to note that when under stress, many people begin to operate almost exclusively in the critical parent role, which often increases the pressure, rather than lessening it.

Nurturing Parent

The nurturing parent ego state is warm, loving, and full of encouragement. These attitudes are vital in the development of intimacy and trust in a relationship.

On the negative side, however, the nurturing parent role may smother the other person with attention, encourage unhealthy dependence, and sometimes create resentment when the person receiving all this feels unable to give equally.

Free Child

A high free child can be delightful: such a person is playful, fun to be with, humorous and lively. Sexually such a person is likely to be creative and enthusiastic.

Too much free child, however, can lead to irresponsibility and disregard to values and morality, as the 'feeling' side of the personality swamps the more sensible reasoning side.

Adapted Child

The adapted child ego state at its best is anxious to get on with other people. The adapted child can be courteous, co-operative and show respect for the thoughts and opinions of others. The advantages of this are self-evident: acceptance, respect and affection.

Too much adapted child ego state, however, can lead to worry and tension — the person may be paralysed in decision making for fear of making the wrong move, and have an exaggerated response to criticism or blame. Overly compliant people are non-assertive, whilst those whose behaviour is rebellious are aggressive.

Adult

The adult ego state is of great advantage to a person: this aspect of your personality deals with problems and difficult situations in a calm and unemotional way. Decisions are made logically and carried through efficiently as the adult uses reason to control his or her world.

Too much adult is a serious disadvantage in relationships with other people: such adult-dominated personalities show little humour, are basically rather boring and dull because they are not in any way risk-takers and lack spontaneity.

Now that you have more information on the qualities of parent, child and adult ego states, assess your own egogram. Is there one ego state that predominates? One that is particularly weak? Can you see any connection between the way you relate to other people and the pattern of your egogram?

You might find it necessary to amend your egogram slightly now that you are more familiar with the qualities of each ego state.

You are now prepared to go on to a better understanding of yourself as a person wanting to build love in your relationship. We developed the following Mature Love Programme to meet the specific needs and requirements of our students and clients. It is therefore a very practical way to assess the strengths and weaknesses of your love.

It's not enough to decide to love more — our program helps you to determine how, where, and in what way. It will answer these questions:

- What changes will I make?
- What will I do to build myself as a loving person?
- What will I do to build my relationships with others?

USING THE MATURE LOVE PROGRAMME

How and Why the Program Evolved

The Mature Love Programme evolved out of forty years of frustration with the many differing definitions and descriptions of love as presented by authors and other experts on the subject. For all these years, it had been difficult to translate into specific action what we had read or heard about love.

So we began to look for an explanation as to why knowledgeable experts disagreed so much. What we began to observe was a pattern of relationships between the authors' highest ego states and their theories. For example, when a particular author wrote a great deal from his/her adult ego state, the descriptions of love would focus on such behaviours as commitment, treating the partner as a best friend, and building communication skills. On the other hand, an author reflecting his/her nurturing parent would make many references to unconditional love, forgiveness, acceptance, tolerance, and the showing of kindness and encouragement. Still another writer would direct attention to the romantic aspects of love, evidencing free child.

All this led to an obvious conclusion: most writers have some good ideas of the truth of love ... and they are all basically right, at least in so far *as it is for them*. After all, writers, as we all do, see the world through their own individual interpretations of reality.

Our next long-term observation was based on what we saw and heard from clients. When we asked them to define love, their words would invariably reflect the highest column in their egograms. For example, people high in nurturing parent would define love as caring, sharing, giving and accepting.

From all this evidence, it became clear that our personal definitions of love are reflections of our own personalities and life experiences.

These observations also led us to see that *all of the ego states are involved in expressions of love.*

Why is this significant? Well, if this is so, then there are clearly many ways to experience, build, give and receive love.

This insight led to remarkable realisations in our clients: those who no longer felt romantic love in themselves or in their partners began to see that they *do* love in a great many ways, and that they are loved in turn in many ways ... not only by their partners, but by other people as well.

Some then began to understand that when romantic love expends its energy and fades, they can *still have romance*. Further, more romance *can be built*, as we will show you in the next pages.

Builders and Preventers There are aspects of each ego state that actively help build deep and rewarding relationships, and others that actively prevent the growth of love. These aspects can be called 'builders' and 'preventers'. In Figure 8.7, these builders and preventers are set out in a table as part of the Mature Love Program to make it easier for you to make your own personal assessment.

Note that a person can have *too much* as well as *too little* of any one ego state, so it is important that you evaluate the significance of each high and low in your egogram. Your aim should be to think about the areas where you need to exert more, or less, energy. For example, if you discover that you do not have many behaviours in the nurturing parent 'builders' section, then you have work to do on your nurturing parent ego state.

Remember, a healthy *balance* of ego states should be your aim.

A guide to understanding the mature love program:

All behaviours listed in the 'builders' section are positive builders of mature love.

All behaviours listed in the 'preventers' section will prevent the building of mature love.

How to use this program:

1. Underline all the behaviours in the 'builders' section which you need to *develop.*

2. Underline all the behaviours in the 'preventers' section which you need to *eliminate.*

3. In the 'plan of action' section write out what you can do to make your behaviour more loving. Be specific. That is: what can you actually do.

Being attentive is not specific enough — 'When I come home from work I will seek out and hug my partner, and find out about his/her day,' is specific. 'I will not turn on the TV,' is specific.

A full and mature love in a marriage will grow as more of the 'building' behaviours in each egostate are developed by each partner and as more of the 'preventing' behaviours in each egostate are gradually eliminated by each partner. Love *feelings* grow with love *behaviours*.

How to Use the Mature Love Programme

1. Practise developing egograms by creating one for each of your parents or parent figures. You might also create some egograms of your friends, siblings, marriage partner or even grandparents. This can be fun: we find students in our School of Marriage course enjoy sharing what they have learned in small group discussions.

2. Now create an egogram for yourself, if you have not already done so. Before you go to the Mature Love Programme explore the areas in which you need to develop. *Always focus on areas where you can grow, rather than on areas where you are already strong.*

    For example, if you find you are high in critical parent, then you may need to develop your nurturing parent. Doing this can reduce your critical parent egostate to the best level for your personality.

3. Now work on the Mature Love Programme as given in Figure 8.7. We suggest you first do one on your partner, (or on a friend or parent if you have no partner). Then do one on yourself.

4. A plan of action is not easy to develop. It will take some thought and energy, especially to turn ideas into specific actions.

5. When you and your partner have completed your Mature Love Programme:

    (a) Exchange sheets with your partner. Read and study what you see. Take notice of how many ways your partner already shows love (usually a surprise to people).

    (b) Talk about yourself with your partner. If you need any help, ask for it.

    (c) Create some small goals for the future.

    (d) Take on only a limited objective.

    (e) Give yourself some time for growth, then return to your sheet and create another objective.

    (f) Establish some long-term goals and behaviour changes.

The Mature Love Programme then, enables you to assess your strengths

EGOSTATE	BUILDERS OF MATURE LOVE IN A MARRIAGE	PLAN OF ACTION	PREVENTERS OF MATURE LOVE IN A MARRIAGE	PLAN OF ACTION
CRITICAL PARENT	Being protective, Disciplining self & partner in a constructive way, Using appropriate confrontation, Maintaining moral standards, Being honest, Maintaining integrity, Maintaining fidelity & loyalty, Being assertive		*Too Little C.P.* Being non-protective, Being non-assertive, Gunny-sacking, Undisciplined, Being disloyal *Too Much C.P.* Accusing and Blaming, Criticising, Being judgmental. All Aggressive Behaviours Being rigid, Self-righteous, Perfectionist	
NURTURING PARENT	Supporting, Encouraging, Caring, Being attentive, Cultivating partner's individuality, Fostering companionship, Showing patience & tolerance, Accepting, Forgiving, Showing kindness, Praising, Giving time, Allowing compromise, Valuing partner highly, Respecting other person, Nurturing, Being empathic, Working for the health of relationship, Providing security, showing interest		*Too Little N.P.* Being non-supportive, Discouraging, Non-caring, Non-attending, Being impatient, Non-accepting, Unforgiving, Being intolerant, Self-centred, Uncompromising, Giving little time to partner, Inattentiveness to partner's awareness *Too Much N.P.* Denying individuality, Over-protecting, Spoiling by giving too much, Creating over-dependency and hindering partner's growth	
ADULT	Being committed, Planning, Taking responsibility, Having realistic expectations, Self-disclosing, Acting on dreams, Leading (when necessary), Treating as best friend, Wanting to solve conflicts, Using communications skills to resolve issues, Willing to assess state of the marriage, Thinks of ways to improve self and relationships		*Too Little Adult* Lacking commitment, Failing to plan, Lacking action, Being irresponsible, Does not lead, Has unrealistic expectations, Takes excessive risks *Too Much Adult* Boring, Dull, Closed, Rigid, Is too cautious, Overworking, Taking too much responsibility	

EGOSTATE	BUILDERS OF MATURE LOVE IN A MARRIAGE	PLAN OF ACTION	PREVENTERS OF MATURE LOVE IN A MARRIAGE	PLAN OF ACTION
ADAPTED CHILD	Cooperating, Sharing, Can be led, Respecting, Accepting limits, Seeking to make compromises, Submitting (when appropriate), Capable of surrendering		*Too Little A.C.* (Rebellious behaviours) Not cooperative, Being self-centred, Uncompromising, Disrespecting, Rebellious, Taunting, Refusing limits, Jealous, Playing 'spiteful' games, Being anti-moral, Acting out, Being aggressive, Polarity-responding (Doing the opposite) *Too Much A.C.* (Compliant behaviours) Losing spontaneity, Over-conforming and laying ground for rebellion and gunny-sacking, Helpless, Overly-dependent, Jealous, Non-assertive, Placating	
FREE CHILD	Expressing affection, Desiring intimacy, Enjoying touching, Is warm, Getting close, Seeking fun and pleasure, Being spontaneous, Being creative, Using imagination, Sexually free, Using humour, Enjoying, Creating romance Romantic Love 'In love' (a temporary experience)		*Too Little F.C.* Cold, Untouching, Withholding affection, Keeping distance, Humourless, Limiting fun and enjoyment, Being non-creative, lacking spontaneity, Little imagination, Sexually inhibited & uncreative, Non-expressive *Too Much F.C.* Parental and societal values and morals taken too lightly. Overly-dependent, Irresponsible	

Figure 8.7: The Mature Love Program

145

and weaknesses as a person and as a partner. It enables you to become directly involved in your personal growth *and* the growth of your marriage or relationship. By recognising in yourself behaviours that are Preventers of Mature Love, you can aim to eliminate them. This will, of course, take courage, perseverance and determination. You will have to be very honest with yourself. Sometimes you will need to take heed of feedback you get from your partner as to the ways you prevent love growing in your relationship. Along with this you will determine what you need to develop to build your love. The Builders of love are set out so that you can work towards developing more and more of these behaviours. You will need to be very specific as you embark on your journey. For example, it's not enough to think 'I'll be more accepting of my partner,' you have to be more accepting by having as your goal 'The next time my partner disagrees with me I'll try to see things from his/her point of view by using the communication skills I've learnt.' Notice that Mature Loving involves all of the Builder Behaviours in all ego states. This is the point of the Mature Love Programme.

When one of our students made out his Mature Love Programme he determined that he was doing rather poorly in the free child behaviours. There wasn't much of what he could call romance, and he had little fun. He therefore established his first goals as follows:

WEEK 1: I will take my wife out for dinner to a very special restaurant

WEEK 2: I will ask my wife to go to a jazz concert with me

WEEK 3: I will give her a full body caress (a light sensual type of massage) lasting at least forty-five minutes

WEEK 4: I will take my wife dancing if she will go (the first time in twelve years)

NOTE: Goals must be as specific as possible for you to make progress.

Each person fills out the program differently: that's to be expected. Recently we collated what a group of students had listed under their Adapted Child Plans of Action. Although students sometimes confuse the ego states, the important thing is to grow and change. Here are some of the examples from the list they made:

- share the housework more
- save money together to buy something
- let my partner choose a movie
- submit to visiting the in-laws when I really don't want to go
- respect my partner's choice of television program
- agree to take up exercise with my partner
- compromise over where we are going to live

- compromise in visiting my partner's friends
- accept the limits of my partner's energy and do what he/she wants to do this weekend

'BUT I STILL WANT A ROMANTIC LOVE IN MY LIFE!'

People often crave a return to romantic love. They cherish the idea that what they once had can be restored with some magic formula — some action on the part of their partners. The feelings of the courtship and honeymoon stage have diminished, perhaps left completely, so they think something must be wrong.

The bad news is that romantic love feelings *always* vanish, or at the least, diminish considerably. Step Two examined why romantic love is so powerful a force — but it also made clear why many of the factors contributing to this powerful feeling are only temporary.

However, there is some *good* news: romantic love can be replaced by something calmer and deeper. Powerful, warm, close, joyous and intimate feelings and experiences are possible. The addictive kind of love may be gone for ever, destroyed by reality — but the love that can then be created has a warmth, power and endurance that makes it much more valuable.

This book is directed towards achieving this deeper love: feeling joyful in your relationships — not always, not every minute — but most of the time.

It is important to realise that this is an *achievable* goal if you are willing to put the effort into it.

THE THREE RS OF MARITAL SUCCESS

These are the three major ingredients needed for the achievement of a deep and rewarding love relationship (see Figure 8.8).

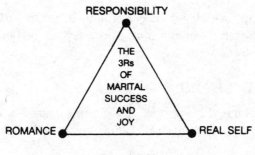

Figure 8.8

Responsibility

The first 'R', responsibility, involves:

- learning from your conflicts and failures, instead of condemning or defending
- learning communication and negotiating skills
- becoming an informed, creative sexual partner
- working at your Mature Love Programme
- taking responsibility for your own capacity to bring joy into your marriage
- being willing to make the effort
- negotiating the kind of relationship you want to have
- learning to think for yourself
- learning to start over again when you fail

Real self

The second 'R', real self, involves:

- discovering who you really are — not what you are to get others' approval
- becoming honest with yourself and your partner
- becoming assertive (*not* aggressive or non-assertive)
- developing self-awareness
- improving yourself
- building self-esteem

Romance

The third 'R', Romance, involves:

- creating ways to have fun, relax and have pleasure together
- being sexually free and creative
- sharing the real you — 'you and me' talk
- encouraging, praising, caring (using your nurturing part to lift your partner's awareness of being esteemed and valued)

Successful and joyous married life is a combination of effort and satisfaction *from* that effort. It is not automatic, not easy, not instant. *But it is possible and achievable!*

'THIS IS ALL TOO HARD'

If you are still thinking to yourself, 'I want that experience of romantic love again and this three 'R' stuff sounds too hard,' you are not at all unusual.

Many years of helping people with their problems has shown that a considerable number of those with a troubled marriage situation prefer to find someone else to 'love', rather than work on the marriage they have at the moment.

> Tom is typical of many people who come to us. He is a leading businessman: a hard-working, over-stressed, extremely successful entrepreneur. Tom has an enormous drive to win, and, in fact, he usually does.
>
> For years the free child in Tom has been neglected. Rarely does he relax at work or at home — wherever he is, business is on his mind. Because the free child has dried up, romance has long since gone from his marriage.
>
> So what does Tom do to nurture this stunted part of his personality? He seeks out a new lover to inject some passion and excitement into his life. This is his prescription for marital boredom ... have an affair and enjoy all the excitement of newness and deception.

The Toms of this world are very prone to use this approach towards solving the problems of a stale marriage. But this course of action backfires: either the marriage continues as an unrewarding, stale, parallel relationship, or there is a complete marital break-up.

There is a better way — to build the free child part of marriage and life in general. Instead of desperately seeking affection and excitement outside the marital home, it can be discovered anew right there.

Tom could have taken another approach, as some discover on their own, or during marital therapy. Here is what one 'Tom' who came to us several years ago did with his life:

1. He built up a new management team in his company to take the responsibility off his shoulders, thus giving himself that vital ingredient, *time.*

2. He bought a yacht so he would be able to have *fun* and do something exciting. His wife started to join him. Sometimes only the two of them went out together, looking for the backwaters where they could anchor, relax and make love when they wanted to.

3. He took a course in couple *communication* with his wife and started to talk about his feelings — telling her things he'd never told anyone. In this way he started to share his *real self.*

4. He began to notice all the opportunities for little *rituals* — meeting her every Friday in the city and taking her out; walking frequently on a very beautiful path surrounded on both sides by trees, flowers and birds.

5. They went to the zoo more frequently, sometimes taking the children.

6. Every summer they took an entire month's holiday — part of it with the children and part of it without them.

7. He began to exercise regularly and thus feel better physically. This had other positive effects: he looked better and also had more energy for lengthy times in the bedroom where he became a more creative lover.

We recently saw Tom again. It was nine years since he had first come to us for guidance. He was no longer the harassed, over-stressed man we had once known. As for his relationship with his wife — as he put it, there is more good feeling between them now than when they first married. Romance has flourished as their relationship has deepened into a joyous and happy partnership.

Summary

In Step Eight we have investigated Love:

- each person's experience and definition of love is different
- the ego states of Transactional Analysis: Child; Parent; Adult
- egograms and how they can be used to understand personality and inter-relationships
- working towards a *balance* of ego states
- introduction to the Mature Love Programme
- how to build mature love
- the three R's of successful and joyous marriage

Step Nine

Intimacy and sex

The greatest joy for many people in marriage is expressed with the word *understand*. When a person tells us about successful relating that word will always appear somewhere: 'He/she really understands me!'

There is a true delight in the realisation that someone knows what is going on inside you — that someone knows the *real person* you are.

When this happens — when you know your partner, and are known in return — it is the result of hard work, maturity and courage. It is the reward for all the time you have both devoted to the search for each other's deepest self.

In this Step we will be exploring *being* together, not just *living* together.

Each of us has a unique self to share — a self made up of our personal experience of living and of our own personal experience of what it is 'to be me'. Therefore your thoughts, feelings, wants, cares, interpretations and desires are different from any other person's.

Other people see our outward shell — we experience our true selves from the inside. Intimacy and love are ways of both *being* and *expressing* the *real self*.

HOW TO RECEIVE LOVE

So far we have only talked about the giving of love, but to understand intimacy there is another part of love — the receiving.

It is not enough to *give* love, there needs to be in each person a *receptive ability* — a willing and open acceptance of the love you are offered. If you cannot receive love, acknowledge it, take it in, become comfortable with it, you will not be able to be intimate.

It is ironic that many of us have more difficulty receiving another person's love than in giving love. This could account for much of the breakdown in marriage, because intimacy is a *mutual giving and receiving* of the mature love experiences.

What Hinders Us from Receiving Love?

1.   It is ironic that the programming we experience as we are growing up can make us just as ineffective at receiving love as giving love. As we grow up many of us come to believe that love is conditional: 'People will only love me if I do/think/believe certain things.'

There are in fact many kinds of programming that inhibit our ability to receive love including the following 'beliefs' or 'programs':

*   I can do it myself — I don't need to depend on anyone else
*   don't trust anyone
*   be suspicious if someone tries to give you something
*   don't open up to others: they might want to control you
*   don't acknowledge love: if you do, you will be indebted to that person
*   people who go around giving things are up to something
*   if I love you, you will take advantage of me
*   my mother loved me so much that she smothered my personality and kept me from being me — I'm not going to let you smother me
*   I don't trust anything that is just given to me
*   I have to work for love; I have to earn it
*   I am *unlovable*
*   if I open up to you, I will be vulnerable

These programs are all from the experiences of childhood. They are all related to the most common *limiting self-belief*. That is, against all evidence to the contrary, a person believes: 'I don't love myself, so how can anyone else love me? I won't even recognise love when I see it because it's impossible. I don't believe it.'

An example of this selective view of life which is based on a refusal to accept that it is possible to be loved is given by Robyn.

Robyn was born last in a family of six children, and grew up with the conviction that her mother had never wanted her and didn't love her. Robyn fought to win her mother's approval and love, but without success. She became convinced that she wasn't worthy of love: that somehow, it was *her* fault that her mother didn't love her.

Now, as an adult, she is scarred by her failure to be loved by her mother. Robyn believes she is not lovable, and even though her partner assures her he *does* love her, she finds this almost impossible to believe. In addition, even the lightest criticism or well-meant advice reduces Robyn to tears and grief. Her attitude is: 'It's me. It's my fault ... that no-one loves me'.

Another case is that of Martin. He had a mother whom he could never ever please, no matter how hard he tried. Martin, therefore, has never felt loved or accepted.

Martin's family had always lived in rented housing, and when his father died Martin decided to make a strenuous effort to win his mother's love by providing her with her own home. He scraped and saved until he had enough money for a down payment on a small house. Martin thought: 'My mother will love me when she sees what I have done for her.'

Martin's mother moved into the house as if it were her right. She didn't show gratitude or affection to Martin for all his efforts on her behalf. Martin is now even more convinced that he is unlovable, because surely his mother would love him if she could. He believes the fault lies with *him:* he does not see that his mother has a cold and unloving personality.

2. Some people see receiving love from another as a form of dependency on their part: a weakening of their position and a letting down of their guard. These people *need* to be in control. They have little of the adapted child ego state in them. One way to do this is to self-disclose very little, so retaining control because they are not known. The result is that they do not know intimacy, nor are they ever understood.

This type of person bottles things up and is closed to other people. Usually they complain of being really 'alone'! Often they have a *longing* (an important word) — they long for someone to be really close to, for someone to be intimate with, for someone to understand them.

Even though they have this deep longing, they will resist receiving love for fear of what might result:
- if I get it, I have to give it too!
- I'm frightened to be dependent on someone else!
- if I rely on you, and you let me down, where will I be then?

3. It is possible to refuse to receive and acknowledge love as a form of *punishment* or *retaliation*. We have often seen this situation when a relationship is in trouble, and one partner realises he or she has not been showing love adequately, and so tries to make amends by starting to do so. Quite frequently the other person refuses to receive the love now being offered: 'Where was the love when I needed it? It's all very well for you to offer it *now* when you think you're going to lose everything ...'

4. The interaction between your parents and yourself can have a strong influence upon your attitude towards love. Examples are:

(a) If your mother and father were over-protective you may be anxious with love: you may have become wary of love because it implies smothering, or being controlled or manipulated by other people.

(b) If your mother and father gave love, but expected a price to be paid in return: in this case love was given manipulatively because you only gained it if you behaved in a certain way, or met certain standards. This teaches you that you don't deserve love unless you've done something to earn it.

5. The perception that giving love is a *duty,* so that when your partner gives you love, it isn't a gift, but merely what a male/female or husband/wife is supposed to give anyway.

   Love often goes unacknowledged because only 'romantic love' is seen as real love. The love from other ego states is not perceived as love, but as a duty.

6. Not acknowledging love when it is given. If you fail to acknowledge the love freely given to you, then you destroy the other person's desire to continue loving. In his or her mind, you are a 'taker'. You value it so little you don't even acknowledge it, let alone give it back.

7. Those people who are the beneficiaries of love but don't give it back — who take it for granted and show little, if any, appreciation of the fact that someone is giving it freely — have very often been spoiled as children, and now have become spoiled adults. And what is the lasting satisfaction in loving someone like that?

You enhance the giving of love by *receiving* it and then *acknowledging* you have done so ... and your appreciation can only encourage the person to love you all the more!

What Can You Say and Do When You Receive Love?

Say things like:

'Every day I think how much I appreciate you loving me.'

'When you went shopping I could tell by the things you bought that you love me.'

'I love the way you love me.'

'Don't ever think I don't value your love.'

'Your love makes me feel secure and happy.'

Do things like:

When your partner looks at you in a special 'I love you' way, complete the circuit between you with an answering look that shows you accept and appreciate what you have been offered. (Some people are much more inclined to 'look' love, rather than say, 'I love you', so you must be aware that a look can carry a valuable message of affection and intimacy.)

When you are held by your partner, just let the love come in ... relax ... take in the warmth and the caring ... try to be there for a long time.

As you work at your Mature Love Programme you will understand that there are many many ways of expressing love and that your partner is actually loving you in many of these ways constantly. Look for what comes from the parent and adult ego states, not just from the child.

The Importance of Trust

To receive love freely, you must be able to *trust*. Trust what?

- trust that you are lovable (that requires you to first love yourself — to value yourself)
- trust that the person has nothing up his or her sleeve, has no ulterior motives and is not trying to manipulate you (unfortunately what appears to be 'love' is sometimes a manipulative tool)
- trust that the intention is not self-serving on the giver's part
- trust that you don't have to pay a price
- trust that you can still be free
- trust that you won't be smothered

DEVELOPING INTIMACY

Intimacy and love are ways of *being* the real self — of *expressing* the real self in loving contact with a beloved person's real self.

Being 'in love' is not the same as intimacy because the 'in love' feeling is not based on the other person being real: we only imagine what that person is. In a sense, we are in love with an illusion, because it takes years to know in any kind of accurate way the real person with whom you share a relationship.

And even after many years your partner may tell you some inner reality which makes you see her/him very differently — a whole new perspective opens up, and you realise that there are still surprises, exciting facets of personality you have the opportunity to explore in the other person.

Intimacy has within it an element of truth. As we grow more aware of our real self and our partner does likewise, we come closer to the truth about ourselves and about each other. Your real self recognises your partner's real self more and more — and there is always more to learn about someone who is growing with you.

People involved in pseudo self relationships can, at best, only be described as 'close' ... we become intimate only on our real self level. Here are some ways of developing your intimacy:

1. Grow more and more towards an awareness of who you really are: discover your real self. You can be more real with someone else only as you pursue self-discovery.

2. Learn more and more about what is going on inside the real self of your partner. Share a meaning at those crucial times when it is really important to understand. It is not enough to just say, 'I understand'; how does your partner know you genuinely do, unless you say what it is you have learned from your partner's self-disclosure? Respect and appreciate what your partner reveals.

3. Ask yourself questions, and reflect and ponder on the answers:
   • what do I really think about this? about that?
   • what do I feel?
   • what do I want?
   • what are my values?
   • what do I think about God/a higher being?
   • why am I here?
   • where am I headed?
   • what is it that I value about my partner?
   • what would life be without him/her?

4. Make out many self-awareness wheels. Each time you make this effort you learn more about your real self.

5. Speak for self: use the word 'I' when describing your awareness. When you say 'you' instead of 'I' your real self is distanced.

6. Share with a trusted friend, counsellor, confidante, but most of all your partner, what is in your awareness. Take criticism constructively.

7. Read literature which helps you reflect on the real you.

8. Write a journal about your inner world.

9. Try to speak in more personal ways, using more straight talk rather than conversational style.

10. Write or tell your beloved your most private thoughts and feelings towards him or her. Overcome the embarrassment of being or sounding 'sentimental'. The letters, notes, birthday cards, Valentine Day cards which people save are usually those in which the real self of another person is written down.

We recently heard of a wife's effort to say 'I love you' by putting notes with this message in her husband's slippers. When he rose during the night and put on his slippers he felt something in them. Thinking it was a cockroach or some other insect, he shook out the notes on to the floor. Only the next morning did he discover that the supposed intruders were actually love notes from his creative wife!

Speaking from the Real Self: an Intimacy Exercise

The following statements come from the real self. If you can state them honestly to another person, then you have created the foundations of the deepest and most rewarding relationship that one person can have with another.

We suggest that you read them alternately to each other as an exercise in intimacy.

1. I want you to know me as I really am. I will not hide or disguise my real self from you. I present myself as I am, without deceptions or apologies.

2. I am true to myself. My self-esteem is based on being honest with myself and by acting out of my real thoughts, feelings and wants.

3. I will express my real thoughts, feelings and wants to you, even if this causes conflict between us. I acknowledge and respect your right to have thoughts, feelings and wants that may not necessarily correspond with mine.

4. I accept that differences and disagreements between us can be used positively for personal growth and understanding. I will not take such disagreements personally, as if they were an attack on me, but will see them as areas of conflict that can be resolved jointly.

5. I will speak for myself; you will speak for yourself. I am in charge of what I think about me; you are in charge of what you think about you. It therefore follows that my feelings of self-worth do not depend on what you think, nor do yours on what I think.

6. I will not hurt you intentionally, although I may cause you pain over something I say or do. I accept that you have no intention to hurt me.

7. I will give what there is in me to give; I accept my own limitations. In the same way, I acknowledge that you also have limitations, and will give to me as you are able.

8. I will work towards personal growth and achievement so that I can reach my potential as a person. I acknowledge that you have the right to develop your own potential as you see fit.

DESTROYING AND DISCOURAGING INTIMACY

We all know, and use, strategies and techniques for keeping ourselves distant from each other. This 'distancing' (both verbal and/or physical) of course makes the growth of intimacy difficult or impossible, and can be accomplished by:

- excessive use of conversation style: 'Let's not get serious — let's keep it light ...'

- a constant whirl of social activities: 'Like to talk if we ever get time ...'
- being too busy with work, study, the children, outside commitments: 'I'm too busy right now ...'
- having excessive weight, poor body hygiene: 'Look, you take me like I am, or not at all ...'
- 'hating' sex: 'I'm tired and I've got a headache ...'
- living out a self-fulfilling prophecy: 'He/she doesn't want to be close to me ...'
- building/moving/changing house: 'We'll talk when everything's over, okay?'
- being aggressive to maintain distance: 'You've made me angry with you!'
- being non-assertive to maintain distance: 'You're absolutely right, so we don't need to discuss it ...'
- poor health/sickness: 'I don't feel well enough right now ...'
- excessive use of alcohol: 'Have another drink ...'
- making sure the children come first (and sometimes that there's lots of them!): 'Do you know what little Jimmy did today ...'
- refusing to discuss: 'I don't want to talk about that ...'

Such techniques and strategies can become habits — ways of operating within a relationship that preclude the development of intimacy. It is obviously better to avoid building these barriers.

Early in marriage some couples begin to open up their real selves to each other. The potential for personal growth and happiness exists: illusions are disappearing, who the other person really is begins to dawn, trust is still alive, and hope is bright for a long and rewarding relationship together.

This is one of the most crucial times in a marriage: when you can develop either an intimate, self-disclosing partnership, or one of the pseudo self types — A-frame, lean-to or parallel, as described in Step 3.

The ideal H-type marriage may start to develop, but during this period of growing self-disclosure it is very vulnerable to the destructive forces let loose by criticising, accusing and blaming.

This is what happens to thousands of people early on in their marriages: honesty is attempted and truth about self is expressed in an open, trusting way. One partner, in effect, says to the other, 'I want you to know me and who I *really* am' — but these efforts to be 'real' are met with behaviour that all but destroys the impulse to be open and honest.

Take the example of Shane and Denise:

Soon after their marriage Shane started to open up his innermost self to Denise. What he told her was nothing really world-shattering, and if her self-esteem had been solid enough she would have taken it as a compliment to her, but because of her insecurity the revelation of Shane's inner self was too much to bear.

Shane told Denise that at times before their wedding he had had some doubts about marrying her. She was not his idea of the beautiful woman he had always imagined he would marry, however he had found her more interesting and attractive than any other woman he had met. Now he realised that he loved her deeply, even though she was not the type he had originally expected to marry.

From her adolescent years Denise had nursed a sense of inadequacy about her looks, so that there was within her high 'emotionality' (a trigger point) on the issue of her appearance. This led Denise to listen *selectively* to Shane's disclosure — she heard what she expected/wanted/feared to hear: 'I don't find you attractive.'

In spite of all Shane's attempts to explain the message he intended her to understand, Denise refused to accept any meaning other than the one she had seized upon.

What effect did this have on Shane and on their marriage? From that point onwards Shane distrusted Denise's interpretations of his innermost thoughts. Being 'real' was too dangerous, so Shane went back to operating out of his pseudo self and the possibility of a truly intimate relationship was blocked. Fifteen years later the marriage ended.

It is sometimes hard to believe that incidents such as the one between Shane and Denise have the potential to destroy the development of intimacy in a relationship, but unfortunately we have seen many examples of this. Too often it takes only one or two instances of misinterpretation or distortion and the marriage never recovers. We often marvel at the fragility of a relationship in this early stage where each person has the choice to grow towards being more real and honest, or to remain unknown in the deepest parts of self.

Intimacy can be destroyed when one person betrays the other, or breaks a confidence:

Penny told her husband the story of a rather wild escapade involving herself and her close friend Jocelyn. This had happened long before marriage, and Penny trusted Trevor not to repeat these now embarrassing details.

Some time later Trevor repeated the story to Jocelyn's husband. The result was the breaking up of a long-standing friendship between the two women. And the result? Penny was taught by that experience never to share herself with Trevor — she could not trust him.

Or take the case of Larry and Beatrice:

Larry freely told Beatrice about the new secretary at work, how several of the staff had taken her out to lunch and how much they had enjoyed her company. Beatrice's weak sense of self immediately produced feelings of threat and anxiety: 'Larry is attracted to (likes) her more than he is attracted to (likes) me!'

Beatrice at once embarked on a program of threats and promised retaliations that would descend on Larry should he ever again lunch with this, or any other, woman.

Larry had been given a short, sharp lesson: never to tell Beatrice anything at all about social life at work.

All of the aggressive behaviours previously discussed will destroy intimacy, and therefore the chances of a deep and satisfying relationship. The use of sarcasm, ridicule, blaming, accusing, withholding, discounting, etc. will eat like acid through the deep bonds that could be forming in a relationship.

One couple that came to us for counselling had these bonds destroyed by the husband's 'mind-reading'. Every time the wife told her husband how she felt or what she thought, he analysed her words, implying with his responses that she was either wrong or inaccurate — he claimed to know more about her than she knew herself! Eventually the slightest suggestion that he was 'mind-reading' made her physically recoil, and the potential for intimacy in the marriage was destroyed.

In another case trust was betrayed under the guise of fun and humour:

Marty told Theresa that he often felt shy at dinner parties and sometimes quite awkward when they were with her friends. For Marty, who was extremely shy, this was a real disclosure and offered to Theresa with full trust.

Next time they were with friends Theresa amused everyone (with the exception of Marty!) by making a joke of the whole thing: 'Imagine, everyone! Marty feels funny with you all! He doesn't feel relaxed ... isn't that a laugh, eh?'

Marty learned, then and there, *never* to open up again, and the possibility of a good intimate relationship with Theresa was effectively destroyed.

Is there anything Marty could do to turn the situation around? Because intimacy is partly built by the resolving of conflict and negative experiences in a relationship, Marty does have the option to take some positive steps. This is what he could do:

• raise the whole matter as an ISSUE
• discuss it with Theresa using COMMUNICATIONS SKILLS
• make a request for CHANGE: 'when I open up to you I want you to keep that confidence'

- have Theresa agree to this new CONTRACT in their relationship

It is extremely important to always remember that when one person opens up and shares the real self that is a very special privilege — a gift for the loved one — and as such needs to be accepted graciously and respected.

But intimacy is more than just opening up and trusting the other person with your innermost thoughts — it is the sum total of two people enjoying and accepting each other in a totally trusting way. Intimacy is something that is *created* and it becomes the bond or glue that holds two people together.

All of the communications skills outlined in Step Four and Step Five are vital to the creation of intimacy — the communication of one real self with another real self.

THE VITAL IMPORTANCE OF TIME

For intimacy to grow it is essential that time together is built into the structure of the relationship. If you want your relationship to develop, not deteriorate, you must give top priority to this issue.

It is naive to think that any relationship can be built to last without the partners experiencing high quality time together *alone*. No matter if there are three young children demanding attention; no matter if both partners have busy and demanding lives — planning time together is absolutely necessary for the health of the relationship, both in the short and long term.

SEX: A WAY OF BEING TOGETHER

In counselling couples we hear a great many complaints about sex, and these are usually quite specific. Moreover, there is a distinct pattern to them: the complaints men make are different from the complaints women make.

This interesting fact has led us to deal with the area of sexual improvement by directing our attention to the differences between men and women when they relate in physical intimacy.

The Most Common Complaints We Hear about Sex

Intimacy between partners is deeply affected by the misunderstandings arising in the sexual area between men and women.

Complaints from women

1. He thinks I should always be willing and able to have sex with him.
2. He touches or kisses me only when he wants sex.

3. He wants to touch me sexually when I'm preparing dinner.

4. He's rough in the way he touches me; (or) he touches me too fast.

5. He goes straight for my breasts or genitals.

6. He goes too fast for me.

7. Once he's had his pleasure he turns over and goes to sleep.

8. He thinks I should always have an orgasm.

9. He thinks he's less of a man because I don't have orgasms.

10. He thinks when I say I'm tired I'm trying to make an excuse.

11. He thinks I'm not normal because I don't orgasm just with him inside me.

12. He can't touch me down there the way I enjoy it.

13. He now wants me to last for hours, since he started reading sex manuals.

14. We always have sex the same way (or in the same place).

15. He never talks to me or says anything loving during our sex times.

16. I enjoy the physical part, but there's no closeness or intimacy.

17. He can't understand why I feel uncomfortable when the children are up or awake.

18. He thinks I'm like a man and should get turned on by just thinking about sex.

19. He's not at all romantic before we get around to lovemaking.

20. We have an argument and then he thinks I'm supposed to hop into bed with him and make love.

21. Our sex life is boring.

22. He's insensitive — a terrible lover and doesn't realise it. How can I tell him?

23. He's too heavy on top of me; (or) he smothers me.

24. He's not spontaneous enough. I like sex to be spontaneous.

Complaints from men

1. She was interested in sex before we had children (or before we married) — but no more.

2. She's always too tired.

3. She just lies there like a log.

4. It's always up to me to initiate lovemaking.

5. She doesn't touch me where (or in the way) I like to be touched.

6. I get bored with having to always do it the same way.

7. She just wants to go on and on because it takes her so long.

8. She thinks once a week is enough.

9. I have to say exactly the right thing or she's not interested.

10. She's too busy for it all day and too tired at night.

11. I have to take all the responsibility for her pleasure.

12. If I try to do anything different or new she just wants to get it over with.

13. If I don't touch her in exactly the right way she turns off.

14. I'm too tired when I get home and she doesn't want sex in the morning.

15. She will never get on top of me because she says that's the way a man does it.

16. I can't last long enough to please her.

17. She doesn't like me seeing her with her clothes off.

18. She keeps saying she's too fat (she isn't) and therefore doesn't feel sexy.

19. She accuses me of looking at other women and thinking they are more attractive than she is.

20. She always wants me to shower before sex.

21. I bought her a sexy nightgown and she was shocked.

22. She won't touch herself and get to know her own body.

23. Everything has to be 'just right' for her to be interested: the time, the place, her mood, what I say. I give up!

What Can Sex Be Like?

Sex is fundamentally a biological/physical survival act — quite simple and basic. It is designed to create and perpetuate our own kind. It is instinctive and powered by enormous drives. To guarantee that procreation will continue to occur, sex is also pleasurable, physically satisfying and relaxing, and it releases the energy which builds up in the human organism.

Beyond that there is even more: as we are physical/emotional/spiritual beings — so, in the physical union, we are also capable of the most intense emotional and spiritual oneness. We call this intimacy: a sexual union in which there is a giving of the total self.

When the total self is there — our emotional expression, nurturing, surrender, our deeper thoughts, our playfulness, our joy — there is no higher expression of love to another person. We are as close as we can be to 'being one' with our beloved.

Sex is a way of being *together.* It is also a way of *being* together — total being. Certainly, it is only one way, but it is, for those who have done the necessary work, the most beautiful and satisfying way to achieve intimacy of one real self with another real self.

Intimate sex is the highest expression of a man/woman relationship. It occurs when you put the effort into building self-awareness, sexual skills and communication skills. A lot of effort and time ... but what an experience it is!

Overcoming the Common Sexual Complaints and Building Intimacy

If you can make the following information part of your understanding, attitudes and action in the sex area of your life, you will move a long way towards a very satisfying sexual relationship.

Sex is a way of 'being' together

Sex is one of the many ways of being together and must be seen as a part of all the other ways. Because it is part of the whole and flows out of all the rest, when you 'go to bed' you can express warmth that has built up from everything else that has happened during the day, week, month, year.

You cannot treat your partner coldly, insensitively, rejectingly, all day or week, and expect him/her to be warm sexually. When sex is seen in isolation from the rest of everyday life, you become not a lover, but an intruder.

Here is an example:

> Jim spends his long working days as a top executive. He is famous in his field, and he is respected for that by the community and his wife, Jane. Jim arrives home late every evening after his usual stressful day, eats dinner and then goes to his study to write reports and make telephone calls. About midnight he makes his way to bed, tired, but stimulated by his day and ready to 'make love' (we use this word facetiously).

> Jane's reaction to this is not a positive and enthusiastic one! For years she has tried her best, but the time has now arrived when she will not be part of it any more.

> Jim's response to Jane refusing to continue is one of hurt: 'I go out every day to give my family a good life. I work very hard. All I want is just a little affection.'

> During counselling Jane said, 'How can I possibly get turned on?' She further revealed that the sex experience, when she did try, lasted only a few minutes.

What is the situation here? Well, besides a great deal of misunderstanding about women, Jim does not realise that sex is only a part of a whole relationship. In fact, the lifestyle he has chosen does not allow time for being with Jane in many of the other ways needed to build an atmosphere or climate for intimate sex.

Alice is a busy wife/mother/career woman. She embraced her demanding profession after completing university in her late thirties. She leaves for the office quite early, as does her husband, Tim. Alice arrives home after six and rushes to prepare dinner for the family and Tim, who usually returns after seven o'clock.

After dinner there are chores, engagements, community meetings. There are other activities, including attending church, during the weekend. In short, Alice and Tim only see each other alone for a short time before retiring. A few times each week they try to fit in a bit of the 'physical stuff' but it's certainly not what it used to be.

Alice and Tim communicate mainly in conversational style — they have neither the time nor the inclination to get down to the real issues that straight/search style talk would induce.

These two are not *being* together much any more. Although they don't realise it, their marriage has become a parallel type and, worse still, is slipping away into even less than that.

What can Alice and Tim do?

For one thing, they have a desperate need to talk over their entire lifestyle. Both career and money have taken higher priority than their relationship, a common experience these days.

- Tim and Alice could discuss their roles. Can Tim take on more of the domestic duties and/or can the children learn to be more responsible and help out?
- They could retreat earlier to the bedroom or another place for some 'you and me' talk — straight style talk — about how they are feeling and what's going on in their inner worlds.
- They could watch a stimulating television program, movie or play together, and then talk about it and how it relates to their inner lives.
- Perhaps they could set aside a time to be together sexually without interruption, even if it means going away all weekend to a quiet place. They could arrange to have short (or long) holidays together more frequently.
- They would benefit by reading the same book or taking the same course together in order to stimulate more thought-provoking conversation.
- Perhaps they could do things together, such as redecorate a house or plan changes to the garden.

In essence, Alice and Tim need to be *together* in more different ways for the sake of *being together* sexually and intimately. Of course, this means there must be compromises. Each will have to give up some time, energy or whatever for the sake of their long-term relationship.

Being together physically must happen, therefore, in an atmosphere of being together happily, humorously, joyfully and closely at other times during a day, week, month. Then, and only then, has physical intimacy the chance of being a union of two hearts, two minds, two bodies, two complete persons.

In such an atmosphere, a sexual union can reach heights of supreme joy.

Sex and physical intercourse is an expression of love and can involve all the ego states

Since the total self can be involved, this means that the more you develop your ego states, the greater your opportunities for deep and rewarding sexual experiences.

- critical parent provides values, loyalty, integrity, faithfulness and sets limits. 'You can trust me ... I am loyal to you ... only you are my sexual partner ...'
- nurturing parent provides sensitivity and caring. This aspect of personality treats the partner as a *total person*, not just as a sexual object. Sexual contact does not always have to be followed by intercourse. 'What you think and feel are important to me ... I care about you ...'
- adult takes responsibility for the other person, recognising that the partner has needs and providing for them. The adult egostate wants to solve problems in a relationship. 'Can you tell me how it feels ... what can I do to give you pleasure?'
- adapted child is able to surrender, to comply, to trust, to give totally. 'I trust you not to hurt me, not to exploit me ...'
- free child ego state is spontaneous enjoyment and creativity. 'Wow! that's terrific ... I love it!'

Too often, people try to keep their sexual life limited to just one style. For example, those that emphasise the adult in their personality will limit the lighthearted and romantic side; those staying in free child will only want fun and pleasure.

It is important to try to involve your *whole* self.

Sex is not just physical intercourse

Countless times we have heard a woman say: 'He can't kiss me or touch me without wanting to go all the way!' This is a major reason why so many women feel like sexual objects, rather than people.

Sex also includes any behaviour between a man and a woman which involves their sensual selves. This can be a loving gaze, a twinkle in the eye, a light touch on the arm, a hug, a kiss, an adoring smile, an expression of affection, a sensual massage, a body caress, a love note, snuggling up to each other, touching knees under the table, undressing together, showering or bathing together, lying together in the sun, sitting with your arm around your partner, holding hands, touching cheeks, eating dinner by candlelight, sharing a sunset together.

All of these can create sexual stirrings — a climate in which passion can flourish. Narrowing the idea of sexual foreplay to that first part of physical sexual contact is far too limited a way to think about sex. The 'foreplay' for a sexual union that occurs at night might well have begun that morning with some of the kinds of attention we mention above.

Men and Women Are Different In Some Crucial Ways

1. Sexual Desire

Men are turned on sexually more easily than women. Furthermore, they are turned on more easily by visual stimuli, including fantasy. Nature also causes a build-up of sexual tension in the healthy male. This build-up actually starts again from the time of ejaculation. In the younger man the sexual tension can return quickly, but with age it takes longer for this to happen.

Women are turned on more by appropriate touching and communication within the context of emotional warmth and love. This is one reason why a woman's desire is blocked so easily by resentment or distrust. Desire is sometimes turned on again by a romantic situation outside her marriage (which she may interpret as love). When a woman turns off her husband because of resentment or loss of respect, she is particularly vulnerable to the attractions of another man who will create an atmosphere of adoration and romance — the very things she feels she lacks in her present relationship.

The responsible couple catch on to their problem before it comes to this, facing it honestly and looking for ways to overcome resentment. Many of the strategies for achieving this are outlined in this book.

2. Sexual response

Men not only turn on faster, but they can also complete the full sexual response sooner. Ejaculation, which is the necessary sexual response for procreation, can occur on penetration or even before. Male orgasm is another matter — that takes longer and requires a man to learn to control ejaculation and allow a fuller involvement of his total self.

While on average the male orgasm is not as strong as in the female, it is a part of the experience of some men — those who are able to take time, build up sexual tension, love being with their partners and surrender to strong sensations. Our experience has been that men who achieve this prefer quality, rather than frequency, of sex. Also, men are not multi-orgasmic as many women are (with the exception of some young men).

Women take longer to reach the peak of excitation where, for many, orgasm occurs. After orgasm, many women who remain high on the plateau stage can have second or even more orgasmic experiences if they wish.

There are women who have great difficulty achieving orgasm — some never do, and perhaps, never can. What men have to remember is that orgasm is not necessarily the goal for many women in lovemaking. Popular literature has put some women in a trap on this subject, because the orgasm has been consistently portrayed as the pinnacle of sex. Women who never achieve orgasm therefore can have problems with both their self-esteem and their sexual performances.

In turn, many men have developed the idea that sex is a 'performance'. This means that both men and women suffer anxiety about sexual performance. But sex is not a contest for big 'O' medals ... it is a way of being together as totally as you can.

3. Influence of environment

Women are more affected by their environment than most men seem to be. A woman's response can be affected by lighting, music, temperature, privacy, the children being settled/out of the way, fragrances, colour of the room — many varying factors.

4. Verbal communication

Women seem to require more spoken expressions of affection, appreciation and shared feelings than men do. The silent male lover often leaves his partner perplexed and feeling unappreciated. She wants feedback — a verbal response to stir the emotional part of her. Men, also, can be highly appreciative of, and turned on by, verbal responses.

5. Touching

Women require more touching — usually the soft, tender, slow and sensitive kinds of touch. A chief complaint of women is that they have never known a man who really knew how to touch them.

A woman has many sensual areas, therefore the more sensory contact she has, accompanied by emotional stimuli, the higher the peak of excitement she will reach and the greater the consequent satisfaction.

Gentle lovers explore and discover the ways to bring their partners to a peak of sexual excitation. The exploration of how, where and when to touch your partner can go on for years.

Never touch your partner in any place where he/she does not want to be touched.

6. Initiation of sex

Biologically, the male is designed to initiate sex. He is more easily turned on and this is often the basis for a woman saying, 'He only has sex on his mind.' But this is Nature's way of ensuring the human species won't die out!

Women, however, often initiate sex when they have a history of happy lovemaking in a long-term relationship which is loving and caring.

Many men are highly excited by the idea of their partners initiating sex: they like to feel wanted and loved just as much as women do. Note that some women have very subtle ways of initiating sex, and men who tune in to their partners recognise the clues.

This area of sex is open to many surprises. The skill of checking out (Step 5) is needed at all times. For example, Susan has subtle ways of initiating sex because she does not feel comfortable being more overt. The clues she gives are so subtle that her husband Sam can confuse them. He has therefore learned to check with Susan by saying things like, 'Am I reading you right when I think you want me to come to bed now?'

The lack of checking cues is dramatically illustrated by the case of this next couple. Be assured that it is a true and accurate story of their relationship.

> Wanda always used to go to bed before her husband Jack. She would lie on her side of the bed and turn her back to the middle. Jack would come to bed, see her lying this way and take it as a cue she was not interested in him sexually. He would lie down on his side, turn his back to the middle, and to go sleep.
>
> This went on for twenty years (yes, twenty years!) before Jack discovered that Wanda behaved this way because she had been taught it was the man's role to initiate sex. And since Jack *didn't*, she assumed he wasn't interested, so she turned her back on him. Her belief was reinforced by the fact that Jack turned his back on *her*.
>
> For twenty years Wanda had wanted to be seduced. For twenty years Jack had believed that she wasn't interested in sex. It was only after counselling that both learned the truth — they both wanted to be together sexually.

7. Erotic language

Many people use erotic language during love play. Some, more commonly women, prefer never to use such language. Others, who would find erotic words offensive outside their sexual lives, find them exciting at the peak of excitement.

In this area sensitivity to your partner is very important.

A Good Sexual Life Involves Knowledge, Skills and Imagination

The ability to procreate comes naturally. More difficult to achieve is an emotionally and physically satisfying sexual life ... for it does not come naturally. There is much to learn about yourself, your partner and the many ways that you can be together sexually. Remember, sexual intimacy is a *joint responsibility*.

Countless books on the subject are available, and we recommend you do your share of reading, preferably together. Most books contain some errors and myths, because research in this area is still in progress, but there is still much useful information. Incidentally, we do not recommend X-rated videos or pornography as the level of sex portrayed in them, is at best, juvenile.

We encourage couples never to make love the same way twice. This advice is a challenge, and stimulates creativity. There are many aspects which can vary — some of these are:

- time of day and length of time together
- place
- lighting
- positions (ways of being together physically)
- speed, pacing
- touching (where, how long, how, when, speed, degree of pressure etc.)
- mutual caressing of entire body, including feet, hands etc.
- movement — unlimited variety (female can also use vaginal musculature)
- thrusting (slow, fast, deep, shallow, circular)
- accessories (vibrator, oils)
- clothing
- mixtures of methods, body positions
- bathing, showering, sauna, spa together
- music (including romantic music)
- fragrances and scents, incense, perfume, flowers
- fantasy
- use of lips, tongue, fingers, hair, breasts, feet, arms
- varied verbal expressions of love and affection

Add to these imagination, which is needed to create the variety of experience.

What Frequency of Sexual Intercourse is Normal?

We are often asked this question, particularly when there is unequal sexual desire and energy in a couple. It is an extremely complex question to answer, since low sexual desire can have literally dozens of causes. This area is currently the focus of research into sexual difficulties.

As a general statement, however, *there is no such thing as normal frequency*. Some couples prefer frequent sex, others do not. There are even some relationships which are quite satisfying, but have no sex.

If the frequency of sexual intercourse is a problem, consider these ideas:

- a common cause of difference of interest is your level of energy. If your physical energy is low, you might raise it with a combination of exercise, improved diet, sleep and proper health habits. Some people, however, have a low energy level by nature
- the most common cause of loss of interest is distancing in your relationship. If this is the case, improving that area should improve your sexual relationship also
- health problems can be the cause. If you suspect this, seek appropriate help
- put the stress on *quality* rather than quantity. Quality includes more lengthy contact time; slower can equal more satisfaction
- employ your imagination: use more of the ways of being together we have suggested. Bear in mind that sex is much, much more than genital connection
- make sure you are not a boring lover
- never say 'yes' when you mean 'no'. Never fake it. Be in touch with your awareness wheel and communicate in an assertive manner (See Step Four)

Summary

In Step Nine we have looked at Intimacy and Sex in Marriage:

- how to receive love
- what hinders us from receiving love
- what to say and do when you receive love
- the importance of trust
- how to develop intimacy (and how to destroy it)
- the vital importance of time
- sex: a way of being together
- the most common complaints about sex
- what sex can be like
- differences between men and women
- the frequency of sex that is 'normal'

Step Ten

Blending your life
with another

How can you blend your life with another, yet be yourself? Now that you have explored all that you can do to be happy in marriage using the previous steps in this book, it is time to consider the demanding experience of blending your life with your partner.

Our individual experiences in relating can vary widely. Really relating can at times be difficult to achieve in marriage and family, because interpersonal events can raise anxiety and thus our defence mechanisms may be used for self-protection. This is a normal reaction. But these walls we raise do more than protect — they also create distance and can destroy relationships that started with love, passion and trust.

Then again, really relating can sometimes seem effortless, uncomplicated and wholly fulfilling, both for a couple and in a family situation. The essential skills to achieve this were discussed in Steps Four to Six. The harmonious way of being together is built on honesty, fairness, and an opening up of the real self. There is very little pseudo-self and false intimacy in this approach to pairing. In this kind of true partnership you can feel close and intimate, while being free to be yourself and to discover the joy of being fully alive. That is why we call it 'really relating'.

This kind of deeply satisfying relationship — usually, but not always, the H-type marriage — can become your life's greatest achievement when you understand how the blending process works. Be warned, however, that for most people this kind of joyful blending does not come without times of conflict. This conflict, to those who practise the skills of really relating, becomes an *opportunity* to understand the other person, or to make changes which will help make closeness feel safe.

Honestly blending is part of the journey of love, which we discussed more fully in Step Eight — the chapter on mature love. Real love is not making believe that you always like your partner, nor is it being habitually 'nice', and it certainly doesn't imply avoiding conflict for the sake of peace. An assertive communicator is respectful of the partner, but also honest and true to self.

In so many ways you and your partner are different. You have different brain functions, personalities, backgrounds, life experiences, family traditions, and personal values. Remember that a key achievement of living is to realise *who you are*, and to *be* who you are — not what someone else wants you to become. But a second key to living in an H-type relationship is to know in some depth who your partner is.

We are not plastic to be moulded. We are people meant to learn two important lessons: firstly, how to love ourselves to the maximum, and to realise what our purpose for being is; and secondly, how to love others, and to learn the hard lessons involved in achieving that. (The character of a person is often reflected in the ability to wrestle with this life goal.)

For many people marriage provides life's greatest challenge — to love another and still be true to self. For those who achieve this it is also life's greatest reward. Those who come to enjoy success at achieving the above have the *patience* to persist, and the courage to take setbacks. They are willing to run the risk of opening their beings to another even though there is a risk of rejection of their ideas and wants.

People who learn the skills of genuine assertive communication realise success far more often than those who use aggression or who withdraw into a wall of silence and dishonesty. Assertive communication is meant to help two people blend their lives. Aggressive and non-assertive communication impedes successful blending and creates distance or pseudo-intimacy. (See Step Four.)

THE BLENDING PROCESS

Blending your life into the life of another takes some time. Indeed, why wouldn't it? As a child you learn to take care of yourself and to behave in your own adapted way in order to cope in as anxiety-free a way as possible with your family life situation. From infancy you are forced to solve the problem of how to get along with others who have the power to hurt or nurture you. The patterns which we develop to deal with these challenges stay with us for life.

Since every individual has a different set of life circumstances to navigate, each of us develop different coping mechanisms and patterns in our own idiosyncratic way. We then attempt to pair with someone who has learned different patterns and ways of surviving life.

This situation can be frustrating, to say the least. One could well say, 'Look, I learned how to cope with my family of origin, so don't push your family of origin stuff on me as well! Enough is enough. Let me be myself.'

From the very start of a courting relationship, most people are trying to simultaneously give of themselves while still retaining their own identity. Unspoken, unwritten and unconscious contracts on how to be with each other start at the beginning.

One couple comes to mind to illustrate the long-lasting effects of those early hours of a relationship:

> Dan and Emily were both enormously attracted to each other, and started to date one lovely, balmy evening. The night ended with a walk along Balmoral Beach, a beautiful and romantic setting in suburban Sydney.
>
> Dan was an interesting conversationalist, and Emily had enjoyed the whole evening. She felt a warm affection for him and automatically reached out to grasp his hand. He rejected her gesture, and moved his hand away.
>
> Emily accepted that, but on their second date she made a spontaneous attempt to take his hand. His reaction was identical — he avoided holding hands with her.
>
> Because of other positive elements in their relationship, Emily persisted with Dan, and they married a year later. Twelve years later into their marriage, Emily and Dan were in marital therapy. The major issue? *Affection.*
>
> At the very beginning of their relationship, Emily had signalled that she accepted Dan's reluctance to show affection by touching. The contract had been unconsciously made that Emily was willing to live with that situation.

Dan and Emily's story illustrates how the blending process can already have hit snags on the first date. In some sense, on the first date Emily had agreed to give up what was important to her. In order to be Dan's partner, her willingness to overlook the lack of affection in the form of touching became a pattern in the relationship, and blending in this area ceased.

For Emily, it seemed like an exciting rewarding experience to commit herself to blending her life with Dan's, but no one had ever managed to communicate to her just how difficult this process of blending really is. Being 'in love' can make us blind, deaf, and very naive in our behaviour. Romantic love might motivate us to form relationships, but it rarely gives us insight into what lies ahead in the journey of blending two lives.

For many others, the process of blending runs into a wall later in the relationship. Frequently this is experienced at the birth of a child, when traditionally the mother takes on a role that leaves her exhausted — she has ceased to become 'starry-eyed' and become 'red-eyed'. Many a husband has been too self-centred to accept the impact of a baby on the blending process, or to help relieve his beleaguered wife.

STEPS ON THE PATH TO BLENDING

Blending two lives into a satisfying experience that makes the journey of life one in which your goals are achieved is a complex task.

1. Leaving the family of origin

The writer of *Genesis* highlights this ancient challenge: 'Therefore shall a man leave his father and his mother, and shall cleave unto his wife and they shall be one flesh.' Even back then, people came from different tribes and the challenge of blending the ideas of the differing families had to be confronted.

In those times, the problem was solved by creating a 'lean-to' marriage. The wife became subservient to the husband. Conflict was minimised, as she gave in to the 'head of the household'. The patriarchal system worked, at the price of the *woman's sense of self.* While some in our culture still theoretically practise this structure of male dominance, a deep look into such a relationship will show that it is usually not anything like the ancient patriarchal system.

The challenge for our time involves leaving home and creating a completely new family based on the value of both people becoming, in each case, his or her real self. Each brings a separate contribution to the relationship and together they must start the long-term blending process, in which each person is fully human, real and valued.

The first challenge, therefore, is to gradually shed the idea that your own family was right, and that it had a unique access to the truth. Instead of re-creating your own family of origin by assimilating the other person into *your* family, you now need *to create a new and unique family based on the value of full respect, both for each other, and for new ideas.*

This is precisely why your ability to communicate from your real self, and to compromise and negotiate, becomes so important (and at times difficult). You are co-creators of a unique relationship that has never before existed. Traditional roles and values need to be discussed and so many other parts of yourself (as shown in Figure 10.1) will need to be talked about and blended.

This task will take years. Commitment becomes not just a word, but a decision to face all that goes into making a relationship in which the self of the other and oneself are both nurtured. The family of origin must be placed in an appropriate perspective and not allowed to 'triangle' into, and control, the new relationship. You are on your own with a partner, and it is your responsibility to learn how to develop togetherness with this person you love, while also developing your own identity — your own real self. In a way, this blending means two people learning how to be together, and how to simultaneously become their real selves.

For some people this task is very difficult, because they bring their

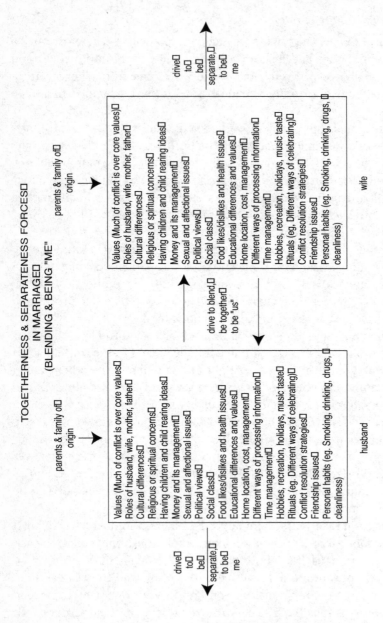

TOGETHERNESS & SEPARATENESS FORCES
IN MARRIAGE
(BLENDING & BEING "ME")

parents & family of origin

parents & family of origin

drive to blend, be together to be "us"

drive to be separate, to be me

drive to be separate, to be me

| Values (Much of conflict is over core values) |
| Roles of husband, wife, mother, father |
| Cultural differences |
| Religious or spiritual concerns |
| Having children and child rearing ideas |
| Money and its management |
| Sexual and affectional issues |
| Political views |
| Social class |
| Food likes/dislikes and health issues |
| Educational differences and values |
| Home location, cost, management |
| Different ways of processing information |
| Time management |
| Hobbies, recreation, holidays, music taste |
| Rituals (eg. Different ways of celebrating) |
| Conflict resolution strategies |
| Friendship issues |
| Personal habits (eg. Smoking, drinking, drugs, cleanliness) |

husband

wife

Figure 10.1: It is necessary for couples to achieve a balance
between these two forces or needs

family of origin into the marriage. Emotionally they have never left home sufficiently to let a partner be his or her real self. An example of this is Con, who, although born in Australia, came from a Mediterranean background. He married Sue, a fourth-generation Australian of English descent.

The conflict they experienced was deadly. There seemed to be no room for her thoughts to be respected. The extent of this finally emerged when, in a counselling session, Con quite blithely said, 'Look, Sue, I've told you many times. If you will simply do things the way I want them done, you will find that it works, and you'll be happy.' Con had not learned to leave his parents. He brought to his marriage all the emotions and beliefs of his family. He had not learned how to think and feel for himself, or to respect his wife's individuality.

2. Thinking for yourself

In order to develop an H-type marriage, you must learn that both you and your partner have a right, and a need, to think for yourselves. Many people naively believe that they do this, whereas in reality they are only reflecting much that they learned in their family of origin and their culture or subculture. We often react automatically, rather than think. In doing so we fall back on what is safe, what we are familiar with, and perhaps what has been believed in our families for many generations.

Far too many families, schools, and other institutions, fail to teach the value of thinking for oneself and to respect the different ideas of other people. As children, we are rewarded for thinking like others. That way we get approval. Further, we are often taught that there is only one way of thinking that is valid, and if we don't think that way, we risk disapproval or isolation. It should not surprise us that as adults we often fail to be open-minded and respectful of the thought processes of others. This illustrates the potency of what we will see as 'togetherness' forces.

Many people go into marriage content to do what they did in their family of origin — to go along with the family, get approval, and everything will be peaceful. Some years into the marriage it may dawn on such a person that this way of operating is not meeting his/her needs. Consequently, conflict unknown in the early days of the coupling arises and the balance is upset.

One of the most interesting and wonderful parts of pairing on a long-term basis is the experience of getting to know someone in depth. *Curiosity* about your partner is a marvellous way of demonstrating love. To have this sense of curiosity, however, you must value and deeply respect the thoughts and life experience of your partner.

In family therapy jargon, we refer to the process of thinking for yourself as one of the ways to *differentiate* from your family of origin. In the early years, all the emotions of our being become attuned to living in the emotional atmosphere of a family. That emotional attunement goes with us for life. In situations which remind us of unfavourable aspects of the family, we react automatically in the emotional self. That reaction can hardly be called thinking. Murray Bowen the American psychiatrist and pioneer family researcher called it 'twitching'. It is an emotional over-reactivity which is automatic — that is, an emotional reflex reaction.

Harry can tell you all about this. When he was growing up, his mother and all the other women in the family were quite controlling. At a young age he learned to react negatively whenever one of those women tried to control him. To this day he over-reacts at the slightest sign of a woman seeking to control him in any way whatsoever.

One of the most essential parts of learning to be in a successful relationship is to find how to deal with these experiences of over-reactivity. Learning to think for yourself, and to respect the thinking of others, is one way to build a calmer being. And to be less reactive in the process.

We must make it clear, however, that it takes a long time for most of us to reach a point where we are not over-reactive to triggers developed in childhood. Becoming free of that family of origin emotional stuff, and building our own sense of self, is a very long process. Murray Bowen, after 30 years of family research, said that you never fully get there. Incidentally, some people think they are not overly-reactive because they don't become outwardly emotional. It is more likely that they have developed instead the ability to withdraw and suppress their emotions.

3. Feeling for yourself

Another part of the blending process is to learn how to develop and to be aware of your own emotional self. This is part of developing self-awareness, a vital aspect of really relating. You cannot relate to another if you are not relating to your inner self. And the more you are aware of what you feel, the more you can relate what is happening with you to another. This is essential for blending with another.

Remember, here we are not talking about your emotional reactivity developed in childhood. We are talking about the whole range of emotions which can be disclosed to others — the many varieties of joy, sadness, love, hate, fear, anger, shame, and so on. The range of the emotions is so great that the English language has over four hundred words to describe them.

Unfortunately, we live in a time when it is very easy to avoid the emotional self with distractions and emotion-deadeners. These include television, newspapers, magazines, alcohol, smoking, drugs (legal and illegal), overwork, gambling, hobbies, sports, music, the internet — countless behaviours that can become addictive. There is too little time left for most of us to think and to feel what is going on in our deeper selves. We are almost an anaesthetised generation. How then can we relate from the core of our real selves? How can we be aware enough to communicate our inner self to another significant person?

It might be necessary, if you want to really relate, to sit still occasionally and reflect about what is going on in your awareness. Use the self-awareness wheel on page 64 as a means to determine what is inside yourself. You are not seeking what you were taught somewhere else by people wanting to program you. What do you sense in your body? What do you feel, think, want? How are you acting or behaving in your present life circumstances? If and when you do value your own awareness then you can value your partner's awareness. No deep blending is possible until you do this. Know yourself and value as well what your partner experiences. This is an important part of loving yourself and your partner.

4. Working at the Blending Process

In case you are not fully aware of how much effort goes into creating the enduring H-type relationship, here is a list of some areas which 'really relaters' have to negotiate:

Values (for example, honesty, punctuality, tidiness, respect, kindness, fidelity, loyalty, gentleness, diligence)

Roles of husband, wife, mother, father etc.

Cultural differences

Religious or spiritual concerns

Having children and child-rearing practices

Money values and management

Sexual issues

Physical contact and display of affection

Political allegiance

Social class issues

Food likes/dislikes and health issues

Educational differences and values

Decisions about home location, cost, decorating, management

Individual ways of thinking and processing information

Time management, hobbies, recreation, holidays, music, entertainment

Rituals (for example, when and how to celebrate Christmas, birthdays, New Year, religious and family occasions)

Conflict resolution strategies

Friendship issues

When you look at this list it can seem overwhelming. Agreeing on many of these issues before the commitment of living together makes the task of really relating less difficult. We are usually drawn to people who have much in common with us, and that is our good fortune. But it is also true that after some time together, conflicting areas will emerge, and that is when we will have to use the following skills to the maximum.

(a) Compromising and Giving

In a good relationship, you must be prepared to give. Sounds easy, doesn't it? Then why do so many find this hard when core issues like those above cause disagreement? The truth is that if it were so easy a matter, very few marriages would fall on the rocks.

The need to compromise, to give something in order to get something, is essential. When you use the intimacy model to resolve conflict, as taught in this book, you will see that there are three important questions to answer. (see page 88) All three questions must be addressed:

- What do you want for yourself?
- What do you want for your partner?
- What do you want for the both of you?

Here is the good news about the use of that intimacy model. Many people are resistant to change until they realise that the partner wants something for them as well as for him/herself. A healthy resolution of conflict is achieved when we actively and earnestly look for ways to give, and at the same time look out for our own interest.

Giving to the other builds your ability to love (In the Mature Love program it is a demonstration of the nurturing parent). Caring for your own concerns is a way of loving yourself and building self-respect.

(b) Acceptance

Blending can only take place with high levels of acceptance from each partner. This act of love is essential, as agreement in every area of a relationship is an unrealistic goal. Acceptance is not the same as agreement with everything that a person is and does. It is a willingness to allow the other person to express in life who he/she is, and to accept his/her unique personality.

Without basic acceptance there can never be successful blending of two people into a long-term H-type relationship. Acceptance allows for the fact that a partner may not be the same as you in many different ways. Research on brain function makes it more clear every day how individual each of us is. For example, there are different kinds of intelligence, and so it is unreasonable and even cruel for one partner to require that the other operate as though he/she has the same type of intelligence.

A person with a scientific mind might be very different from a person with high levels of interpersonal intelligence. Blending of two people with this match can be fraught with great conflict until each accepts that neither of them is wrong — they are just very different. There can be so much richness in a relationship where these kinds of dissimilarities exist, but only when it is accepted by both that this diversity can be turned into a very interesting life journey together. Perhaps there will be some times of difficult conflict, but that in itself can create an opportunity for stretching the love and maturity of each person.

One marriage therapist wisely asked her clients to imagine: 'What would it be like to live with you every day?' How would you respond to that? Perhaps it would make you get on the other side of the paddock, as suggested in Figure 5.1.

Any time that you have to imagine what it would be like to be in your partner's position, it should also encourage you to explore the possible feelings of that person — a separate entity to you.

The blending process will always be facilitated by practising a measure of empathy. What does empathy do? It diminishes the tendency we all have to jump to conclusions. It slows you down in the harmful practice of blaming — and nothing prevents blending like this habit of blaming. That vice is often paramount in relationship destruction.

Life is not easy. We all appreciate someone being with us in our bad times as well as our good times. You will assist the development of long and enduring love when you are there for your partner in the trying times.

(c) Listening with Understanding

As marriage counsellors we often hear people complain about not being heard and understood. In fact, people who become involved in extramarital affairs often say that they could talk for hours and were understood by the other person. This is one way of highlighting the extent to which people will go in order to experience understanding of their innermost selves. Sadly, it is a fact that so many of us never felt understood as a child. There is in many children a deep loneliness because of this.

When people find a partner there is often an unconscious rule placed on the relationship: 'I expect you to listen to me and to understand my hurt, pain, longing, joy, aspirations, passion, search for the one and only. You are the one I have chosen to listen to me and to have a sense of what makes me tick.'

We cannot say it too strongly: if you want to blend with your partner, *listen, listen, listen*. And, although it is not easy, you must try to understand what your partner is attempting to say to you.

Transmitting what is in the depth of you into the understanding of another is very difficult. It takes time and much soul-searching. You must become aware of your own self, and try to clarify what is there. Then you must patiently try to communicate this heart-felt content to your partner.

Listening to your partner takes empathy, acceptance, respect, giving, courage and much love, but this is really relating in action.

(d) Balancing Togetherness and Separateness Forces

In order to examine this huge issue, we need to go back to Step Three, where we brought into focus the issue of our *roots* and the drives towards togetherness and individuality. It is these two forces which complicate the blending process.

- The togetherness force compels us to blend with another, to spend time with people significant to us, and to make the adaptive changes necessary to build a relationship.
- The separateness force drives us to retain our identity, to discover our real self, and to have time and space for ourself.

There is a need to balance these two forces. One is not more important or significant than the other. They are both essential aspects of an enduring H-type relationship.

In Figure 10.1 we have attempted to picture what is necessary to blend. You don't have to read very much in that Figure to see that there is an enormous amount to blend together. The togetherness force will drive us to do exactly that. We want to get along on the many issues that create a harmonious marital team. The separateness force, however, will pull against that in many areas. We will each want our own way. That, once again, is why *compromise, acceptance and empathy* are so important as you apply the conflict resolution method of Step Six.

Let us look at an issue that comes up often today. It is the concern about whether to have children, and how many to have. Adding a child to a relationship is a strong commitment to togetherness. This is a situation where the forces of togetherness can compete with the forces of individuality. For that reason, the couple has to come to some mutually acceptable agreement on this matter or the blending process will be seriously impeded, if not destroyed.

You might look at the list in Figure 10.1 and see other areas which people have to resolve. They are often *not* resolved just by copying what your family of origin did, or by following some tradition. The force of individuality and separateness compels people to be more true to self these days. Thus a major emphasis of this book is on effective communication as a means to break through conflict in a mutually satisfying way.

At this point you might challenge yourself and make a list of some of the issues over which you have had difficulty in the past or with which you are still having difficulty. What will have to happen for you to reach mutual agreement and continue to blend your life with your partner's? Any time the issue is a hard one to overcome and you have reached an impasse, it might be helpful to use a self-awareness wheel, followed by discussion, using the format found on page 88.

Before going any further, we would like to give you a better idea of the positive and negative aspects of both the togetherness forces and the separateness forces. This understanding could help you work at achieving a balance which will meet both your needs.

Positive Aspects of Togetherness Forces:

1.   You think of others first.
2.   Cooperation is a high priority.
3.   You enjoy being with others.
4.   You seek unity of purpose.
5.   You seek security in sameness and agreement.
6.   Your loyalty to the other is a high priority.
7.   You work for the approval of others.

Negative Aspects of Togetherness Forces:

1.   Disagreement threatens security and causes high levels of emotional reactivity.
2.   You can lose your sense of self as separate and unique.
3.   Differences are discouraged, and boredom can emerge.
4.   Blaming of others increases.
5.   You become overly responsible for the happiness of others.

As you have read through the above list, you might have noticed how much you value the togetherness aspects of a relationship. Life is such, however, that it is quite easy to get out of balance and become resentful. Blending your life with another, therefore, has many possible pitfalls as well as blessings, and these need to be understood. Hopefully, the above list will help you have a better picture of where some of your unease comes in your relationship. The balance has to be addressed, and indeed it is one of the lifelong issues which cannot be escaped. It is simply a part of life.

Positive Aspects of Separateness Force:

1.   You think, feel, want and act for self.
2.   Responsibility for yourself is a high priority.
3.   You speak for self.
4.   You self-explore, and develop your own beliefs.
5.   You are emotionally separate and differentiated from your family of origin.

6.   The approval of others is not a driving force.

7.   There is a freedom within to develop your real self.

Negative Aspects of Separateness Force:

1.   Self-centredness can take over.

2.   You can cut off from others and become isolated.

3.   It is possible to develop rebelliousness and egotism, and maybe arrogance.

4.   There can be a preoccupation with talking about yourself.

5.   You risk being more concerned about yourself than others.

6.   You can close off from external contributions to your life.

Once again, notice that balance is important. As you blend your life with another person there is much to think about. As marriage therapists, we come into contact with many couples who are struggling and cannot figure out what is troubling the relationship. This often causes people to pin the blame on the other person, when in fact they are wrestling with common, ordinary human problems, which can be solved once they are understood.

Getting the balance right is illustrated with the story of Jane. After four years of marriage, with one child, Jane's husband Bob decided he had had enough. Her reliance on her mother, and to some extent her father as well, brings to mind all of the above descriptions of the blending process. She had not really left her family of origin emotionally. Daily telephone calls to her mother were filled with advice about how to live her life. Her mother's approval was continually sought. Jane's sense of being a separate self was weak. Her husband's opinions and feelings were not valued and respected.

Jane covered up the resulting insecurity by being nice, but she always wanted to be the centre of her husband's attention. In fact, his attention to their child was actually a threat to Jane, and she found herself resenting this. The end result was that Bob did not respect Jane, and the resulting distance between them resulted in a marriage breakdown.

Jane had not developed a sense of her own self prior to the marriage, because her mother was a very controlling person who did not foster Jane's independence and individuality. Only when the marriage had broken down, and Jane had marital therapy, did Jane realise all of this. She went on to develop a sense of her separate self.

Why had blending with her husband stalled after only a short time in the marriage? Because she herself had failed to achieve balance between the forces of togetherness and separateness with her family of origin.

Later, in one-to-one talks with her parents, Jane gained the strength to become an autonomous person with confidence and self-reliance. Not that this achievement was easy, as Jane's mother had a dependence on her own children and mother in the same way as Jane had a dependence on her.

What often happens in marriage is a misbalance of separateness and togetherness. For example, Henry was reared in a family that was fragmented and distant. He longed for the day when he would have a partner with whom he would spend all his free time. When he met his 'soul mate', Melba, they became inseparable.

While Melba had hobbies, sport and friends, Henry had done all that, and now wanted to be with Melba all the time. Living out of a childhood deficit, being with her was all that really mattered to him.

At first, Melba loved the exclusive attention. Henry gave the relationship every bit of his energy. She thought it nice to be loved that way. Needless to say, it all became too much for her after a year of being together. Melba wanted more separateness. She wanted to spend more time at sports activities and with her women friends. His anxiety about her distancing took hold, and he put pressure on her to be with him.

When Melba resisted by enjoying her sport and the company of her friends, Henry's jealousy and suspicion mounted. Obviously Henry urgently needed the communication skills as set out in Steps Four and Five.

For their marriage to survive, Henry had to give Melba space. The forces of togetherness needed to be balanced by the forces of separateness. Henry must come to the realisation that there was something in it for him if Melba had a balance that was more satisfying to her. As it was, she was becoming resentful, and time together was increasingly filled with arguing — which is often an unconscious space producer.

Fortunately for the marriage, Henry came to an understanding of the blending process, and how he had tried to heal his childhood loneliness in a self-defeating way. Melba's time apart was enjoyed more, and their time together pleasant. Happily, Henry also found his friends again, once he realised that he was depriving himself of a more balanced life.

Relationships are complex. The points made in this Step and in the previous Steps make it obvious just why that is so. The bottom line is that some of what is involved in the blending process must be carefully studied, understood, and practised, during the entire course of a relationship.

Summary

In Step 10 we looked at Blending Your Life with Another:

- the need to blend your life with another and yet be true to yourself
- blending takes time, often many years
- blending is a complex task which involves learning to think for yourself, know your own feelings and negotiate differences
- the gentle art of balancing the forces of Togetherness and Separateness

How to go about working on your marriage

I n Steps One to Ten we have examined romantic love, the development of your unique 'real self', your relationships with other people, understanding yourself and your partner, constructive ways to resolve conflict, the source and power of your emotions, the growth of mature love, the building of intimacy and trust and the blending process. In Step Eleven we will take the information you have gained and the skills you have learned and show you how to apply them to your own relationships.

WHAT IT MEANS TO WORK ON A MARRIAGE

Each person is unique: each marriage/relationship is unique. Because of this, the ways to improve a partnership are many and varied. The way you and your partner go about working on your relationship will be different to the way another couple might. One important point, however, is that *both* partners should be involved.

To illustrate this, we will use Judy's case, which is typical of many couples we have counselled over the years.

Judy spent the first twelve years of her marriage with the idea that if she did everything to make her husband happy, gave him all he wanted and needed — a tidy house, the children ready for bed when he arrived home, herself neat and attractive — all would be well.

Although some of this was appropriate and fits with part of the Mature Love Programme, Judy was taken for granted. Her husband happily took all she had to give, disregarding any need or wants she might have in the process.

After years of working singlehandedly at her marriage in this self-sacrificing way, Judy began to realise that she was missing out on important experiences. Intimacy in her marriage was almost completely absent, and as her children grew up she had less and less opportunity to express her feelings.

Judy's efforts to work for a more intimate relationship met with resistance from her husband. Her increasing awareness of her real self created marital unhappiness as her husband hid behind his pseudo self, refusing to change or grow. And Judy couldn't go back to the parallel marriage that had existed before, as once she had started to develop as a person it was almost impossible to reverse the process.

Today, Judy's story is being repeated over and over again. So what is the point of working at a marriage if this is what happens?

Firstly, we must establish what really working at a marriage means:

To Work At a Marriage Means ...

1. To decide that you will work at the three Rs of marriage.

2. To think — not just emote — but really try to *think* about what is happening in your marriage and what *you can do* to improve it.

3. To decide that you will *learn* about yourself and grow more mature by successfully dealing with the intricacies of your own unique relationship.

4. To *learn* to start over again with your partner when you slip or fail.

TAKE CARE: These four points will fail to produce a mutually satisfying relationship *unless both* people take responsibility.

MISTAKES PEOPLE MAKE WHEN CONFLICT ARISES

Attempts to change a marriage usually start during the conflict stage as individual differences emerge. When the issues between the two partners are not resolved, and become problems, a number of behaviour patterns appear. Common ones are:

1. Attempting to solve problems too fast — as the old saying goes, 'more haste, less speed' — and this particularly applies to relationships. Here, going slow will ultimately lead to faster and more effective problem solving. The rule is, 'Go slow in order to go fast.'

2. Narrowing the 'solution' to a simple action or formula, such as: 'All you have to do is be nicer and then everything will be all right' or 'If you would just let me know what you're feeling I could get closer to you.'

3. One partner (sometimes both!) expecting the *other one* to do all the changing. As marriage is an extremely complex interaction of complex individuals, both partners must play a role in resolving differences

(although the positive growth of one usually helps both).

4. Increasing aggressive behaviour: although not necessarily involving physical violence, there is an increase in shouting, emotional over-reaction, anger, jealousy — or possibly withdrawal (hidden aggression).

5. Deciding: 'If we can't solve our problems, then no-one else can.'

6. Expecting that: 'Because we're in love, these issues and problems will automatically go away.'

7. Thinking (but not saying): 'I married the wrong person! We're not compatible!' The error here is to stress 'compatibility' rather than combatability — the learned ability to deal assertively and cleanly with issues.

8. Acting to achieve a short-term gain, rather than concentrating on a long-term gain. For example, avoiding an issue; seeking peace at any price; frightening the other person into submission. Each of these short-term gains is actually a *loss* — the person 'wins' a particular battle, but will eventually lose the war.

9. Taking the position, 'I am right — you are wrong', instead of, 'We experience reality, life, this problem — differently'.

10. Analysing your partner, 'You are this way because ...' and therefore not taking responsibility for *your* part in the problem.

DESTRUCTIVE WAYS OF TRYING TO CHANGE A RELATIONSHIP

When things start to go wrong in a relationship and conflict occurs, stress is the result. Stress brings out the aggressive and coercive part of the critical parent ego state, which simply creates *more* stress.

Trying to *force* the other person to change is a time-honoured method: we learn this when we are small — from parents who show us change is brought about by punishment when they discipline us; from teachers who reward good behaviour and deal severely with bad behaviour. So it is that we are trained from an extremely early age that behaviour that belongs to the critical parent ego state can provide an effective way of changing people.

Criticism is *not* an effective way to change the behaviour of another person. The person who is critical is trying to coerce a change in the other person by pointing out flaws, faults and wrong behaviour. Is this effective? No! When self-esteem is reduced by such an attack it affects not only the person's ability to change, but even his or her ability to see the problem itself as the anxiety caused by the criticism brings self-defence mechanisms into play.

In these situations, one person is trying to change the other person, *not change the relationship*. If the relationship is to change, this requires both people to change in some way — a daunting prospect for some. It's less demanding to instruct your partner to change, than to consider that *you* should be changing too!

Nagging is another technique used by one partner in an effort to change the other. Like the constant irritating drip of a leaking tap, nagging, haggling and whining infuriate and provoke. It is better to have a full-blown complaint that starts and stops, and is therefore much easier to deal with, than to endure a constant barrage of wearisome fault-finding and complaints.

Another method used to create change is withdrawal. 'If I withdraw myself, the other person will be shocked by the significance of my absence.' This withdrawal technique is often carried out by the 'silent treatment'.

Yet another technique is withholding: one partner withholds something the other person values: money, sex, opportunities to be together, going out — the list is endless.

Stronger than withdrawing or withholding is *deprivation*. One partner completely removes something of great value to the other partner, depriving him or her of affection, sexual relations — anything of deep importance to that person.

In some relationships the principle is: 'Punish them enough and they will change.' The most extreme form of this method is physical violence. The majority of murders occur in family disputes where this technique had led to complete loss of control and subsequent tragedy.

At the opposite end of the scale of physical violence is the avoiding of conflict by over-submissiveness. There is no power struggle — one person simply gives up and over-submits or over-co-operates. This is a very dangerous technique, since the person who is so over-accommodating is also building up resentment and dislike because he or she is acting against true feelings. The end result is often a complete breakdown of the relationship as this person says, 'I'm not interested any more ... I couldn't care less.'

The range of self-defence mechanisms can be used by one partner to, for example, deny there is a problem at all ('You just want to make trouble ...'); to rationalise the issue away ('It's just because we don't have enough money ...'). Self-defence mechanisms are used to bury the issues so that blame or fault can be put somewhere else.

All these methods involve the pseudo self — they are all ego-saving and face-saving techniques used to avoid taking an honest look at the real situation and the real self. They are coercive and manipulative methods of dealing with conflict and stress, and, in the end, they are all self-defeating. It is pointless to try to change the other person in the relationship and not look at yourself.

TAKE CARE: These destructive ways to try to bring about change in a relationship will kill the ability to trust and destroy the ability to respect. Eventually, this will lead to a loss of affection because trust and respect are basic to being able to be warm, open, affectionate and sexually responsive.

CONSTRUCTIVE WAYS OF BRINGING ABOUT CHANGE IN A RELATIONSHIP

1. Look at yourself. Is there something you can change in yourself? Is there room to develop your more honest and genuine real self in some area?

2. Determine if there is something on your part which is causing emotional over-reactivity (see Step Seven). *Calm* is needed to sort out problems — if you find you can't achieve calmness, you probably have work to do on yourself.

    NOTE: Problems must *never* be worked on when there is emotional reactivity present, because thinking processes stop in the heat of emotion.

3. Try to determine as specifically as possible what you would like to see changed in your relationship. During the course of your discussion the issue may change, turning out to be something different to the issue you thought you had. (But be sure to relate it back to the starting point.) If this happens it is a positive step as it gives a starting place for dealing with the issue.

4. Make out an Awareness Wheel and then present your issue and the *specific request for change*. Particularly note the word 'specific'. To say, 'I'd like you to be a happy person' is a pure waste of energy. That is not a request for change — it's an attack! A request for change is something like this: 'When I come home at night I would like you to drop what you're doing and pay me five minutes attention.'

    'During dinner I would like the television turned off and the family to sit down together.'

    'On Friday night every week I would like us to be together, just the two of us.'

5. Notice that requests for change are *always* made when there is a complaint. *Never, never* make a complaint or criticism unless you are prepared to take responsibility for being specific about what you would like to see changed.

6. During this whole process use the conflict resolution skills outlined in Steps Four to Six.

7. When you reach an agreement finish with a gesture of affection.

WHAT YOU CANNOT CHANGE IN A RELATIONSHIP

Before we look at the many, many areas in which you can experience change in your relationship, it is necessary to come to terms with what *cannot change*. Too many people waste their lives trying to change the unchangeable, thus ignoring or destroying opportunities for improvement that do exist. This is the wisdom we all need ... to recognise what should, and could, be changed.

Here are some of the things that cannot be changed, no matter how hard we try:

A person's nature:

We all have a different nature, and an important part of this is how our thinking functions. Each of us has different brain characteristics and we will always have these differences. This is what explains the creative genius of Mozart, Beethoven, Einstein, Edison, Rembrandt ... and why *you* think differently to the person next to you.

The interesting point is that how we think affects how we solve problems. Some people think flexibly, seeing many options; others think inflexibly, convinced there is only one way to do something. Some people are good at details; others have an innate ability to grasp the whole.

In marriage these different ways of thinking can complement each other, or they can clash.

You cannot change the ways you and your partner each think, but you can learn to understand and accept the differences. In fact, these differences can even be an advantage. For example, a partnership where one person thinks in detail and the other sees the sweep of the whole situation can provide the framework for a great team.

Life experiences:

Life experiences are the second thing you cannot change. Some of us have had easy, happy childhoods. Others have been very hurt. We have learned different customs, languages, rules, religious concepts, expectations and when we come together as partners we each bring this history of life experiences.

Each of us therefore has to adapt and adjust to our partner's ways. This can be difficult, as we are often taught in our families that our way is the *right* way, and we act accordingly in our relationships.

There are, of course, no *right* ways: there are *different* ways of living.

Physical appearance:

Physical appearance is another thing that cannot really be changed. We can slow down the ageing process — we can keep ourselves fit and well groomed — but age will eventually cause wrinkles, cellulite, weight gain, greying of the hair, loss of firmness of the body ...

Unfortunately we are often attracted to a person because of beauty or handsomeness. We may be captivated by some single factor — eyes, figure, muscle development — or some combination of attractive features.

Neither you nor your partner can hang on to youth forever. This is why it is so important to recognise and develop many more reasons for loving than mere physical ones.

The past:

Another unchangeable thing is the *past.* What has happened, has happened — what's gone, is gone. Going over the past and criticising yourself or your partner prevents you from dealing with the present. Never say, 'If only you had ...' or, 'If only we had ...'

People who live in the past experience depression; people who live in the future create anxiety; but people who live in the present can know life.

WHAT YOU CAN CHANGE IN A RELATIONSHIP

Happily, there are many areas where change can occur in a marriage. You are in charge of many of these, and that is why you can be optimistic about improving your relationship and moving closer and closer to an H-type marriage.

The first and most important area of change concerns your attitudes and behaviour. You can do much about your own bad habits, irritating behaviours, neglectfulness, poor use of time, insensitivity, hurting behaviour, poor communication skills, lack of awareness of self and others — all of these are involved in and necessary for working on the three R's of marriage.

Any discord in your marriage offers a challenge for you to learn. And as you do that, as you grow and change, this will often be the impetus that your partner needs to grow in turn. The example you give of someone growing in personal esteem, confidence and inner peace may be the indirect cause of change in your partner too.

The next step is to explore many ways of enriching your marriage as you work at the three R's — responsibility, real self and romance. Here are some specific items to work upon:

1. Developing Self-awareness:

To deepen and develop an interesting marriage, self-awareness is crucial. Without it there is little possibility for intimate experience, as straight style talk is rare and the real self is not known. Lack of self-awareness encourages pseudo self behaviour and shallow conversational style talk.

Much change is possible when you become more *self* aware. Of course, as this can be difficult to achieve and because many people find it threatening, your drive to do this must be strong.

Nigel's experience is a good illustration of the importance of self-awareness:

> Nigel first came to us for counselling when his wife Bernice became deeply depressed and refused to get close to him any longer. Nigel and Bernice were involved in joint counselling for a time as well as in a communication course for couples. Nigel followed this with individual counselling, and he was encouraged to enter discussions with his mother to reduce his emotional over-reactiveness springing from his family of origin.

> There was a steady improvement in the marriage, particularly after they both attended our School of Marriage Course (from which this book grew).

> Nigel has now become far more self-aware and Bernice has overcome her depression and developed into an assertive person. Their marriage provides each with rewarding and enjoyable experiences as they work together to develop trust and intimacy. When we saw them recently, Nigel said: 'I'm simply not the same person I was before, and neither is Bernice. I couldn't have believed we could have such a great relationship as we have now.'

2. Expectations:

Most people enter marriage with the firm expectation that they will somehow be more successful than their parents — after all, they have seen all the flaws of their own families, so they won't make the same mistakes again!

The problem is that two things go with each person into a union: first, the models and examples of each person's own family; second, the genes inherited from the parents which can make the individual rather more like one (or both) parents than he/she would like to admit.

This means that achieving a 'better' marriage is not easy, as there will have to be an active fight against the mistaken expectations, bad habits and all the bad lessons learned in the past.

There are two things you *can* expect: first, that you and your partner are not perfect — on the contrary, in many ways you are each sure to be far from perfect. And second, that you both have a lot to learn which is brand new — your families probably never taught you most of the skills needed to form an H-type relationship with all its potential for growth.

3. Self-development and self-improvement:

One of the most important things you can change is *you* — there are so many ways that you can improve and develop yourself.

All of this makes you much more interesting. So many people are boring to their partners because they have never changed and never grown. They are, essentially, exactly the same at fifty as they were at twenty. Life together is routine and predictable as marriage provides an endless repetition of the same with only minor variations.

Change can be exciting, interesting, *alive*!

4. Reprogramming:

Although you cannot change how you were originally programmed, you certainly can re-evaluate and create *new* programs.

> Edna, for example, had a strong program that could be titled 'Move on if things ever get too tough'. With two marriages behind her (obviously each had got 'too tough') she came to us for counselling about her third marriage.
>
> When Edna realised how she had been blindly obeying a program that encouraged her to run away from painful situations, she was able to work on re-programming herself to constructively work on difficult problems, rather than evade them. Edna is now happily working at, and enjoying, her third marriage.

You, too, can change such kinds of damaging programming.

5. The mature love programme:

The Mature Love Programme gives you an endless number of ways to change your relationship. There are many ideas available there which can increase your *love actions* and *feelings*. All this says that love can be increased — you can change if you act before you lose incentive or sink into despair.

Don't let love die of malnourishment or neglect — *feed it daily with loving actions*.

6. Educate yourself about marriage:

One of the most complex human experiences is marriage, and in this book we have highlighted how much can be involved in creating a successful marriage.

We see people daily changing their marriages by gaining more information. This makes sense: would you try to sail a yacht across the ocean without learning navigation skills? Not likely! Yet millions of people sail into marriage without learning any of the skills required.

Shipwrecked marriages are everywhere because people know too little to take them through rough seas or find smooth waters.

7. Special events:

Smart lovers seek special ways of being together, setting everything else aside and concentrating upon being together *exclusively*. This may involve going into the country, or to the beach, or spending a weekend away once in a while. It might be a world cruise together or trekking in the Himalayas!

Such couples do not take another couple along in order to *avoid* each other! If you find yourself doing this, you may need to work at your communication skills and at developing curiosity about each other.

8. Develop sexual relating skills:

In Step Nine we outlined many of the sexual relating skills which can contribute to change in a relationship. While the knowledge of how to procreate is quite instinctive and can be understood quite rapidly, the knowledge of how to be with each other in a really intimate and satisfying way is developed over many years.

In most of the great marriages we see, people's sexual enjoyment increases, not decreases. These couples have worked at *being together* in many ways, and topped it off with enjoying being together sexually. Such couples *make* love to make *love*.

9. Perspective:

You, your partner, every person in the world, has experienced life differently from the time of conception. Our counselling has led us to marvel at the enormous variety of life experiences, even within the same family. And, quite apart from this, there are cultural, language, religious, educational and philosophical differences. Even the way each person thinks is individual — each of us has a unique brain function.

So why is this significant?

It is significant because no one will ever see all of reality precisely as you do ... even the person who is your special choice of a life partner.

What often makes marriage so interesting is your partner's uniqueness ... his or her 'differentness' from you.

Try to see life and reality from the perspective of your partner — enjoy, appreciate, learn and benefit from another's point of view and way of seeing. (Remember the ball in the paddock in Step 5.)

10. Priorities in life:

To improve your life and your relationships, you must change priorities so as to give time to what is *really* important to you. Ask yourself: 'Is my marriage more important than television, or the newspaper, or sport?' Look at how you allocate your time — it is often a good way to measure your true priorities.

In counselling we have often heard the wife and children express how low down the list of the husband's priorities they feel they have been placed. Husbands in turn can be convinced that their wives have placed the children above them as far as importance is concerned.

Those couples who recognise that the top priority should always be the relationship between them are building a long-lasting foundation for themselves and for their children.

11. Self-esteem:

How much you value yourself — your self-esteem — is vital in the giving and receiving of love. If you have low self-esteem, this can be changed. Indeed, one of the most positive steps you can take is to become a more assertive communicator, as outlined in Step Four.

12. Develop common interests:

Frequently, couples who find their marriage has deteriorated do too little together and have interests that are too few or too dissimilar. There are often many reasons behind this failure to develop common interests, including the need of one (or both) to be distanced from the other, the desire to actually *avoid* the other, or the custom of spending little time with the opposite sex.

If you believe you and your partner lack common interests, then each of you should make a list of all your present areas of interest, as well as those you would like to develop in the future. See which of these interests you can share together.

Remember, marriage should involve many ways of *being together*.

13. Change in roles:

Much marital conflict centres on roles. In the traditional marriage forged over centuries, the role of women was submissive and confined to household duties, while the role of men was dominant and had its main sphere of action outside the home. In many cultures this sharp separation of roles still exists.

Today, our Western culture is in a transitional stage, with these once clearly defined roles increasingly in a state of flux. There is a blurring of the division of duties and responsibilities, as women and men try to establish new and more elastic roles in society.

Because of this, it is common for people to develop a sense of unfairness and resentment about what they see as the failure of others to take equal responsibility or to give equal respect.

This means that you need to use your communication skills to negotiate differences over roles. It is just one more area which makes modern marriage more difficult, but at the same time it offers more freedom, fulfilment and growth to both sexes.

14. Change of contract:

In Step Seven three types of contracts were identified as figuring in relationships: the spoken contract, the unspoken contract and the unconscious contract.

The first, the spoken contract, is interesting, because even though the expectation may have been clearly stated, people change their wants in life. The contract that seemed quite reasonable before marriage becomes a source of unhappiness afterwards. For example, perhaps the man clearly says before marriage, 'My career has priority over everything else,' and his partner agrees that this is reasonable. But, as time goes by, the woman discovers that she is caught in a trap of loneliness, and the contract she agreed to originally has become a source of tension and anxiety.

If the contract no longer 'fits' — if one person finds it unsatisfactory and wants to change it, then a new agreement must be negotiated. If this doesn't happen, then the contract will be a constant source of conflict and anxiety.

More subtle marital conflict is often caused by people becoming aware of the third kind of agreement, the unconscious contract. This realisation can be positive, as the couple grow in understanding of their relationship and begin to improve it; it can also be negative when the awareness makes clear that the two have a fundamental difference of serious magnitude.

Resolution of problems about contracts is very much helped by the adult ego state.

It is important to realise that many relationships do successfully change or modify contracts — they do not have to be the source of serious conflict.

15. Change in communications skills:

It is impossible to learn too much about communication skills. Steps Four, Five and Six concentrate upon the essentials of communication, but these skills need practice! practice! practice!

Communication is the key to all that is good in really relating.

16. Work on over-reactivity:

As outlined in Step Seven, emotional over-reaction not only confuses the issue, it makes matters worse. In marital conflict such over-reaction contaminates your thoughts and makes conflict resolution difficult, if not impossible.

Understanding, and hence overcoming, your emotional triggers will help you calm down and approach differences with your partner in a constructive way.

You cannot avoid some differences with your partner, but you can avoid clouding the issue with emotional over-reaction.

17. Reduce life stress:

When two people in a relationship are under stress, the marriage, no matter how suited the two may be, will also undergo stress. In counselling we have seen the relationships of many people who are quite ideally suited crash because of stress, particularly in the early child-rearing years.

These early years, when the foundations for the future of the relationship are being built, are also often the time of maximum stress. A new family, a new car, a new home — so much to pay for, so little energy, so little knowledge of how to handle these stresses — can lead to a breakdown of the relationship.

Wisdom is needed to reduce stresses. Do you both really need all those material things in order to be satisfied and fulfilled? What you do need is each other and time to build your relationship. Don't let the debts, commitments and responsibilities mount up until they are too large for you to handle. The debt trap is one of the best destroyers of a marriage.

If you find yourself in this stressed situation, reduce whatever stress you can and increase time for yourselves.

A warning: we have too often seen a couple build a big new home and celebrate moving in with a separation!

18. Time and life management:

How you use time is how you use your life — we all have the same numbers of hours in a day. And you can change how you are using time so as to have more for your partner.

One couple we counselled never had time together because of the lifestyle they had adopted. This lifestyle was so busy, so stressful, that they had no energy or time left over to nurture themselves or each other. He was swept up with the demands of his business career; she was totally consumed with her career in art. When he approached her sexually, often at one or two in the morning, it naturally seemed like an intrusion. Basically, they had too few ways of being together.

They saved their marriage, but only by radical lifestyle surgery that put the emphasis where it should always have been — on their relationship.

19. Curiosity:

You can change from lack of interest in what makes your partner tick to great curiosity. Of course, to do this — to appreciate how your partner is different from you — requires love for the other person.

It can be fascinating to learn about your partner's childhood experiences, embarrassing moments, unique ways of thinking, interests, ideas, beliefs. Remember, no one is the same — every person is different.

20. Rituals:

Many people enrich their lives with rituals: repetitive occasions and experiences to look forward to.

As a couple or a family you can celebrate birthdays, anniversaries, family reunions, national holidays — there are any number of excuses for getting together with your extended family.

You can meet with valued friends on a regular basis to talk, play cards or enjoy sports.

A yearly holiday to some loved or romantic place not only gives time for rest and relaxation, it can also provide a storehouse of happy memories together.

21. Eliminate or reduce fear:

Fear can be a major cause in the decline of a relationship, so it is important to recognise that it exists. As we grow up our unique fears are developed, fears that will later cause difficulties in our relationships. There can be fear of people in general, of getting close, of intimacy, of disclosing one's innermost thoughts and feelings, of surrendering, of sexual behaviour, of facing life — the list goes on and on.

Perhaps the most basic fear is the fear to admit your fear. And it is helpful to know that most people are frightened of something, although they usually refuse to admit it.

We are constantly amazed at the progress people make by simply admitting their fear of something. By expressing it, by disclosing it to your partner, you rob the fear of much of its force.

And obviously, if the fear you have hinders the building of an H-type intimate relationship, then it is particularly important that you deal with it.

22. Humour:

Humour can be found in almost everything — in our School of Marriage courses, we get the greatest laughter response when we portray a typical marriage dispute!

Most marital arguments have elements in them which are laughable. It is instructive to tape record your arguments and see how often you are both irrational, and how often you can smile at a dispute that at the time seemed vitally important.

Many marriage disputes are quite trivial. In a year's time, a month's time, possibly even an hour's time, you will view the argument with tolerant amusement.

Often we have asked couples on the verge of splitting up just what their arguments are about — and they cannot remember! Their conflict has changed from deciding on an issue to a raw struggle for power — an 'I win/you lose' approach.

When life is just too stressful, find a way to laugh. Humour is a saving grace, and can often rescue you from the most serious situation.

23. Self-limiting beliefs:

We all have many beliefs which limit us from achieving our best potential. For example:

> SHE: 'I'm not as attractive as the other women in our group so I know he will never love me as much as I want him to.'

> HE: 'I'm really a failure because I don't earn as much as the other men in my family, so my wife will always be disappointed in me.'

During counselling we have heard literally thousands of such self-limiting thoughts, almost always arising from the harsh critical parent ego state.

Such thoughts will limit your personal growth because they distract you from your many positive features and inhibit you. Don't let your over-critical self stop you from growth and achievement!

24. Accepting your partner's idiosyncrasies:

Every person has behaviours which are unique, unusual, different. Many of us are quite unaware of these little quirks we have. A person may, for example, talk out of the side of his mouth, and never be aware he does it.

You should try to accept your partner's individual little habits and behaviours, as he or she accepts yours (we all have them!)

Sometimes, since these idiosyncrasies are habitual and the person is unaware of them, it can be useful to point them out (take care to be constructive) in order to give the person the opportunity of control.

25. Boundaries can be changed:

Jessica and Graham had a bedroom that anyone could enter at any time. Everyone in the family, including the cat and dog, was part of whatever went on in that room because they could gather there any time they pleased.

Jessica objected: 'Where were the boundaries?' Graham accused her of being selfish and not believing in 'one big happy family'.

How did Jessica feel? As far as Graham was concerned she couldn't see that she was any more important or special than the children, the dog or the cat — after all, he treated them all the same.

Counselling helped Graham understand that his family was composed of a whole series of A-frame relationships, in which everyone was too dependent and territory was constantly being violated.

When Graham understood that Jessica needed boundaries — that she required some privacy and the security of her own 'space' he agreed to limits. The result? Jessica at long last felt she had a special place in Graham's life.

26. Develop your spiritual self:

Many people are in search of something or someone to calm the inner core of their being. They have a restlessness, a lack of meaning in their lives, a sense of going nowhere.

Many people pursue things that they think will satisfy them, only to find in the end that they are empty. Fame, friends, university degrees, relationships, material possessions ... we can have them all and still feel unhappy.

This inner dissatisfaction is often translated into: 'I have the wrong partner in life.' This is a mistake: the answer lies in yourself.

Many find that in the long run there is a real need to satisfy this inner spiritual self — to find calm. We have often observed that when one partner finds a spiritual 'centre' the pressure is off the other person, because the peace the troubled partner has found dissolves the dissatisfaction that had been wrongly blamed on the relationship.

27. Intention:

Perhaps your first intention in marriage was easy gratification — 'I'll enjoy myself!' This doesn't take into account the personal growth opportunities that await you. Your free child ego state says, 'I want to have fun,' but your adult egostate says, 'Nothing that is worthwhile comes without work.'

There are no spectators in the successful marriage game ... only participants! Make the effort, and win!

28. Tape record your discussions:

We have seen remarkable changes occur in people simply by listening to their discussions, marital disputes and overly emotional scenes. The first time we had a couple do this, many years ago, the husband came in saying, 'I am really boring. I go on and on like a broken tape recorder. I just never heard myself like others do.'

Clients often say, 'While I listened to the tape I realised how critical I am of my wife/husband.'

29. Respect:

Learn a new respect for your partner's point of view. Every cell of your partner's body is different from yours. Your partner has a different brain function — unique ways of thinking. Love means that you respect and appreciate those differences. No one can be like you because no one else, including your partner, is the same.

30. Say 'I love you':

Every day, in some way say 'I love you', either in word or by special actions (keeping in mind the many ways this can be done using the

Mature Love Programme). We once had a client tell his wife, 'I told you twenty-three years ago that I loved you and until I change my mind I'll not tell you again.' She did not seem amused by the comment.

HOW LONG DOES IT TAKE TO CREATE A SATISFYING MARRIAGE?

As we described in Step One, a marriage can progress through four distinct stages:

STAGE ONE: Courtship

STAGE TWO: Honeymoon

STAGE THREE: Conflict

STAGE FOUR: Resolution

Every marriage that goes into the conflict stage is caught up with the question, 'How long? Just how long will this painful time last?'

It seems the answer could depend on countless factors, but in truth, *it depends on you.*

In Step 3 we outlined four types of marriage:

- The A-frame marriage
- The lean-to marriage
- The parallel-type marriage
- The H-type marriage

We believe that in this age and in the future, there will be more and more people wanting H-type marriages. Some may, of course, settle for another structure because it is easier, or because they feel incapable or don't know how to grow into enough of their real selves to have an H-type marriage.

Our counselling has shown us that stale marriages are rife. Everywhere there are marriages built on pseudo self and pseudo intimacy. The marvel is not that there are so many divorces but that so many stay in marriages which offer so little fullfilment.

The great strength of the H-type marriage is that it encourages each person to be 'real' — to be whole, fulfilled, mature and challenging in a positive way. Each partner is thus in touch with more of his/her real self and with all the exciting potentials of personal growth and achievement that can result from this.

Creating an H-type marriage, however, takes hard work, the development of skills, the qualities of patience and courage, and faith in the processes and outcomes of growth.

So how long before you reach this treasured goal? How long before your relationship reaches the rewards and delights of Stage Four?

For some it is a short time — two, five, seven years. Many couples find, however, that it takes much longer to reach something like an H-type relationship. But take heart! Bear in mind that the H-type marriage is an *ideal:* we are never fully real, never fully developed as a self, and life is a *process* of personal development, and therefore relationship development.

Remember, the journey is full of self-discovery and personal growth for both partners; and the achievement is more than worth the effort.

Here is an example of the evolution of a marriage:

> Elsa and Harry had been married for three years when we first saw them in counselling. Never had a marriage begun with a more dramatic 'falling in love' basis. Well suited in every way, they were connected by the most powerful and overwhelming feelings of romantic love — feelings so strong that they felt their love would continue forever, unchanged and untended.
>
> Both Elsa and Harry plunged into their respective careers, in each case experiencing great success. They had many of the romantic love experiences we discussed in Step Two, they had material success … life was a delight.
>
> Yet, after three years of inattention to the importance of their relationship — it was on the rocks! Taken for granted, it had drifted, deteriorated, and finally fallen to pieces.

How did this happen? Wasn't the kind of love they had enough to carry them through? No! Because while both Elsa and Harry had worked hard and long at their careers, they had paid little attention to their relationship. These otherwise successful people had paid no heed to the development of a mature and lasting love between them: it was a concept quite foreign to them both.

During counselling Elsa and Harry made the same complaints about the other: their romantic love relationship had become a 'parallel' type marriage that had left them both feeling starved of love, affection, touching, encouragement — all the positive rewards that an H-type relationship contains.

Elsa and Harry found they had three choices. They could continue as before in a parallel-type relationship and hope to survive together somehow. They could divorce, or, they could embark on the development of mature love and the building of an H-type relationship.

They decided that each was too valuable to lose, and that the potential relationship they could work towards was worth any amount of time and effort. They are now embarked on the journey towards a relationship based on the three Rs of marriage and they have the hope that concentrated effort will bear fruit. The quality of their relationship is improving, and the promise of future contentment and opportunities for personal growth encourages their efforts.

Remember, marriage is not just a ceremony, a legal state. Marriage is a process — one which can take years to achieve its most satisfying and rewarding stage. A deep relationship is never static — it never stops growing, improving, changing — and mature love can grow as you both grow.

STARTING OVER AGAIN

We often hear this kind of lament: 'I've been hurt by my partner and I just can't forget the past ... I don't known if there's any way we can start over again.'

Many times during the process of marriage we can feel despair and defeat — it all seems too hard. For that reason, we have to learn the art of starting again.

Starting over isn't just an occasion where you say, 'Okay, let's wipe the slate clean and start again.' The concept implies the learning of whole new attitudes and the use of new skills.

The Importance of Forgiveness

It is easy to concentrate on grudges stored up over the years: to dwell on past hurts and allow resentment to poison your partnership. But if you forgive, you leave your resentments behind and have the opportunity to move ahead in your relationship.

Some people live for the present, getting all they can out of today and then moving on to tomorrow. Others hold on to the hurtful experiences of the past, often quite insignificant things — some of which may have occurred five, ten, fifteen, even twenty years ago! During counselling we have come across many cases of 'long storage' resentments: in one a man kept recalling how hurt he had been when his wife put some of his prized possessions out in the garage, and this had happened thirty years ago!

Some people delight in putting past hurts into a 'museum' so that they can visit them whenever they feel depressed or when someone has hurt them. Assembling such a collection of bitter memories and then examining it at regular intervals is not going to make forgiveness a viable concept — on the contrary, such a 'museum' leads to increased feelings of resentment and hurt.

How to forgive:

Forgiveness begins with an acknowledgement of your ability to hurt others: it is not a one-way street — people hurt you, and you hurt them. It is important to recognise this in order to let go of the hurts that build resentment.

An occasion for forgiveness is when one person owns that he/she has hurt another; 'I own that I hurt you and I'm sorry.'

The forgiving person then extends some kind of mercy in behaviour and/or words: 'I'm letting you off the hook … I'm not going to hold it against you forever … it's over, it's past business.'

The forgiving person also accepts that the present is the only reality — that there is no point in living in the past or hoping for the future. No one can change the past or live in the future — the now is the important thing.

Is He/She Really Sorry?

It is healthy to have some scepticism when the offending person repeats behaviour damaging to the relationship over and over again.

Some people say, 'I'm sorry!' to be let off the hook. Alcoholics, for example, may beg forgiveness regularly: 'I'm sorry, I'll never do it again …' and then repeat the behaviour. We can all use this ploy to avoid discomfort. We aren't sorry, and we don't intend to change, but it's convenient to say so, as it makes things so much easier.

Consider this: when you ask for forgiveness, are you genuinely saying, 'What can I change about myself so that I don't do that again?' Or are you just using a ploy to avoid an issue/problem/conflict?

As discussed in earlier Steps, the family of origin can provide us with certain programmed responses to situations, so that when we are reminded of the past we 'twitch' in a reflex reaction. Unless we are willing to examine the programs we have learned in our family framework, we will always be saying 'I'm sorry', but not doing anything to avoid the same problem in the future.

Why is it so hard to forgive?

1. Some people develop a strategy that says: 'I'm just waiting for you to hurt me because I'll throw it in the gunny sack and when the time is right, when the occasion is convenient … I'll make you suffer!'

   In this case, holding on to the past gives the person ammunition to use against his/her partner. This is a destructive method which distracts your partner from the real problem and/or redirects attention from yourself.

2. Creating familiar and comfortable territory: many people recreate the atmosphere in which they feel most at home so, for example, a person who has been brought up in a family where issues were argued vehemently, but never resolved, is likely to create that confrontational approach because that is home territory and it feels comfortable.

3. Injustice collecting: this approach belongs to people who do not (or

cannot) enjoy life. They think, 'I might as well feel *really* miserable ...' He or she collects injustices: opportunities to feel depressed, guilty, wrong. Such people *live in the past* and use it to feed their dark feelings.

4. Failing to come to grips with the amount of pain one's partner feels in life: if you do not acknowledge or even realise the amount of pain your partner has experienced in the course of living, then you are missing an opportunity to grow closer. To acknowledge that hurt allows you to draw closer to someone else: 'I have been hurt, my partner has been hurt. We are together today partly because of that pain in the past. We share therefore we understand.'

5. Playing games: as Eric Berne pointed out in his best seller *Games People Play*, there is always a personal payoff for people who play 'games'. One way to overcome low self-esteem is to play games such as 'I'm better than you', where the aim is to pull others down in order to build up an image of self-worth. It is interesting to listen to people gossiping and to observe how many end up feeling better after they have spent some time tearing others down.

    Many do not forgive so that they can continue to play a 'victim game'. Over and over such a person will say, 'Look how many times you have hurt me!' Calling up incidents over many years is a 'poor me' victim game. Sometimes it takes the form of, 'if it weren't for you I'd be happy!' Living in the past is a vital part of the victim game.

6. Fear: 'I'm afraid to forgive you, because if I do you might hurt me again, so I'm not going to trust you.'

When a person has been hurt by another, it is very difficult to be trusting. But in order to start again, trust is essential. Some risk is involved, but the greatest risk is to take no risk at all.

In order to start over again, trust is absolutely essential. And achieving it is not easy ... it takes maturity and healthy self-esteem.

What does forgiveness do?

The ability to forgive gets our relationship going again. It gives us the opportunities to try out new skills, to build something together that will be mutually rewarding.

Forgiveness allows us to find the relationship that has eluded us so many times in the past because we haven't known how to achieve it. It lets us make a fresh start, using our former mistakes as rich learning experiences to help us build the future.

What to Do When You Can't Achieve Resolution

Many people try to create marital harmony by resolving differences as they appear along life's way, but they experience repeated disappointment. They begin to see the writing on the wall — the more they try to change, the more everything seems to stay the same.

At this point it is important to recall what we have emphasised in the previous section. A successful marriage can take a long time to build, especially an H-type marriage, which is the emerging ideal in our culture. Don't give up! Learning to live happily with someone else is a long-term project, and each person probably brought to the partnership things that can cause problems.

Go over all the sections of this book again. Learn your lessons well, remembering that the mastering of communication skills can take time, as can the many skills required for intimacy.

Don't be one of those people who gives up too soon and either settles for one of the pseudo self type marriages or heads for the divorce courts. Our society unfortunately teaches us too many lessons about easy gratification: 'If it doesn't come easily, it must be wrong.'

And a warning: if you don't learn your lessons *now* you will only take all your hangups and problems into your next relationship. We often see people who have had a series of 'serious' relationships — four, five, six — and they are *still* trying to find the easy way. These people have not learned the lessons you've read about in this book.

So what can you do if things are still not working out? Here are some possible ways of making progress:

1. Take a course in couples communication, or in interpersonal skills. We use the Minnesota Couples Communication program, in conjunction with our own program as outlined in this book. The Minnesota Couples Communication program is available in English-speaking countries and you may be able to find one running somewhere near you. If not, there are many other useful marriage and parenting communication courses. As well, a course in problem solving or conflict resolution might be available in your area.

2. Pursue a course in marriage. Our own School of Marriage usually has 100 to 150 people enrolled, which we believe indicates that the stigma of doing such courses is vanishing. The reality is that each of us *needs* to learn about the complexities of living with another person.

3. Seek out necessary counselling from a qualified person. Often your friends will have had good experiences in this area and be able to refer you to a competent person in the field. However, make sure that the person has qualifications in marriage counselling.

And remember, don't wait too long! Most people go to professional helpers too late. A skilled marital therapist will teach you many things about yourself and your relationship. If you have already tried counselling and felt the therapist did not have the necessary skills to help you, try someone else. There are many competent people available with whom you may be able to have a more positive counselling experience.

DIVORCE

Is divorce a failure? The answer to this is sometimes 'yes' and sometimes 'no' — it all depends on what effort you have made to take responsibility for your growth and to learn about how relationships work.

It is probably better not to think in black and white terms, but to consider the concept as a continuum, with 'failure' as one extreme and 'success' as the other. Then we can think of ourselves as being more on the success end, rather than the failure end.

An important point is that you can *learn* from failure. When people look back they can often see that they acted irresponsibly or in a self-defeating way. For these people, success can be seen as coming later in that being able to see a past pattern of failure changes the way they act in the present.

Bill and Jean present an example of success *and* failure — their relationship taught him nothing, so for him it was a failure, but Jean learned and achieved a great deal, so for her it was a success.

Bill and Jean's marriage began as a passionate romance. Bill was 'handsome'; Jean was 'lovely to look at' (their words). Jean already had two children by a first marriage. Bill had experienced a short-term marriage in which his wife had left him.

Their marriage turned sour very soon after their first child was born. Jean was under stress and was exhausted, so she was no longer able to make Bill 'number one' in everything. He bitterly resented the change and in attempting to remain the centre of her attention, he tried to create a lean-to type union.

His words at this point are memorable: 'If you do what I want and take care of my needs I'll be happy. And if *I'm* happy, we'll both find it easy to be happy.'

Jean saw that this meant giving up the real parts of her self and becoming a non-self. She was far too assertive to do this, so Bill called in the big gun — his father, a man who had ruled the roost in his home.

The resulting triangle was explosive. Bill's overemotionality and his father's example of male dominance took over the situation. When they came to one of us for counselling, Bill was determined to change Jean to his way of thinking, in the same way as his father had managed to do with his mother. And, as Bill knew nothing of the years of training and growth that a qualified counsellor undergoes to become objective, he believed a male marriage counsellor would support his point of view.

Counselling soon showed that Bill was not ready to take responsibility for his actions. Soon after, a separation occurred, followed by a divorce.

For Bill, this divorce is a failure, since he has still not learned anything important about building a relationship. He has much work to do to be differentiated from the emotionality of his family of origin. When he enters another relationship, conflict will once again emerge, since he takes the same potential problems with him, and a similar solution will be attempted.

Jean, on the other hand, has courageously taken the risk of being a self-supporting parent with three children. For her, many lessons have been learned because she is *willing to learn*. In this way her divorce is not a failure, but has allowed her to achieve some personal growth and understanding.

Jean learned well that the greatest risk is to take no risk at all.

When is Divorce a Failure?

People nearly always feel some sense of failure when a divorce eventuates and brings all of their dreams to an end ... it is difficult to see it any other way.

Often the source of failure was the choice of partner. Romantic love is blind to so many things and people get into many traps out of sheer emotional need and the drive of their biological selves.

Nevertheless, it is almost uncanny how so many of us choose a partner who is appropriate to us — the unconscious self often finds the right kind of person.

When can it be said that a person has failed in at least some respects?

1. When you have not really tried all the means available to create marital satisfaction.

2. When you have not attempted to diligently develop your *real self*. If you leave a marriage without working on your own deficiencies you will inevitably take them into a new relationship. Worse, you will not only take your hangups along with you, you will also take new ones developed by the broken marriage.

3. When you have not learned skills necessary for a satisfying marriage.

4. When you think you can blame everything on the other person.

5. When, in the process of leaving a marriage, you are deceitful — when even in divorce you cannot be honest and assertive.

6. When you need defences like denial and rationalisation to justify your role in the breakdown. If your partner tried to get your attention and create change for some time and you just denied the existence of problems, it can mean that you lack self-esteem and cannot face yourself.

7. In essence, when you have not learned some of the valuable lessons important to marital joy and success. In our terms, when you have not worked at the three Rs of marriage you have let yourself and your partner down.

Summary

In Step Eleven we outlined How to Go About Working On Your Marriage:

- what it means to work on a marriage
- the mistakes people make when conflict arises
- destructive ways of trying to change a relationship
- what you cannot change
- what you can change
- how long does it take to create a satisfying marriage?
- starting over again — the importance of forgiveness
- what to do if you can't achieve resolution of problems
- when is divorce a failure?

How to apply 'really relating' to your problems

There are some serious relationship problems which occur when people ignore using many of the skills covered in this book. The following common behaviours can cause many of the problems to occur:

1. When people keep to themselves what they are really thinking, feeling, wanting, deeply desiring, longing for — secrets which block the free flow of love.

2. When people compensate for what they are missing by going outside the relationship to meet those needs.

3. When people retaliate against the partner (many times at a quite unconscious level) in order to pay that person back.

4. When unhappiness in a relationship is dealt with by manipulation, or by threats and sometimes violence.

5. When people attempt to short-cut the process of solving basic problems in order to get what they need or want in some other indirect way.

6. When people involve their children or family in an attempt to force the other person to comply.

7. When the partner is not attentive enough to listen to or to notice the other's hurt.

8. When people resort to analysis of the other person, either as a way to fit in or to 'help' that person change. Analysis of a partner is too often a way to 'cut that person down to size' — a way of control, not love.

9. When people resign themselves to unfavourable aspects of a relationship, which they then secretly resent and put into their 'gunny

sack' of hurts and resentments. In time a loss of positive feeling towards the partner will occur.

10. When people use relating and problem solving methods which appear to work in the short term, but will devastate good will in the long term. For example, conflict avoidance is a common short term solution which fails in the long term.

The following pages highlight common relationship problems and suggest how to employ Really Relating skills.

WHEN THE PARTNER WON'T RELATE

One of the most common statements heard from couples experiencing a crumbling of their commitment is, 'We have grown apart'. In reality, people in this predicament have often not grown at all because they have failed to nurture romance and to build a mature love relationship.

Our marriage courses include many such couples who have moved from growing apart to a satisfying relationship they previously thought impossible. However, there are always participants who do the course alone because their partners refuse to be involved. This refusal of one partner to be involved in constructive examination of the relationship is often justified by the statement 'We don't need outside help — we ought to be able to do this on our own'. (See Rationalising and Denial pages 40–43).

Should you have a partner who resists involvement in changing and improving your relationship together, you might consider the following points if you want to become an agent of change:

1. Fear is the most common cause of not relating, but it is unlikely the resisting partner will admit, 'I'm afraid to relate with you'. The usual way of coping with fear is to withdraw or to cover it up with anger. It is important to note that fear might be caused by past experiences in the relationship (see pages 158–160) so you must be honest with yourself and ask how you might have contributed to the problem or reinforced a fear which your partner developed in childhood.

2. Stand back and look at your role in the problem. Have you been overly analytical? Critical? Smothering? Know-it-all? Over-controlling? Jealous?

3. Perhaps your partner has never seen a good example of how people can relate. As you grow, you have an opportunity to demonstrate healthy examples of relating.

4. If you have found in your egogram (pages 136–141) and the Mature Love Programme (page 141–147) that you have behaviours which fall into the category of Too Much Critical Parent, or Too Little Free Child.

5. If you have been over-reacting emotionally, this might have put your partner off. Step 7 is required reading as it helps you explore the reasons behind your emotionality. You cannot push your partner away and bring him or her close at the same time.

6. Predictability is another vital factor because your partner needs to know that your patterns of behaviour are consistent. If a person self-discloses, there needs to be a knowledge that it is safe ... not safe one day and unsafe the next.

Responses that encourage/destroy growth:

It is important to highlight a relationship destroyer which frequently occurs when a once-closed partner starts to self-disclose. The relationship can be destroyed — or strengthened — by the response he or she receives to this self-disclosure. An accusatory response is the surest way to close down a partner who is risking a new behaviour.

Your partner owns up to a particular weakness or pattern of behaviour or inadequacy:

Destructive response:

'That's right. That's what I've been telling you for years ...'

'I knew it all along — but you wouldn't listen to me ...'

'I always said you were just like your father/mother ...'

Constructive response:

'I really appreciate you telling me that ...' (See page 76 regarding keeping some thoughts to yourself)

We suggest that when a long-awaited awareness develops in a partner and this behaviour is owned and admitted, that you use the skill of sharing a meaning (pages 78–79) and then thank your partner for trusting you with that information. This will help to encourage and stimulate further self-disclosure (see page 144 Nurturing Parent Love).

I DON'T WANT CHILDREN

For many couples, one of the most deeply emotional and potentially destructive issues concerns children. We have referred to this issue in item 13 of the pre-marriage check list (page 9) and in the sections on contracts (pages 116–119 and 198).

The issue of whether to have children or not is so emotionally charged that extensive psychotherapy may be required to allow a couple to reach a resolution to the problem. In some cases one partner may make a dishonest agreement for the purpose of keeping the peace. In a scenario that is all too frequent, a reluctant partner gives in to the person wanting the child, then makes that person pay for it from that time onwards. Even worse is when an innocent child is made a scapegoat for the resentment and anger that the unwilling partner feels.

This is not to say that such conflict cannot occasionally end with a happy result. Many of us know cases where a previously reluctant partner becomes a marvellous parent when the child is born, but this is too serious a question to leave to luck.

Ideally, the question of children should be carefully considered before making a commitment to marriage. Should the issue of children not be resolved before marriage then a masterful use of conflict resolution skills (Steps 4–6) may be essential. In many cases professional assistance is necessary because the problems in this area often involve unresolved issues from childhood or previous relationships.

A further complication occurs when re-marriage results in a 'blended' family. In this case, the addition of a new child should be considered only when other conflicts have been resolved (see the following points on the 'curdled' family).

Children deserve the very best that we can offer them of ourselves. They deserve to be wanted and to have the utmost of your nurturing parent love.

RELATING WITH CHILDREN

Many people who are learning the communication skills in this book ask us, 'Do I use these skills with my children?' The emphatic answer is 'Yes!'

No matter the age of the child, he or she will begin to learn how to be an assertive communicator if you are a positive role model and use these skills yourself (see Steps 4, 5, 6).

It is interesting that when children begin to put words together they will quite naturally speak for themselves, using 'I' and 'me', but as they grow older many will start to use 'you' talk. If you set the example of 'speaking for self' (pages 56–57) you will help your child retain and use this important communication skill.

A child's self-awareness can be developed through use of the Awareness Wheel. For example, you can invite disclosure and ask 'Tell me what you see and hear on your walk' or 'I'd like to know what it is you really want and how you feel about that.' (See pages 64–67)

Other useful techniques include: Sharing a Meaning (pages 78–79) which not only results in mutual understanding, but has side benefits of building trust and self-worth; Checking Out (pages 77–78) which can even be used by young children, where, for example, a three year old should be able to ask, 'Are you cross with me?' and be given an honest answer; choice of Style of Communication (pages 81–90) where Heavy Control should be avoided, instead developing a Conversational Style and, of course, Search and Straight Styles where an issue is to be discussed/resolved.

Encourage your child to speak to you by paying attention (pages 90–94) and have a clear idea of what helps or hinders disclosure (pages 71–77).

THE CURDLED FAMILY

When two people marry and at least one has a child from a previous relationship, the name usually given to such a grouping is a 'blended' family. Unfortunately, many such families do not operate harmoniously, and therefore might be described as 'curdled' families.

Issues that make/maintain a 'curdled' family:

1. Discipline: Issues such as the following must be discussed and agreed upon: Does the natural parent *only* discipline his/her child? All the time? In some situations only? What role does the step parent play in discipline? Do both parents discipline all the children at appropriate times?

2. Personal space: Does the visiting child have some place in the home that can be called his/her own? A room? Bed? Shelf? Play Box? (Important to giving a sense of belonging)

3. Togetherness: Do you always want to do things together? Does one partner sometimes want to do things with his/her children alone? (We recommend this if done in moderation) Do all the children have to be together in play? Do you expect them to like each other? (This is unrealistic)

4. Values: Inevitably you will have differing values from your partner, some of which provide the potential for conflict. Areas where values differ might be centred on such things as the children's television viewing or what are acceptable standards of behaviour and manner. Ideally you will have used the pre-marriage check list (page 9) to really know your own values and those of your partner. When values differ in a relationship, it is important to be accepting and tolerant of other ways of living and to resolve conflicts assertively and constructively.

5. Relationships: Children do not ask (usually) to be part of a re-constituted family — it just happens to them. The important rule is to 'go slow' and be careful not to push children (or your new partner) into relationships with step-parents, step-children or a new extended family.

6. Rituals: All families have rituals that relate to what to do on birthdays, at Christmas, on other special days and how to behave in certain situations. It is important not to expect the members of a newly blended family to automatically follow the rituals brought from other families. Tolerance and an attitude that there may be other ways of doing things will help resolve impending conflict in this area.

7. Access to natural parent: In most cases it is crucial that children have an on-going relationship with the parent with whom they do not live. The significance of the family of origin to the individuals means that the maintenance of an emotional connection with a natural parent is extremely important.

8. Habits: We all have habits and they are part of what makes us an individual, however some can be unpleasant, unsociable or extremely irritating. Partners may be able to resolve conflict in this area with assertive communication skills, but problems often arise when the step-children have habits that annoy the step-parent (or vice versa). The basic rule is that this issue must be resolved between the people involved — the natural parent must not triangle into the situation. Each person should be assertive and respect the other's point of view. A Request for Change (page 88) should be made, using Search and Straight Styles of communication (pages 85–90).

A curdled family can be avoided and a harmonious family life achieved by the use of ALL the communication skills, awareness of the lessons Ball in the Paddock demonstrates (pages 69–70) and the clear understanding that it takes *time* for your step-family to grow into a blended family.

MARRIAGE THE SECOND AND THIRD TIME AROUND

People look for ways to 'solve' their loneliness, so when a relationship ends the tendency is often to fill the empty place as soon as possible — to find a new partner as a solution to an inner pain.

The danger is that you will find someone who seems to have what you have been missing, and therefore you fail to know the whole person. Also, if you are in this situation you need to consider that you may find a new partner, but you take the old 'you' into this new relationship. We all have blind spots and it is difficult to have a clear eyed self-perspective. The tendency is often to believe that you will be happy if you find the 'right' person this time, but of course effective, rewarding relationships depend upon the contributions of *both* people. (See the Three R's of Marital Success pages 147–148 and the Mature Love Programme pages 141–147).

THE EX-PARTNER

A major area of concern after divorce is the relationship with the ex-partner. Issues arise such as anger, jealousy, relationships with children and (if your former partner remarries) the new spouse, as well as custody, child support, maintenance and visitation rights.

Many people find communication with an ex-partner extremely difficult, but our experience has shown that there are steps to be taken that will make the task easier.

1. Allow considerable time for healing to occur. A massive dose of patience is often appropriate.

2. Accept reality — the marriage is over. The mature and positive thing is to work for a happier future. Hatred can cost you your health and peace of mind and it can alienate your children from their other parent and from their extended family.

3. Try to forgive. Go back to pages 205–207 and apply them to your current life situation.

4. Make efforts to build relationships between your former spouse and your children. When people turn their children against the 'ex' it very often backfires on them in the long term. By making this effort to build relationships you also teach relating skills to your children by being an example.

5. Do not triangle between your children and your ex-partner. They are responsible for their own relating and you should not act as a mediator. It is just too easy to over-react emotionally when you are in a triangle situation (see page 97).

6. Attempt to normalise the relationship with your former partner, behaving with him or her as you would with a friend. Remember, though, you will never be together the way you once were.

7. If the 'ex' has a new partner, try to build a normal relationship with that person. Blaming someone else for the failure will hinder your own development. Another positive result of normalising this relationship is that conflict will be avoided at family events (such as wedding ceremonies, birthdays etc.) where it is appropriate for both natural parents to be present.

Rebound relationships

When a significant emotionally satisfying relationship ends and an inner emptiness and/or loneliness is felt, people often seek another meaningful relationship to overcome the pain. This inner void, the broken heart, the hollow place is often denied. This denial is only one of the defence mechanisms which can come into operation and enable a person not to feel discounted.

As many of you know one of the most effective but dangerous ways to feel good again is to 'fall in love' with someone else. And this is precisely what many people do. Sure, it can make the pain go away, but just how much perspective do you have? The answer is normally — exactly zero.

While some might not carry this rebound to the extent of developing a romantic love, they do become overly involved in a relationship which they are not ready for at all.

Whether you become emotionally entangled again or not, there are some reasons for being very cautious of many potential traps at this point. We could recount story after story of lives ruined during this very vulnerable time when a person is so needy.

John is a good example. When his wife of fourteen years left him for a former love, he went into shock. This was all too unbelievable. Basically he thought their relationship was sound and that they were working together towards a future when they would not be so busy with careers and would have more time for each other.

Little did he know that she had a longing to be with her first love — and longings are very powerful forces which can drive people into situations far worse than they are already experiencing.

As it turned out John came into her life originally when she was on the rebound from her first love. So she rebounds back to that first love. What does John do? You guessed it? He rebounds into a relationship wherein the woman tells him she just wants to be a friend. Little did John realise that at that time he was in a very vulnerable state, one which eventually led him into a new commitment which was worse than loneliness.

When a heart-felt relationship ends, there is a need for time to learn what kind of person you are without a deeply felt involvement. It is so simple to find a new person who cares, at least while there is none of the stress which is a natural part of building a new life with someone. Deception, however, is often rife. The new person doesn't seem like the former partner. It seems so easy to talk and be understood. You can be led to believe that you are now *really relating*. Well maybe you are. But conflict will emerge and then what will be different for you? (See pages 113–116, 170–171)

If you are going to date or get involved with others after the breakup of a serious relationship or marriage, go slowly. Haste makes more than waste — it can destroy you. Take the time to experience other relationships. See how it feels to be with different people. The danger of instant gratification is always there when you are bereft and vulnerable. Need blinds to reality. Distance, time, self-examination, learning, growth, healing — these experiences can bring the wisdom to enable you to find someone with whom you can genuinely relate.

The affair

In the written history of the human race affairs have existed as far back as we know. Two of the Ten Commandments address the inclination of people to this behaviour: 'Thou shalt not covet … thy neighbour's wife' and 'Thou shalt not commit adultery'. Biblical history is replete with stories of adultery and the consequences of those affairs. Times have changed little since then and in fact the sexual revolution accelerated by the 'pill' and other birth control methods plus women's increasing financial independence have probably contributed to increasing the frequency of affairs.

If you sat where we have, listening to the disasters growing out of this common human experience, you would probably be impressed with some of the following:

The power of sexual drives is never to be denied. Nature will not be deprived of the need to reproduce and survive. And people will go to almost any length to have sexual satisfaction.

Sex, furthermore, is easily confused with love and relating. In a person's search for someone with whom they can experience a spiritual union, the physical union can become a false substitute. Many affairs are, in reality, a search for a partner with whom a genuine intimacy can be experienced. Seldom does a true intimacy develop out of an affair but this doesn't stop people from trying.

Most affairs are never revealed and the relationship dies a natural death. On the other hand, when a partner discovers that there is an affair, the rejection and emotional reaction often cements that temporary involvement into something more permanent.

Since affairs rarely help a person find someone with whom they can really relate, it is not a satisfactory way to solve the deeper needs of the human psyche.

When an affair is revealed or discovered it often spells the end of a relationship but it is often the catalyst for a very much improved marriage. Since it usually is a non-verbal way of saying 'something is missing in our relationship', the wise person will first seek to forgive (see pages 205–207) and then proceed to discover ways of rebuilding. Bear in mind that it is no time for games and if a partner persists with an affair or will not deal honestly forgiveness is not appropriate.

Relationships do not often grow in a straight line. There are successes and failures, periods of going ahead and periods of going no place or even backwards. An affair is a going backward experience. Dealing with the relationship problems which existed beforehand and after the fact are often an opportunity for honest soul-searching and increasing self-disclosure and intimacy.

Finally, an affair is often a way of acting on some deep and unfinished business carried from the past. In part that helps explain the frequency of people having one affair and never again repeating the experience. Obviously many people learn that there is a vast difference between an affair and a permanent and honest relationship. Affairs often involve a great deal of game playing. Marriage is lived out with little opportunity for such deception and requires the involvement of your total self.

Here are some important things to bear in mind when an affair occurs:

1. The anger of the partner must be expressed. Recognise also that the anger can reappear for years even after the relationship has become successful. Allow the anger. It heals the aggrieved when expressed and makes one depressed when not expressed.

2. The perpetrator of the affair might need therapy to deal with personal problems carried over from childhood.

3. When forgiveness is sought and achieved, the integrity of that is measured by future efforts to remain true to one's commitment.

4. Every effort should be made to learn how to create a satisfying relationship as this book teaches throughout.

5. Healing usually does not come overnight. Be patient. Take your time. Go slow to go fast.

6. Marriage therapy is usually needed but get a referral to someone highly qualified, non-judgemental, and mature.

Conclusions

This book has set before you challenges to learn — to learn for the rest of your life the joy of REALLY RELATING. We are well aware that this is an ideal for which we strive. There is always room for more growth — for knowing and understanding better someone with whom you want to really relate. Fear not! Such a goal gives many of us a powerful reason for living. People often die simply because they have no more goals.

If you adopt some of the challenges, skills, ideas of this book you will always have some reasons to live. Why?

Because Being Real — Being Your Self — Really Loving — Really Being Loved — Really Relating makes the adventure of life truly happy.

Index

A-frame marriage 35-6, 128, 201, 203
abandonment, fear of 29, 104
acceptance 29-30, 92-3, 102, 180, 182
actions 65
adapted child 134, 140, 146
addiction 20
adopted people 27, 112
adult ego state 134, 140-1
affairs 221-2
aggressive communication 51-4, 123
   assertive communication and 57
   characteristics of 54, 59
   intimacy and 160
anger 35, 65, 110, 123-7, 213, 222
anxiety 30, 160
assertive communication 45, 54-7, 60
   benefits of 54-5
   blending lives 173
   expressing anger 126-7
   how it differs 57
   how to be 55-6
   value of 61
assumptions 102

balance and blending 176, 182-5
ball in paddock exercise 69-71, 181, 217
behaviour, relationship problems and 212-3
   see also communication
belonging 26
Berne, Dr Eric 132, 207
blending lives 172
   process 173-4
   steps towards 175-85
body sensations 65
bonding 17
boundaries 201
Bowen, Murray 26-7, 178
builders of mature love 142, 144, 146, 180
   see also mature love programme
burnout, anger from 125-6

calm 191
career 8
change 188
   constructive ways of 191-2
   destructive ways of trying 189-91
   request for 135, 160, 191
   what you can 193-203
   what you cannot 192-3
checking out 77-8, 215
child ego state 133-4
childhood

   coping strategy and 25-6
   ego states and 133-5
   emotions 178-9
   programming 26-9, 103-5, 195
   receiving love and 152-4
   relationship change and 192-3
children 8, 214-15
   former partners and 218
   relating with 215-16
   rules and 120
   second marriages and 104, 216
   unresolved conflict and 98-9
closeness 106
common interests 7, 9, 197
communication 45-63
   listening and 90-4
   sex and 168
   skills 45-6, 71-81, 122, 160, 198, 208
   styles 81-90, 215
      see also aggressive communication
      assertive communication
      non-assertive communication
      self-awareness wheel
compensation 42, 43
compromising 180, 182
confidence 50, 54
conflict
   A-frame marriage and 35
   mistakes when it arises 188-9
   reason behind 103-7
   unresolved 95-101, 208
conflict resolution 9, 12-13, 107-8, 182
   steps to 101-3
contracts 161
   changes in 198
   emotions and 116-19
conversational communication style 81-2, 158, 216
   see also communication
coping strategy 25-6, 29-31
costs of living 3
counselling 208
courtship 11
cover-up, anger as 124
crazy-makers 122-3
critical parent 131, 132, 133, 135, 139-40, 143, 213
criticism 189-90
curdled family 216-17
curiosity 177, 199

deception 220
denial 41, 213
dependency 35, 128, 152
deprivation 190
discipline 216
disclosure
    difficulties of 73-6
    excessive 76-7, 158-9
    partner, encouraging 71-7, 214
    self 35, 68, 75
discussions, recording 202
displaced aggression 53-4
        see also aggressive communication
displacement 41-2
    of anger 124
distancing 26, 95-6, 105, 106
divorce 209-11, 218
dominant partner 36
double binds 122-3
Dusay, Dr John 136

education 2, 3
ego states 132-4
    analysing egograms 139-41
    constructing egograms 136-9
    mature love programme and 141-2,
        144-6
    personal interaction and 135-6, 154
    recognising different 134-5
    sex and 166
egograms 136-9, 143, 144-6
    analysing 139-41
elusiveness 20, 128
emotion 109
    controlling 198
    language and 102
    reasons for strong 111-26, 178
empathy 92, 181, 182
equality 2-3
erotic language 169
ex-partners 218
expectations 117, 194
eye contact 73

family of origin 3
    blending and 182, 184, 185
    childhood programming 25-9
    conflict and 103-6
    emotions and 111-16, 178-9
    H-type marriage and 39-40
    leaving 175-7
    real self and 33, 175
    receiving love and 152-4
    rules and emotions 119-20
fears 29-30, 206, 213
    disclosure and 74
    eliminating or reducing 200

feelings 64-5, 178-9
    death of 96-7
forgiveness 205-8, 218, 221
free child 133, 140, 149, 202, 213
friendship 9

game playing 98, 236
Games People Play (Berne) 132, 207
genograms 112-16
giving 102-3, 151, 180
gunny sack 50-1, 63, 68, 125, 212-13

H-type marriage 23, 38-9, 44, 62, 128, 158,
    172, 203
    blending and 179, 180
    why few develop this 39-42
habits 217
healing 220, 222
heavy control communication style 84-5,
    215
        see also communication
hidden agendas 4
honesty 158
honeymoon 11
humour 200-1

illusions 19
imagination 170
in-laws 105-6
        see also family of origin
indentification 42-3
individuals 3-4, 23
    blending lives 172, 182
    coping strategy 25-6, 29-31
    family of origin and 28
inner critic 50
insecurity 106
intentions 202
interruptions 74
intimacy 18, 151
    destroying 157-61
    developing 155-7
issues 45, 61, 69, 160
    awareness wheel and 64-7
    children and 216
    defining and conflict resolution 101
    what are they? 62-3

jealousy 32, 104-5, 110, 127-9
Jung, Carl 34
justified anger 126-7
        see also anger

language
    emotive 102
    erotic 169
lean-to marriage 36, 128, 203
light control communication style 82

see also communication
limited awareness 89-90
listening 90-4, 181
loneliness 4, 217
love 7, 11, 14, 16, 147
    being in love 14, 16, 18-19
    giving 202-3
    mature love and 131
    personal definitions and experience of 130-1
    receiving 151-5
    sex and 166
        see also mature love programme; romance; romantic love

manipulation, anger as 125
marriage
    changes in 2-4, 197
    courses in 208
    creating a satisfying 203-5
    education self about 195
    myths about 11
    negative reasons for 4-7
    positive reasons for 7-9
    pre-marriage checklist 9-10
    really relating in 10
    second 104, 217
    stages of 11-13, 203
    starting over 205-9
    three Rs of success 147-8, 193, 204, 217
    types of 23, 34-44, 203
    why do it? 1-2
    working on 187-8
mature love programme 131-2, 195, 203, 217
    builders and preventers of 142-3, 180
    ego states and 133-41, 144-6
    how it developed 141-3
    romance and 142
    transactional analysis and 132-5
    using the programme 143
        see also love; romantic love
Minnesota Couples Communication Programme 63, 208
mutual understanding 78-81, 85, 91-4, 181

nagging 190
nature 25, 192
non-assertive communication 46-50
    characteristics 50-1, 58
        see also communication
non-verbal aggression 52
        see also aggressive communication
nurturing parent 133, 140, 180

orgasm 167-8
over-reactivity *see* emotions

pain 206
pairing 17
parallel-type marriage 37-8, 203, 204
parent ego state 133
participation 93-4
partners
    change and 188, 201
    disclosure and 71-7, 158-9
    ex 218
    mature love programme and 143
    respect for 202
    submissive or dominant 36
    won't relate 213-4
passive aggression 52-3
        see also aggressive communication
past 193
payoff 48-9
personal space 73, 201, 216
perspectives 69-71, 196
physical appearance 193
physical environment
    disclosure and 73
    sex and 168
power struggles 37, 99-101
preventers of mature love 142, 144, 146
        see also mature love programme
priorities 196-7
privacy 201
        see also personal space
problems *see* issues
projection 43
pseudo self 31
    characteristics of 32-3
    intimacy and 155
    jealousy and 127-8
    relationship change and 190
        see also real self; self
punishment 153, 190

rationalising 41
reaction formation 42
        see also emotions
real self 32
    barriers to developing 40-3
    blending and 175
    characteristics of 33
    developing 33-5, 193-4, 203
    drive to be 43-4
    marital success and 148
        see also pseudo self; self
rebound relationships 219-20
regression 42
rejection 30
relating
    children and 214-16
    curdled families 216-17

ex-partner and 218
partner won't 213-14
problem behaviour 212-13
repeat marriages 217
three ways of 46-56
   see also communication
repressing 41
responding 93, 213-14
   sexually 167
responsibility 148
right to be heard 94
rituals 43, 200, 217
role changes 2-4, 197
romance 142, 147-8
romantic love 14, 15-16, 128, 130, 147, 154
   advantages and disadvantages 21-2
   power of 17-22
      see also love; mature love
      programme
rules and emotions 119-22

scapegoating 107
   anger as 125
search style of communication 85-7, 216
      see also communication
self
   communication and 50, 54
   components of 24-6
   dissatisfaction with 124
   sense of 23-4
   sharing 152
   speaking for 45, 56-7, 102, 156, 157
   thinking for 177-8
      see also pseudo self; real self
self-awareness wheel 64-6
   anger and 127
   change and 191, 193-4
   child's 215
   doing it 67
   feelings 179
   intimacy and 156
   putting it to work 68
   search and straight communication
   styles 86
   setting procedures for 68-9
self-defence mechanisms 40-3, 128, 190
self-development 195
self-discovery 204
self-esteem 19, 29-30, 50, 54, 55, 106, 152,
   160, 197
self-fulfilling prophecies 98
self-image 4, 8, 61
self-limiting belief 48, 201
self-respect 50, 54, 61
senses 64
separateness

balancing with togetherness 182-5
blending and 176
negative and positive aspects of 183-4
sex 151, 161, 196
   complaints about 161-3
   good sexual life 170
   initiating 169
   men and women, differences 167-9
   overcoming complaints 164-7
   what it can be like 163-4
sexual desire 20-1, 167, 221
sexual intercourse 166-7, 171
sexual response 167-8
sharing a meaning 78-81, 93, 215
silence 94
skills
   communication 45-6, 71-81, 122, 160,
   198, 208
   sexual 170
sleep deprivation, anger and 126
sorry 206
special events 196
spiritual self 34, 202
spoken contracts 116
starting over 205-9
stopping 102
straight style of communication 85, 87-8,
   216
      see also communication
stress 199
      see also emotions
sublimation 42
submissive partner 36, 190
      see also partners
survival program 25, 29-31
   H-type marriage and 39-40

tension release, anger as 125
thoughts 65
time 74, 161
   blending and 173
   creating satisfying marriages and 203-5
   managing 199
togetherness 27
   balancing with separateness 182-5
   blending and 176
   children and 216
   negative and positive aspects of 183
   sex and 164-6
touching 168, 174
tradition 2
transactional analysis 132-41
triangling 97, 105, 218
trust 74, 155
   intimacy and 155-60
twitching 178

unconscious contracts 116, 118, 198
    see also contracts
unhappiness 126
unspoken contracts 117-18
    see also contracts

values 7, 9, 179, 216
verbal aggression 51-2
    see also aggressive behaviour
violence 53, 190

wants 65
wholeness 18
withdrawing 26, 111, 190, 213
withholding 190
women
    complaints about sex 161-2
    equality and 2-3
    overcoming 164-7